RUNNING AGAINST THE MACHINE

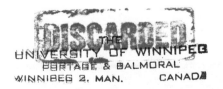

The Mailer - Breslin Campaign

Edited by PETER MANSO

RUNNING AGAINST THE MACHINE

1969

DOUBLEDAY AND COMPANY, INC.

Garden City, New York

RUNNING AGAINST THE MACHINE
*was published simultaneously in a hardcover edition
by Doubleday & Company, Inc.*

Acknowledgment is made to the following for permission to reprint their copyrighted material:

WPIX-TV For material from "Democratic Mayoral Candidates Debate" used through the courtesy of the WPIX Community Affairs Department.

NEW YORK DAILY NEWS For "The Bore Buster" by William Reel. Courtesy of the Sunday News, New York's Picture Newspaper.

THE NEW YORK TIMES For "In the Nation: Mailer with His Hair Combed" by Tom Wicker; "Million Advance for Mailer Seen" by Henry Raymont; "Mailer Plays a Night Club Date in Mayoral Quest" by Sidney E. Zion; "Observer: Cheers for Politerates" by Russell Baker; "Why Are We in New York?" by Norman Mailer. Copyright © 1969 by The New York Times Company. Reprinted by permission.

WASHINGTON STAR SYNDICATE, Inc. For "Talking Tactics" by Mary McGrory. Copyright © 1969 by New York Post. Reprinted by permission of Washington Star Syndicate, Inc.

NEW YORK POST For "An Odd Couple" by James A. Wechsler; "Victory in Defeat" by James A. Wechsler; "Be My Guest, Norman Mailer" by James Wechsler; "$ Million for Mailer's Next." Copyright © 1969, New York Post Corp. Reprinted by permission of New York Post.

STERLING LORD AGENCY For "I Run to Win" by Jimmy Breslin; "The City Politic: Running Other People's Lives" by Jimmy Breslin; "The City Politic: And Furthermore, I promise . . ." by Jimmy Breslin. Copyright © 1969 by Jimmy Breslin. Appeared in New York Magazine. Reprinted by permission of The Sterling Lord Agency.

THE CONDÉ NAST PUBLICATIONS INC. For "Shoot-for-the-Moon Mailer" by Leticia Kent. Reprinted from Vogue. Copyright © 1969 by the Condé Nast Publications Inc.

G. P. PUTNAM'S SONS For poem from ADVERTISEMENTS FOR MYSELF by Norman Mailer. Copyright © 1959 by Norman Mailer. Reprinted by permission of G. P. Putnam's Sons.

This is not my book for I didn't write it and was not present to edit it, although I think the editing work is more than fair. Since I figure in this book with some prominence, however, I expect it would do no harm to write a dedication and so I say that I wish to dedicate this collection to the hard-working staff and the enthusiastic volunteers of the Mailer-Breslin Campaign. To the extent we were successful much of the credit can be given to the long hours they put in, to the extent we failed the candidate can appropriate his full and thorough share.

Norman Mailer
July 22, 1969

CONTENTS

INTRODUCTION – PETER MANSO

This book offers a number of perspectives on the Mailer-Breslin campaign. It divides itself rather neatly into five parts: the first is made up of essays and speeches by the candidates, while the final section consists of pieces by their associates, observers, and sometime critics. In between one finds the campaign position papers and a sampling from the never too encouraging New York press. Then too, there is a miscellany of ads, handouts, and fliers. A balance, a structure, even a certain fair-mindedness was meant to inform the collection, and one can rest happily with the thought that in its variety and shifts the volume as a whole suggests the extraordinary seven-week curve of the campaign.

The reader will doubtless note the absence of any summary précis or post-mortem. This should not be surprising; in fact it might even be said to have been inevitable. For the campaign was more than engaging and left a vacuum in its wake, and no one directly involved, certainly not your editor, is sufficiently fresh at this point to attempt its history or reading. So the reader is asked to put aside his bad habits—that urban urge for the finite and immediately answerable—and to ferret for himself the style of the ideas put forth on this collection. He is asked to use his imagination—to sense the energy, the rightness and wrongness of Mailer and Breslin, and to speculate, as well, on the New York that created their campaign.

The campaign, needless to say, was a philosophical campaign. It proceeded from a body of ideas that had as their end something other than the success of the candidates. In the course of the seven-week run remarkably few compromises were made; mainly the ideas held. In fact they developed, grew one out of the other and so proved the soundness of the original argument—that the time had come for New Yorkers to assume responsibility for their city and their individual destinies. Working with the notion day after day, one came to give it a lot of affection for it not only justified one's efforts but was so alive in giving the campaign its zap.

Mailer ran as a "left-conservative." The phrase is intriguing, the density and unexpectedness of it, but it confused a good many who saw it as yet another Mailerism and, a confirmation of their abiding sense that neither Mailer nor any of his crew had any business in Gracie Mansion. You could see the suspicions it created on people's faces, a momentary confusion quickly turning to smirk. The refusal to follow its argument was probably more than a reflex to the legendary Mailer, or even to the turns of the phrase itself. Among those of the city who pride themselves on their reasonableness it was simply a paradox, an insult to one's sense of proportion, one's perspective and balance. It demanded too much, raised more questions than it answered. It seemed too philosophical, perhaps just cute . . .

But it would do no harm to ask what we mean by "left conservatism." Neither the electorate nor the press sufficiently considered the question during the course of the campaign, and this says something about the habits of both. It also says a great deal about the city and its politics. One tends to use the terms "left" and "right" as straightforward labels that work in our interest. It could be argued that in New York this is generally not the case. For the center has set the two in quick opposition and made a false dialectic of our lives. It has scared us, encouraged an indifference to all but the middle way—and this, surely, has not brought us very far. Rather it has removed New York from itself, brought on a listlessness and alienation that often seem terminal. And no wonder, for the Establishment has depressed the emotional element of all ideology. It has refused human ends as the core of its argument. Scarifying in equal measure the hysterical right and the black left, it has bullied people into knowing the quality of their lives through cant and category rather than by the mood and turn of their gut.

And so concretely I would suggest that the center's polarization of the left and right, its terrorizing, has been a form of brainwashing that seriously interfered with the city's understanding of Mailer and Breslin. It made impossible any mating of the ideas implicit to their plank.

"Unfixing old interests at once" was for Burke "a thing apt to breed a black and sullen discontent"—an unloosening of all sanctions and a return to some anarchic state of nature. Conservatism has thus stood for the skeptical side of man's nature, seeing about itself man's basic rapaciousness, his sin, and frailty. Traditionally it finds its treasures in the past, in prescription and custom. In our own day, it has dreamed a dream of frontier independence; from the Populists through Goldwater and Buckley, it has distrusted and declaimed both the programs and procedures of big government. In the face of "New Dealism" or "creeping Federalism" it has reacted against the forces of modern life, its restrictions and anonymity, and demanded that individuals have the right to determine their own destinies. Unfortunately, however, it has failed to understand the corollaries of its position . . .

The left, on the other hand, has always defended the efficacy of institutional government. Steeped in the principles of the French Enlightenment, it held faith in man's reason and perfectibility, and its rationalism led to the conviction that society's worth is a function of government, and government itself a product of man's intelligence. And it believed that government was ever-improving, its democratic values bulwark against injustice and loss of personal liberties. It would free the individual from the restraints of traditional, organic societies and endow him with a "voice" in his government—it would establish the principle of "the consent of the governed" as the basis of the equitable life. As a democratic institution, government could therefore only be a benevolent, progressive institution.

History, however, has proven a few of these assumptions wrong. Industrialism, centralized government, and the left, aligning itself too narrowly with the interests of particular groups, failed to understand the dangers inherent to this centralization. While appropriate to the depression of the thirties, the New Deal has become an embracing ideology that has gone a long way toward standardizing life styles. With its ineffectual federal assistance programs it has too often become an end in itself. So while granting the obvious necessity of government services to the poor, to blacks and others, one must also say that the worst features of the left have made it an extension of modern life itself—sterile, rigid, and authoritarian. With its institutional taint, it belies the notion of a varied society, and so provides no ready solution for the ills that beset us.

With its insistence on "individualism" the right therefore has something to offer, the potential, perhaps, for reinvigorating our lives. At the same time, of course, it has been bigoted, selfish, and worse in its disregard of the many people powerless to effect their lives, people who have only crime and addiction as exercises of wit and freedom. So the left has its point—that the poor must be given the power to reinstate themselves. But without strings attached. Their style and the refinement of that style must be their own, not dictated, however graciously, from above. For whenever we tell someone something is untrue, impractical, or impossible, whenever we tell him how to live, we invoke authority and such authority will surely, inevitably, minimize a man in his own eyes. It will remove him from the springs of his talent and sullen his mood. And then our problems will worsen, New York and the nation will move closer to outright disaster.

Now while such a thumbnail sketch may hardly be the stuff of political analysis it serves the argument. For the essential point is that the people of New York City have been victimized by the center. A center which has not allowed them margin for their own discoveries and mistakes. And so there must be an alternative, otherwise the anomie deepens and you've got, as Breslin says, shotguns on Park Avenue and Vietnam in the streets. Left-conservatism, drawing on the best of the right and the best of the left, comes as close to such an alternative as anything I know.

While a philosophical notion, to be sure, left-conservatism, is a simple one because it insists that politics be an extension of our personal lives and that existence is nothing if not for individual responsibility and action. At bottom it requires every man to gauge the success or failure of his life by the extent to which he knows that life and all that it might be. It calls for democracy but a democracy which is nothing if not pluralistic. In effect, it is everything that the center is not.

The relevance of this excursus is confirmed by the press clippings reprinted in this volume. The contention is that the Establishment has not only terrorized the city into abjuring all "extremes" but controls the press as well. And so the clippings of section two are meant to suggest as much about New York as about the campaign. For during those hot weeks in May, in its treatment of Mailer and

Breslin and the other candidates, one came to see the press as one of the more committed forces of the city's interests. Rather than cover Mailer and Breslin regularly, on a day-by-day basis, take seriously their position papers, their notions of the fifty-first state and neighborhood control—their left-conservatism—the papers sniped, ridiculed, or merely ignored what was probably the most dynamic if not popular campaign of the primary. To wit: those two small fillers, appearing in the *Times* and the *Post* on May 13, announcing the advance on Mailer's moonshot book. Their point, of course, was that the campaign was rolling in money. Actually our pockets were flat, our debts mounting, and potential campaign contributors could hardly have been spurred by news of the candidate as the richest of America's authors. So those two items hurt, and as with Mary McGrory's *Post* column of the following week, one could only conclude a gossipy, spoiler's meanness as their intent. The reader is of course invited to make his own conclusions.

The position papers included in section three were released regularly in an attempt to expand and publicize the possibilities of the fifty-first state. While some of their suggestions could doubtless be implemented at present—various interests willing—they are of a package insofar as they rest on the notion of the city becoming a state. Their recommendations on housing, crime, and education, and even transportation, assume that New Yorkers can only begin to solve their ills by controlling their lives, their neighborhoods, and their money. The assumption underlies ideas large and small and lends a coherence to the papers as well as the campaign. Hopefully the papers make this clear.

Like other phases of the campaign, the position papers were a group effort. They involved the candidates and a staff of researchers as well as their authors. They cannot be regarded as the work of a single person. And so it would not be irregular to thank all those who contributed their time and talent. This I now do.

Peter Manso
July 1969

RUNNING AGAINST THE MACHINE

PART ONE

The Candidates

WHY ARE WE IN NEW YORK?

NORMAN MAILER

The New York Times Magazine, May 18, 1969

How is one to speak of the illness of a city? A clear day can come, a morning in early May like the pride of June. The streets are cool, the buildings have come out of shadow, and silences are broken by the voices of children. It is as if the neighborhood has slept in the winding sheet of the past. Forty years go by—one can recollect the milkman and the clop of a horse. It is a great day. Everyone speaks of the delight of the day on the way to work. It is hard on such mornings to believe that New York is the victim "etherized upon a table."

Yet by afternoon the city is incarcerated once more. Haze covers the sky, a grim, formless glare blazes back from the horizon. The city has become unbalanced again. By the time work is done, New Yorkers push through the acrid, lung-rotting air and work their way home, avoiding each other's eyes in the subway. Later, near midnight, thinking of a walk to buy the *Times,* they hesitate—in the darkness a familiar sense of dread returns, the streets are not quite safe, the sense of waiting for some apocalyptic fire, some night of long knives hangs over the city. We recognize one more time that the city is ill, that our own New York, the Empire City, is not too far from death.

Recollect: When we were children, we were told air was invisible, and it was. Now we see it shift and thicken, move in gray depression over a stricken sky. Now we grow used to living with colds all year, and viruses suggestive of the plague. Tempers shorten in our hideous air. The sick get sicker, the violent more violent. The frayed tissue of New York manners seems ready to splatter on every city street.

It is the first problem of the city, our atrocious air. People do not die dramatically like the one-day victims of Donora, rather they dwindle imperceptibly, die five years before their time, ten years before, cough or sneeze helplessly into the middle of someone else's good mood, stroll about with the hot iron of future asthma manacled to their lungs. The air pollution in New York is so bad, and gives so much promise of getting worse, that there is no solution to any other problem until the air is relieved of its poisonous ingestions. New York has conceivably the worst air of any city in the universe today—certainly it is the worst air in the most technologically developed nation in the world, which is to say it is the air of the future if the future is not shifted from its program. Once Los Angeles was famous for the liver-yellow of her smog; we have surpassed her.

That is our pervasive ill. It is fed by a host of tributary ills which flow into the air, fed first by our traffic, renowned through the world for its incapacity to move. Midtown Manhattan is next to impenetrable by vehicle from midday to evening—the average rate of advance is, in fact, six miles an hour, about the speed of a horse at a walk. Once free of the center, there is the threat of hour-long tie-ups at every bridge, tunnel, and expressway if even a single car breaks down in a lane. In the course of a year, people lose weeks of working time through the sum of minutes and quarter-hours of waiting to crawl forward in traffic. Tempers blow with lost schedules, work suffers everywhere. All the while stalled cars gun their motors while waiting in place, pumping carbon monoxide into air already laden with caustic sulphur dioxide from fuel oil we burn to make electricity.

Given this daily burden, this air pollution, noise pollution, stagnant transport, all-but-crippled subways, routes of new transportation twenty years unbuilt—every New Yorker sallies forth into an environment which strips him before noon of his good cheer, his charity, his calm nerve, and his ability to discipline his anger.

Yet, beneath that mood of pestilential clangor, something worse is ticking away—our deeper sense of a concealed and continuing human horror. If there are eight million people in New York, one million live on welfare, no, the figure is higher now, it will be one million two hundred thousand by the end of the year. Not a tenth of these welfare cases will ever be available for work; they are women and children first, then too old, too sick, too addicted, too illiterate, too unskilled, too ignorant of English. Fatherless families and motherless families live at the end of an umbilical financial cord which perpetuates them in an embryonic economic state. Welfare is the single largest item in the city budget—two years ago it surpassed the figure we reserve for education, yet it comes down to payments of no more than $3800 a year for a family of four. Each member of that family is able to spend a dollar a day for food, at most $1.25 a day.

Still, it is worse than that. If one of eight people in New York is on welfare, half as many again might just as well be on welfare because their minimum wage brings in no more than such a check. So the natural incentive is to cease working. Close to $1.5 billion is spent on welfare now. The figure will go up. Manpower Training, in contrast, spends about a twenty-fifth as much. Looking to skill the poor for work, it will train as many as 4000 men a year, and place perhaps 10,000 men out of 100,000 applicants in bad jobs without foreseeable future, the only jobs indeed available for the untrained. Sometimes in the Job Corps it cost $13,000 to train a man for a job where he might be able to make $6000 a year if he could find a job, but the skills he had learned were not related to the jobs he might return to at home. Poverty lies upon the city like a layer of smog.

Our housing offers its unhappy figures. If we have calculated that it is necessary to build 7500 new low-income apartments a year, merely to keep on the same terms with the problem, we end in fact with 4000 units constructed. Never mind how most of it looks— those grim, high-rise, new-slum prisons on every city horizon. Face rather the fact that we lose near to the same number of units a year as old buildings which could have been saved run down into a state requiring condemnation. Of the $100,000,000 the city spends each budget year for new housing, $20,000,000 goes into demolition. If four times as much were spent by present methods on low- and middle-income housing, 36,000 new and rehabilitated units could be provided a year, but housing needs would still be huge and un-met—the average family could wait twenty-five years to benefit from the program.

Our finances are intolerable. If New York State delivers $17 billion in income tax and $5 billion in corporate taxes to the federal government, it is conservative to assume that $14 billion of the total of $22 billion has come from the people of New York City. But our city budget is about $7.5 billion: of that sum only $3 billion derives from the state and from Washington. New York must find another $4.5 billion in real estate and other local taxes. Consider then: We pay $14 billion in income tax to the federal government and to Albany: back comes $3 billion. We put out five dollars for every dollar which returns. So we live in vistas of ironbound civic poverty. Four of those lost five dollars are going to places like Vietnam and Malmstrom in North Dakota where the ABM will find a site, or dollars are going to interstate highways which pass through regions we probably will never visit. In relation to the federal government, the city is like a sharecropper who lives forever in debt at the company store.

Yes, everything is wrong. The vocations of the past disintegrate. Jewish teachers who went into the education system twenty years ago to have security for themselves and to disseminate enlightenment among the children of the poor, now feel no security in their work, and are rejected in their liberal sociological style of teaching. The collective ego of their life style is shattered. They are forced to comprehend that there are black people who would rather be taught by other black people than by experts. The need for authenticity has become the real desire in education. "Who am I? What is the meaning of my skin, my passion, my dread, my fury, my dream of glories undreamed, my very need for bread?"—these questions are now become so powerful they bring the pumps of blood up to pressure and leave murder in the heart. What can education be in the womb of a dying city but a fury to discover for oneself whether one is victim or potential hero, stupid or too bright for old pedagogical ways? Rage at the frustration of the effort to find a style became the rage at the root of the uproar in the schools last year, and the rage will be there until the schools are free to discover a new way to learn. Let us not be arrogant toward the ignorant—their sensitivity is often too deep to dare the knowledge of numbers of the curlicue within a letter. Picasso, age of eleven, could still not do arithmetic because the figure 7 looked like a nose upside down to him.

Among the poor, genius may stay buried behind the mask of the most implacable stupidity, for if genius can have no issue in a man's life, he must conceal it, and protect it, reserve it for his seed, or his blessing, or, all else gone, for his curse. No wonder we live with dread in our heart, and the nicest of the middle class still padlock their doors against the curse. We are like a Biblical city which has fallen from grace. Our parks deteriorate, and after duty our police go home to suburbs beyond the city—they come back to govern us from without. And municipal employees drift in the endless administrative bogs of Wagnerian systems of apathy and attrition. Work gets done at the rate of work accomplished by a draft army in peacetime at a sullen out-of-the-way post. The Poverty Program staggers from the brilliance of its embezzlements. But, of course, if you were a bright young black man, might you not want to steal a million from the feds?

Here, let us take ourselves to the problem. It goes beyond the Durham gang. Our first problem is that no one alive in New York can answer with honesty the question: Can New York be saved? None of us can know. It is possible people will emigrate from New York in greater and greater numbers, and administration will collapse under insufferable weights, order will be restored from without. Then, everyone who can afford it will redouble his efforts to go, and New York will end as the first asylum of the megacity of the technological future. We who leave will carry with us the infection of the cowardice and apathy, the sense of defeat of the terminal years. We will move into other cities similarly affected or into a countryside wary of us, for we are then packers and peddlers from an expiring social world. So our first problem is to find whether we can find a way to rally our morale.

Part of the tragedy, part of the unbelievable oncoming demise of

New York is that none of us can simply believe it. We were always the best and the strongest of cities, and our people were vital to the teeth. Knock them down eight times and they would get up with that look in the eye which suggests the fight has barely begun. We were the city of optimists. It is probably why we settled so deep into our mistakes. We simply couldn't believe that we weren't inexhaustible as a race—an unspoken race of New Yorkers.

Now all our problems have the magnitude of junkie problems—they are so coexistent with our life that New Yorkers do not try to solve them but escape them. Our fix is to put the blame on the blacks and Puerto Ricans. But everybody knows that nobody can really know where the blame resides. Nobody but a candidate for mayor. It is the only way he can have the optimism to run. So the prospective candidate writing these words has the heart to consider entering the Democratic primary on June 17 because he thinks he sees a way out of the swamp: better, he believes he glimpses a royal road.

The face of the solution may reside in the notion that the left has been absolutely right on some critical problems of our time, and the conservatives have been altogether correct about one enormous matter—which is that the federal government has no business whatever in local affairs. The style of New York life has shifted since the Second World War (along with the rest of the American cities) from a scene of local neighborhoods and personalities to a large dull impersonal style of life which deadens us with its architecture, its highways, its abstract welfare, and its bureaucratic reflex to look for government solutions which come into the city from without (and do not work). So the old confidence that the problems of our life were roughly equal to our abilities has been lost. Our authority has been handed over to the federal power. We expect our economic solutions, our habitats, yes, even our entertainments, to derive from that remote abstract power, remote as the other end of a television tube. We are like wards in an orphan asylum. The shaping of the style of our lives is removed from us—we pay for huge military adventures and social experiments so separated from our direct control that we do not even know where to begin to look to criticize the lack of our power to criticize. We cannot—the words are now a cliché, the life has gone out of them—we cannot forge our destiny. So our condition is spiritless. We wait for abstract impersonal powers to save us, we despise the abstractness of those powers, we loathe ourselves for our own apathy. Orphans.

Who is to say that the religious heart is not right to think the need of every man and woman alive may be to die in a state of grace, a grace which for atheists and agnostics may reside in the basic art of having done one's best, of having found some part of a destiny to approach, and having worked for the view of it? New York will not begin to be saved until its men and women begin to believe that it must become the greatest city in the world, the most magnificent, most creative, most extraordinary, most just, dazzling, bewildering and balanced of cities. The demand upon us has come down to nothing less than that.

How can be begin? By the most brutal view, New York City is today a legislative pail of dismembered organs strewn from Washington to Albany. We are without a comprehensive function or a skin. We cannot begin until we find a function which will become our skin. It is simple: Our city must become a state. We must look to become a state of the United States separate from New York State; the fifty-first, in fact, of the United States. New York City State, or The State of New York City. It is strange on the tongue, but not so strange.

Think on the problem of this separation. People across the state are oriented toward Buffalo or Albany or Rochester or Montreal or Toronto or Boston or Cleveland. They do not think in great numbers of coming to New York City to make their life. In fact the good farmers and small-town workers of New York State rather detest us. They hear of the evils of our city with quiet thin-lipped glee; in the state legislature they rush to compound those evils. Every time the city needs a program which the state must approve, the city returns with a part of its package—the rest has been lost in deals, compromises, and imposts. The connection of New York City to New York State is a marriage of misery, incompatibility, and abominable old quarrels.

While the separation could hardly be as advantageous to New York State as it would be for the city, it might nonetheless begin the development of what has been hitherto a culturally undernourished hinterland, a typically colorless national tract.

But we will not weep for New York State—look, rather, to the direct advantages to ourselves. We have, for example, received no money so far for improving our city transit lines, yet the highway program for America in 1968 was $5 billion. Of this, New York State received at least $350 million for its roads. New York City received not a dollar from Washington or Albany for reconstruction of its six thousand miles of streets and avenues.

As a city-state we could speak to the federal government in the unmistakable tones of a state. If so many hundreds of millions go to Pennsylvania and Oklahoma and Colorado and Maine for their highway programs, then we could claim that a comparable amount is required for our transportation problems which can better be solved by the construction of new rapid transit. Add the moneys attainable by an increased ability as the fifty-first state to press for more equitable return on our taxes. Repeat: we give to Washington and Albany almost five tax dollars for every dollar which returns; Mississippi, while declaiming the virtues and inviolability of states' rights, still gets four federal dollars for every income-tax dollar she pays up.

As the center of the financial and communications industries, as the first victim of a nuclear war, the new State of the City of New York would not have the influence of one state in fifty-one, but rather would exist as one of the two or three states whose force and influence could be felt upon every change in the country's policy. With the power implicit in this grip, it may not be excessive to assume that divorce from Albany would produce an extra billion in real savings and natural efficiency, and still another billion (not to mention massive allocations for transit problems) could derive from our direct relation with the federal government: The first shift in our ability to solve our problems might have begun.

It would not, however, be nearly enough. The ills of New York cannot be solved by money. New York will be ill until it is magnificent. For New York must be ready to show the way to the rest of Western civilization. Until it does, it will be no more than the first victim of the technological revolution no matter how much money it receives in its budget. Money bears the same relation to social solutions that water does to blood.

Yet the beginning of a city-state and the tonic of a potential budget of 8 or 9 or 10 billion dollars would offer a base on which to build. Where then could we take it? How would be build?

We could direct our effort first against the present thickets of the City Charter. The Charter is a formidable document. There are some who would say it is a hideous document. Taken in combination with the laws of New York State, it is a legal mat guaranteed to deaden the nerve of every living inquiry. The Charter in combination with the institutional and municipal baggage surrounding it is guaranteed to inhibit any honest man from erecting a building, beginning an enterprise, organizing a new union, searching for a sensible variety of living zone, or speaking up for local control in education. It would strangle any honest mayor who approached the suffocations of air pollution or traffic, tried to build workable on-the-job training, faced the most immediate problems of law and order, attacked our shortage of housing or in general even tried to conceive of a new breath of civic effort. There is no way at present to circumvent the thicket without looking to power brokers in the trade unions, the Mafia, and real estate.

Only if the people of New York City were to deliver an overwhelming mandate for a city-state could anything be done about the thicket. Then the legal charter of the new state could rewrite the means by which men and women could work to make changes in the intimate details of their neighborhoods and their lives.

Such a new document would most happily be built upon one concept so fundamental that all others would depend upon it. This concept might state that power would return to the neighborhoods.

Power to the neighborhoods! In the new city-state, every opportunity would be offered to neighborhoods to vote to become townships, villages, hamlets, sub-boroughs, tracts, or small cities, at which legal point they would be funded directly by the fifty-first state. Many of these neighborhoods would manage their own municipal

services, their police, sanitation, fire protection, education, parks, or
like very small towns, they could, if they wished, combine services
with other neighborhoods. Each neighborhood would thus begin to
outline the style of its local government by the choice of its services.

It may be recognized that we are at this point not yet vastly
different from a patch of suburbs and townships in Westchester or
Jersey. The real significance of power to the neighborhoods is that
people could come together and constitute themselves upon any
principle. Neighborhoods which once existed as separate towns or
districts, like Jamaica or New Utrecht or Gravesend, might wish to
become towns again upon just such a historic base. Other neighborhoods with a sense of unity provided by their geography like Bay
Ridge, Park Slope, Washington Heights, Yorkville, Fordham Road,
Riverdale, Jackson Heights, Canarsie or Corona might be able without undue discussion to draw their natural lines.

Poorer neighborhoods would obviously look to establish themselves
upon their immediate problems, rather than upon historical or geographical tradition. So Harlem, Bedford-Stuyvesant and the Barrio
in East Harlem might be the first to vote for power to their own
neighborhoods so that they might be in position to administer their
own poverty program, own welfare, their own education systems, and
their own—if they so voted—police and sanitation and fire protection for which they would proceed to pay out of their funds. They
would then be able to hire their own people for their own neighborhood jobs and services. Their own teachers and communities would,
if they desired, control their own schools. Their own union could
rebuild their own slums. Black Power would be a political reality
for Harlem and Bedford-Stuyvesant. Black people and, to the extent
they desired, Puerto Rican people, could make separate but thoroughgoing attacks upon their economic problems, since direct neighborhood funding would be available to begin every variety of economic
enterprise. Black militants interested in such communal forms of
economic activity as running their own factories could begin to build
economies, new unions and new trades in their neighborhoods.

Power to the neighborhoods would mean that any neighborhood
could constitute itself on any principle, whether spiritual, emotional,
economical, ideological or idealistic. Even prejudicial principles could

serve as the base—if one were willing to pay. It could, for example, be established in the charter of the city-state that no principle of exclusion by race or religion would be tolerated in the neighborhoods unless each such neighborhood was willing to offer a stiff and proper premium for this desire in their taxes.

In reaction to this, each and every liberal, Negro and white, who would detest the relinquishment of the principle that no prejudice was allowed by law, might also consider the loss of the dream of integration as the greatest loss in the work of their lives. They would now be free to create neighborhoods which would incorporate on the very base of integration itself—Integration City might be the name of the first neighborhood to stand on the recapture of the old dream. Perhaps it might even exist where now is Stuyvesant Town.

On the other hand, people who wished anonymity or isolation from their neighbors could always choose large anonymous areas, neighborhoods only in name, or indeed could live in those undifferentiated parts of the city which chose no neighborhood for themselves at all. The critical point to conceive is that no neighborhood would come into existence because the mayoralty so dictated. To the extent that they had been conditioned for years by the notion that the government was the only agency large enough and therefore effective enough to solve their problems, so to that extent would many people be reluctant to move to solutions which came from themselves.

To the degree, however, that we have lost faith in the power of the government to conduct our lives, so too would the principle of power to the neighborhoods begin to thrive, so too would the first spiritual problem of the twentieth century—alienation from the self —be given a tool by which to rediscover oneself.

In New York, which is to say, in the twentieth century, one can never know whether the world is vastly more or less violent than it seems. Nor can we discover which actions in our lives are authentic or which belong to the art of the put-on. Conceive that society has come to the point where tolerance of others' ideas has no meaning unless there is benumbed acceptance of the fact that we must accept their lives. If there are young people who believe that human liberty is blockaded until they have the right to take off their clothes in the street—and more! and more!—make love on the hood of an automobile—there are others who think it is a sin against the eyes of the Lord to even contemplate the act in one's mind. Both could now begin to build communities on their separate faith—a spectrum which might run from Compulsory Free Love to Mandatory Attendance in Church on Sunday! Grant us to recognize that wherever there is a common desire among people vital enough to keep a community alive, then there must be also the presence of a clue that some kind of real life resides in the desire. Others may eventually discern how.

Contained beneath the surface of the notion is a recognition that the twentieth century has lost its way—the religious do not know if they believe in God, or even if God is not dead; the materialist works through the gloomy evidence of socialism and bureaucracy; the traditionalist is hardly aware any longer of a battlefield where the past may be defended; the technician—if sensitive—must wonder if the world he fashions is evil, insane, or rational; the student rebellion stares into the philosophical gulf of such questions as the nature of culture and the student' responsibility to it; the blacks cannot be certain if they are fundamentally deprived, or a people of genius, or both. The answers are unknown because the questions all collide in the vast empty arena of the mass media where no price has ever to be paid for your opinion. So nobody can be certain of his value—one cannot even explore the validity of one's smallest belief. To wake up in New York with a new idea is to be plunged into impotence by noon, plunged into that baleful sense of boredom which hints of dread and future violence.

So the cry of Power to the Neighborhoods may yet be heard. For even as marriage reveals the balance between one's dream of pleasure and one's small real purchase upon it, even as marriage is the mirror of one's habits, and the immersion of the ego into the acid of the critic, so life in the kind of neighborhood which contains one's belief of a possible society is a form of marriage between one's social philosophy and one's private contract with the world. The need is deeper than we could expect, for we are modern, which is to say we can never locate our roots without a voyage of discovery.

Perhaps then it can be recognized that power to the neighborhoods is a most peculiar relocation of the old political directions. It speaks from the left across the divide to conservatism. Speaking from the left, it says that a city cannot survive unless the poor are recognized, until their problems are underlined as not directly of their own making; so their recovery must be based upon more than their own private efforts, must be based in fact upon their being capitalized by the city-state in order that the initial construction of their community economics, whether socialist or capitalist or both, can begin.

Yet with power in the neighborhoods, so also could there be on-the-job training in carpentry, stone-masonry, plumbing, plastering, electrical work, and painting. With a pool of such newly skilled workers, paid by the neighborhood, the possibility is present to rebuild a slum area *room by room.*

Better! The occupant of an apartment who desires better housing could go to work himself on his own apartment, using neighborhood labor and funds, patching, plastering, painting, installing new wiring and plumbing—as the tenant made progress he could be given funds to continue, could own the pride of having improved his housing in part through his own efforts.

So power to these poor neighborhoods still speaks to conservative principles, for it recognizes that a man must have the opportunity to work out his own destiny, or he will never know the dimensions of himself, he will be alienated from any sense of whether he is acting for good or evil. It goes further. Power to all neighborhoods recognizes that we cannot work at our destiny without a contest—that most specific neighborhood which welcomes or rejects our effort, and so gives a mirror to the value of our striving, and the distortion of our prejudice. Perhaps it even recognizes the deepest of conservative principles—that a man has a right to live his life in such a way that he may know if he is dying in a state of grace. Our lives, directed by abstract outside forces, have lost that possibility most of all. It is a notion on which to hit the campaign trail.

Which is where we go now—into the campaign: to talk in the days ahead of what power to the neighborhoods will mean. We will go down the steps of the position papers and talk of jobs and housing and welfare, of education, municipal unions and law and order, finance, the names of laws, the statistics of the budget, the problems of traffic and transportation. There will be a paucity of metaphor and a taste of stale saliva to the debates, for voters are hard-working people who trust the plain more than the poetic. How then can Mailer and Breslin, two writers with reputations notorious enough for four, ever hope to convince the voting hand of the electorate? What would they do if, miracle of political explosions, they were to win?

Well, they might cry like Mario Procaccino, for they would never have a good time again; but they would serve, they would learn on the job, they would conduct their education in public. They would be obliged to. And indeed the supposition could remain that they might even do well, better than the men before them. How else could they have the confidence to run? They might either have supposed that the Lord was not dead but behind them or they must have felt such guilt about the years of their lives that only the long running duties of office could satisfy the list of their dues.

As for the fact that they were literary men—that might be the first asset of all. They would know how to talk to the people— they would be forced to govern by the fine art of the voice. Exposed by their own confession as amateurs they might even attract the skill of the city to their service, for the community would be forced to swim in full recognition of the depth of the soup. And best of all, what a tentative confidence would reign in the eye of New York that her literary men, used to dealing with the proportions of worlds hitherto created only in the mind, might now have a sensitive nose for the balances and the battles, the tugs, the pushing, the heaves of that city whose declaration of new birth was implicit in the extraordinary fact that *him,* Mailer! and *him,* Breslin! had been voted in.

Sweet Sunday, dear friends, and take a chance. We are out on the lottery of the years.

RUNNING OTHER PEOPLE'S LIVES

JIMMY BRESLIN

The City Politic
New York, April 21, 1969

The trouble is everywhere. It is on the streets and in the apart-
ment-house elevators and on television and in hospital emergency
rooms, and anywhere you go and anything you do, even the simple
business of stopping at a friend's house for a drink on Saturday
night, brings you across these pieces of trouble in the city of
New York in 1969.

The flatbed truck in the traffic in front of us swayed along
Atlantic Avenue in Brooklyn, at the part where the Long Island
Rail Road tracks climb out of the rutted street and turn into an
El. Garbage is in piles at the foot of the El pillars and abandoned
cars line the curbs. Gas stations and commercial laundries, their
fronts cloaked in steam, break up the rows of collapsing brownstones and firetrap frame tenements. Many of the windows of
the houses are broken. The holes have been stuffed with rags
against the last cold of the winter.

The flatbed truck was loaded with wooden packing crates. They
were six feet high and were lashed down by thick chains. At a
red light, when we came up behind the truck, we could read the
stenciled addresses on the crates.

TO: USOM
BANGKOK, THAILAND

USOM is the United States Operations Mission, and it is the
civilian phase of the military effort in Southeast Asia.

The light changed and the truck started up. It had come through

East New York and Brownsville, where children set fires in the night in the empty buildings. Now the truck was going past Nostrand Avenue and Bedford and Clinton and Lafayette and the other streets of the Bedford-Stuyvesant. A woman I knew named Virginia lived on Lafayette. In the summer, her fourteen-year-old nephew came up from North Carolina to stay with her. She sent him to the store one afternoon. She heard noises from the street and looked out her second-floor window. A pack of neighborhood kids were around her nephew. Virginia yelled down at them. With a shout the kids fell on her nephew and one of them put a knife into the nephew and the kids ran down the block and Virginia screamed while she watched her nephew die on the sidewalk.

The truck came past these streets of the Bedford-Stuyvesant, this sprawling section which fights to survive and has the power, if it does not survive, to cut the legs off the city without anybody realizing it. The flatbed truck with its six-foot-high crates for Bangkok, Thailand, kept running through the streets of Brooklyn and down to the docks, and a little bit more of the city dripped away on a freighter going to Asia.

We turned off at Hicks Street, in Brooklyn Heights, and went to John Doar's house for a drink. John Doar is the president of the Board of Education. Now, we have had many presidents on this board. Mrs. Rose Shapiro was the last president. She is a woman who belongs in a knitting shop. John Doar is different. He was in the business of human rights seven and ten years ago in the South, when anybody was eligible to get hurt and people put a lead pipe or a gun where their temper was. But now, in New York, Doar feels the danger is invisible and impersonal, but much more serious to many more people. All of us, perhaps.

"I've been in Albany for the last week," he was saying.

"How did it go?" he was asked.

"I don't know," he said. "You've got the same old thing. You've got white people standing around and trying to decide things for a school system that is 52 per cent black and Puerto Rican. The political constituency of the schools is one thing. White people and unions. But the parents and students in the school system are black and Puerto Rican."

"What do they want to do in Albany?"

"There's talk of replacing us with a three- or five-man paid commission appointed by the mayor and passed on the City Council. Shanker wants to get rid of this board, that's for sure. Galamison and myself. Then this new commission would hire a replacement for Bernie Donovan as superintendent."

"Where will that leave anything?"

"Locally elected school boards is the heart of decentralization and that's what we have been working on. But now it looks like they might give Shanker what he wants."

"What kind of help can you get?"

"I don't know. I could use some political leaders, I guess."

The drink turned sour. John Doar walking through hallways in Albany to see politicians who run the business of the city of New York; white politicians pressured by Albert Shanker and his trade union associates, men who feel their responsibility to the city begins and ends with road building.

There are 1.1 million students in the New York City school system. The 1968–69 school year has been a wound. White people borrow to get children into private schools. The competition for space in the few public high schools that work is incredible. There are six thousand applications for Bronx Science next fall. The number of non-white students in the lower grades of grammar school is so much higher than 52 per cent that projections leave you shaken.

For the beginning of a start toward a solution, the decision is to come from such as Perry Duryea, who lives in Montauk Point; Earl Brydges of Niagara Falls; and John Marchi, who is a product of the times when Staten Island was farther away from New York than Niagara. And the major lobby is led by Albert Shanker, who lives in Pearl River.

They meet in Albany and discuss their own interests. The schools and the pupils are in places they never see, East New York and the South Bronx. These are the neighborhoods John Doar knows of. And he knows that if you let the education system continue, let it keep sending a few hundred thousand helplessly uneducated kids into the flow of the city each year, there can be only one result.

"They'll destroy the city and when you destroy the city, you're starting to destroy the country," John Doar was saying.

On the drive back to Queens, we passed a school in the Ocean Hill-Brownsville district. One of the teachers in the school was telling me the other day about a pigeon who flew into his fourth-grade classroom. The kids jumped up. The teacher said that maybe the class could make a pet out of the pigeon. One of the kids started tiptoeing toward the bird. "No, let's kill him," the kid said.

I RUN TO WIN

JIMMY BRESLIN

New York, May 5, 1969

Some time ago, I made a basic decision about the way in which I was going to live the little of life available to me. The idea was to place myself in the presence of only those people who give off the warm, friendly vibrations which soothe the coating on my nerves. Life never was long enough to provide time for enemies. Nor is it long enough for people who bore me, or for me to stand around boring and antagonizing others, or for all of us, the others and me, to get into these half-friendly, half-sour fender-bumpings of egos and personalities and ideas, a process which turns a day into a contest when it really should be a series of hours serving your pleasure.

So I gave up jobs which made me uncomfortable. I wrote a book and sold it for a movie without seeing one person involved. I began avoiding any bar or restaurant where there was the slightest chance of people becoming picky and arguing. I reduced conversation, even on the telephone, to the people I like and who like me. One night, my wife had a group of people for dinner and I was not sure of the vibrations around me at the table so I said, "Excuse me, I have to go to bed. I have paresis." It worked wonderfully. I began to do things like this all the time and I wound up doing only what I liked when I liked doing it and always with the people I liked and who liked me.

"Do you want to go out to dinner tonight?" my wife asked me.
"Where?" I said.

"Well, I don't know. We'll go with my sister and her husband."

"Oh, I don't know," I said. "I don't think he had a good time with us last week and he might be a little cold tonight. I'm afraid he might strip my nerves. I'd rather just stay home."

"All right," she said.

So we stayed home. During the night I said hello on the telephone to Jerry Finkelstein, Jack O'Neill, Burton Roberts, and Thomas Rand. We all talked nice to each other and I could feel the coating on my nerves being stroked and soothed. On Sunday I went into the office in my house and I spoke to nobody and saw nobody all day. So it was one of the most terrific weekends.

The first phone call on Monday morning was at seven o'clock.

"He's asleep," I heard my wife mumble.

"Wake him up?" she mumbled.

She kicked me and I reached over for the phone.

"Somebody named Joe Ferris," she said. "He needs your correct voting registration for the petitions. *What* petitions?"

I sat up in bed, with the phone in one hand and my head against the wall and my eyes closed.

"What petitions?" my wife said again.

I knew what petitions Joe Ferris was talking about. I knew about them, but I never thought it would come to the point of an early morning phone call about them. You see, when it started, I was only in this thing for pleasant conversation with nice people.

"Hello," I said to Joe Ferris. I was afraid he would send cold waves through the phone.

"I've got to be at the printer with the petitions this morning," Joe Ferris said. "So what I need is the exact way your name and address appears on the voting rolls. We don't want to have any petitions thrown out on a technicality. Because they're going to be looking for mistakes. Particularly when they see how much support you and Norman are going to get. That's all I've been hearing around town. You and Norman. I think you've got a tremendous chance."

"I'll get the information and call you back," I said to Joe Ferris. He gave me his phone number and I told him I was writing it down, but I wasn't. Maybe if I forgot his number and never called him back, he wouldn't bother to call me any more.

"What petitions?" my wife said when I hung up.

"Nothing," I said. I put my face in the pillow. Well, to tell you what happened, I really don't know what happened, but I was in a place called the Abbey Tavern on Third Avenue and Twenty-sixth Street at four o'clock one afternoon, when it was empty and I wouldn't have to talk to anybody I didn't know, and Jack Newfield came in. Jack Newfield is a political writer. He writes for *The Village Voice* and *Life* magazine and he does books and we got to know and like each other during the Bobby Kennedy campaigns last spring. Anyway, I'm having coffee with Jack Newfield and he says, "Did you hear me on the radio the other night? I endorsed you. I endorsed Norman Mailer for mayor and you for president of the City Council in the Democratic primary." I did two things. I laughed. Then I sipped the coffee. While I did it, I was saying to myself, "Why is Mailer on the top of the ticket?"

And a couple of days later, I had lunch in Limerick's, on Second Avenue and Thirty-second Street, and here was Newfield and Gloria Steinem, and she likes me and I like her, and Peter Maas, and he is all right with me, too, and we got to talking some more and they kept saying Norman Mailer and I should run in the Democratic primary and finally I said, "Has anybody talked to Norman?"

"No, not recently," Gloria said.

"Give me a dime," I said.

I went to the phone and called Norman. While I was dialing, I began to compromise myself. Norman went to college, I thought. *Maybe it's only right that he's the mayor and I'm the president of the City Council. But that's the only reason. He has a Harvard diploma. On ability, I should be mayor.*

"Norman?"

"Jimmy, how are you?"

"Norman, let's run."

"I know, they spoke to me. But I have to clean up some business first. I think we could make a great team. Now here's what I'm doing. I'm going to Provincetown for a week to think this over.

Maybe we can get together for a night before I go. Then when I come back, we can make up our minds."

"All right," I said.

So two nights later there were about forty people in the top floor of Mailer's house in Brooklyn Heights. They were talking about the terrible condition the city was in, and of the incredible group of candidates the Democrats had in the mayoralty primary, which is on June 17. Norman Mailer began to talk about the right and the left mixing their flames together and forming a great coalition of orange flame with a hot center and I looked out the window at the harbor, down at a brightly lit freighter sitting in the black water under the window, and I was uneasy about Mailer's political theories. I was uncertain of the vibrations. Then I turned around and said something about there being nine candidates for mayor and if New York tradition was upheld, the one who got in front in the race would be indicted. When I saw Norman Mailer laughing at what I said, I decided that he was very smart at politics. When I saw the others laugh, I felt my nerves purring.

Then he began to talk casually, as if everybody knew it and had been discussing it for weeks, about there being no such thing as integration and that the only way things could improve would be with a black community governing itself. "We need a black mayor," Mailer said. "I'll be the white mayor and they have to elect a black mayor for themselves. Just give them the money and the power and let them run themselves. We have no right to talk to these people any more. We lost that a long time ago. They don't want us. The only thing white people have done for the blacks is betray them."

There hasn't been a person with the ability to say this in my time in this city. I began to think a little harder about the prospects of Mailer and me running the city.

We had another night at Mailer's, with a smaller group, and he brought up the idea of a "Sweet Sunday," one day a month in which everything in the city is brought to a halt so human beings can rest and talk to each other and the air can purify itself. When he got onto the idea of New York taking the steps to become a state, he had me all the way. The business of running this city is done by lobster peddlers from Montauk and old Republicans from Niagara Falls and some Midwesterners-come-to-Washington-with-great-old-Dick such as the preposterous George Romney. I didn't know what would come out of these couple of nights, but I knew we had talked about more things than most of these people running in the Democratic primary had thought of in their lives.

Mailer was leaving for Provincetown the next morning, and we agreed to talk on the phone in a few days.

I stayed around the city and somewhere in here I had a drink with Hugh Carey. He is a congressman from Brooklyn and he is listed as a candidate for mayor. I told Carey I was proud the way he turned down a chance to make a lot of headlines with an investigation into the case of Willie Smith, a poverty worker in New York who had been convicted of great crimes in the newspapers. Carey announced that Willie Smith not only was clear, but also was doing a fine job for the poor. Endorsing the poor is not a very good way of getting votes these days. So I thanked Carey.

"What did you want me to do?" Hugh Carey said.

"Well, I just wanted you to know," I said.

"I wish to God I'd been right on the war when I should have been," he said. He had, from 1965 until only a short time ago, been a Brooklyn Irish Catholic Hawk, of which there are no talons sharper. But now he could look at you over a drink and tell you openly that he had been wrong. "It's the only thing in my life I'm ashamed of," he said. "And I'm going to go in and tell every mother in this city that I was wrong and that we're wasting their sons."

Pretty good, I thought. Let's have another drink.

"How's it look for you?" I asked.

"Well, it's up to The Wag," he said.

"The Wag?" I said.

"The Wag. Bob Wagner."

"What the hell has he got to do with it?"

"Look, if he comes back and runs and I can get on the ticket with him, then in a year he'll run for the Senate against Goodell and I can take over the city and we'll start putting the type of people in . . ."

Well, I told him then what I'm putting down here now. If Robert Wagner, who spent twelve years in City Hall as the representative of everybody in New York except the people who had to live in the city while he let it creak and sag, if this dumpy, narrow man named Robert Wagner, by merely considering stepping back into politics, could have a Hugh Carey thinking about running on the ticket below him, then there was something I didn't like about Hugh Carey. Not as a guy, but as a politician who would run a city which is as wounded and tormented as New York.

You see, the condition of the city of New York at this time reminds me of the middleweight champion fight between the late Marcel Cerdan and Tony Zale. Zale was old and doing it from memory and Cerdan was a bustling, sort of classy alley fighter and Cerdan went to the body in the first round and never brought his punches up. At the start of each round, when you looked at Zale's face, you saw only this proud, fierce man. There were no marks to show what was happening. But Tony Zale was coming apart from the punches that did not leave any marks and at the end of the eleventh round Tony was along the ropes and Cerdan stepped back and Tony crumbled and he was on the floor, looking out into the night air, his face unmarked, his body dead, his career gone. In New York today, the face of the city, Manhattan, is proud and glittering. But Manhattan is not the city. New York really is a sprawl of neighborhoods which pile into one another. And it is down in the neighborhoods, down in the schools that are in the neighborhoods, where this city is cut and slashed and bleeding from someplace deep inside. The South Bronx is gone. East New York and Brownsville are gone. Jamaica is up for grabs. The largest public education system in the world may be gone already. The air we breathe is so bad that on a warm day the city is a big Donora. In Manhattan, the lights seem brighter and the theatre crowds swirl through the streets and the girls swing in and out of office buildings in packs and it is all splendor and nobody sees the body punches that are going to make the city sag to its knees one day so very soon. The last thing, then, that New York can afford at this time is a politician thinking in normal politicians'

terms. The city is beyond that. The city of New York either gets
an imagination, or the city dies.

A day or so after seeing Carey, I came into Toots Shor's on the
late side of the afternoon, when the place is between-shifts empty.
Paul Screvane was finishing lunch. He was sitting with Shor. I tried
a cautious drink. The vibrations among the three of us were all
right. I settled down to talk with them. For weeks, Screvane had
wanted to announce his candidacy for mayor. But he had been
waiting until he heard what Wagner was going to do.

"Why wait?" I said.

"Well, because all the financial support I normally would get
would go to Wagner," Screvane said.

"Well, what's he going to do?" I asked.

"I've called him for a week. I'm waiting to hear from him right
now," Screvane said. "He's next door in the 21 Club. He knows
I'm here. I'll just wait."

Screvane waited. He waited while Wagner came out of the 21,
walked slowly down the sidewalk to Shor's, stopped and chatted
with somebody in front of Shor's, nodded to Shor's doorman, probably looked through the doors and saw Screvane inside, and then
ambled off.

"That's a real nice guy," I said to Screvane.

He said nothing. A few minutes later, the headwaiter handed him
the phone. Screvane came back muttering, "Wagner just had his
secretary call me. 'Where will you be at seven and at nine tonight
in case Mr. Wagner wants to get in touch with you?' How do you
like that?"

"Why don't you just say the hell with this guy and go ahead
and announce you're in it?" I said.

Shor slapped his hand on the table. "Go ahead," he said.

"The hell with it," Screvane said. He got up and went to the
phone. He came back smiling. "All right, I called my secretary
and told her to start calling the papers and television for a press
conference tomorrow morning at eleven o'clock."

"Terrific," I said.

"Are you going to be there?" Screvane said.

"Absolutely," I said.

Well, what happened was, I walked out of the place feeling so good about Paul Screvane standing up and not letting somebody push him around, and this is the way it should be because Screvane is a tough, extremely competent man and nobody should try to take advantage of him. Well, I felt so good about all of this that two hours later I called up Norman Mailer and I said, "Norman, the hell with it. Let's make up our minds right now."

"We're doing it," he said.

The Village Voice promptly came out with pictures of Mailer and myself on the front page. The type underneath the pictures said that we were "thinking" of running for office.

I don't know about the rest of the paper's circulation, but I know of two people who looked at the front page very closely.

One was Paul Screvane.

The other was my wife. "This is a joke, of course," she said.

"Oh, sure," I said.

"Well, if you're that sick for publicity," she said.

There were a couple of calls at the house in the next day or so and my wife handled them, although not too well. "The publicity stunt is tying up our phones," she said. "I don't want these phones tied up. I have real estate people calling me from the Hamptons. We're going away on a vacation this year. We haven't had one in three years."

"Uh huh," I said. I was looking over the messages she had taken during the day. One was from Gloria Steinem. I knew what that was about. She had a meeting scheduled with some good, young Puerto Rican guys who were interested in politics and wanted to see what Mailer and I looked like. There would be no warm, friendly vibrations from them. These guys would snarl and snap a little, particularly if I said something stupid. So what? I'd learn something from them while I was at it.

So now here we come to this one morning, and this is how I got into what I am into, and I am in bed with my face in the pillows and I am trying very hard to forget Joe Ferris' phone number, and the phone rings again and my wife answers it.

"Yes," she says.

"Oh, I don't know if he's doing that."

"You know that he's doing that? How do you know?"

"Gloria Steinem said *what?"*

"You're going to write a *story?* Here, you better talk to him."

She handed me the phone. "This is Sarah Davidson from the Boston *Globe* and she is going to write a nice big story for the first page about you and Mailer running for office. Tell her to make sure she puts in that you're a dirty bastard."

I take the phone and I say hello to Sarah Davidson. A gentle, restrained, cautious politician's hello.

"Sarah, dear, how are you, baby? When are we going to get together for a drink?"

Ten minutes later, the call that makes the whole thing official comes.

"Gabe Pressman," my wife muttered.

"Oh, he's just a friend of mine, you know," I said.

"Hello, Gabe, how are you, baby?" I said.

"Running? Well, we *have* been talking about it. You know what I mean, Gabe. How many times did we speak about this over a drink? You know how thin the talent is in this city. Look at the names. Scheuer. He says he's going to spend a million dollars for his primary campaign. Well, let me tell you, Gabe. Scheuer has to spend a million-two, just to get known in his own *neighborhood.* And look at these other guys. Mario Procaccino. How do you like it? How do you like the Democratic Party going with Mario Procaccino for mayor in an election? Mario for waiter, yes. For mayor? Good Lord. And the guys they got running in my column, the City Council president, hell, we can't afford to have a thing like this.

"Wagner? Forget Wagner. He's an old man. He won't win a primary."

"Shut up," my wife said.

I held the phone away. "Hey, what are you telling me to shut up for?"

"I said shut up," she said.

I went back to the phone. "Lindsay? Gabe, you know better

than I do that Lindsay came into this city like a commuter. He doesn't . . ."

"Shut up," she said again.

"What do you mean, shut up?" I said.

"Because he's going to put down what you say and make you sound like a sour dope."

"What do you mean? Gabe and I are good friends."

"You're not supposed to give long answers to a reporter," she said. "You're going to make yourself look like a jerk and the whole family is going to suffer because of it."

I'm holding the phone against the pillow so Gabe Pressman won't hear.

"Hey, this is a friend of mine calling up. It isn't like an interview. This is personal."

"No it isn't. He'll put down everything you say. He's unethical."

"What do you mean he's unethical? Gabe Pressman is not. He's a friend."

"Hey," she said, "all reporters are unethical. Who knows better than you? You wrote the book."

I made a date to meet Pressman and a camera crew at noon. When I hung up, the phone rang immediately. It was Alice Krakauer, who is handling the scheduling for our college appearances. She told me to write down a date for City College. While I was doing this, my wife got up, got dressed and went out of the bedroom. She called up to me from the first door. "I'm going with my sister to look at houses. We'll be back tomorrow. When I come back, if the phone rings once with this business, I'll have to ask you to leave."

She left. I got up and started for the subway. At the newsstand, the woman said, "Don't I see your picture some place? Are you running for something?"

I stood there and thought for a moment. Thought very deeply. *Newsstand Dealer for Mailer and Breslin!* My right hand shot out so fast the woman nearly fell over backward.

"Hi, I'm Jimmy Breslin," I said to her.

AND FURTHERMORE, I PROMISE . . .

JIMMY BRESLIN

The City Politic
New York, June 16, 1969

It must be 10:30 at night now, and the small noises, the chair creaking, a man knocking his pipe into a tin ashtray, come right through me. I am standing in this hot, narrow room one flight over a Chinese restaurant on Eighty-seventh Street and Broadway. The room is the headquarters of a Reform Democratic club and they are interviewing candidates in the Democratic primary. Harrison Goldin, who is running for controller, has just answered questions and left. His wife is with him. She is wearing a huge button which says, GOLDIN—THE YOUNG DYNAMO. Myself, if I had my way, I'd have my people wear big buttons saying, BRESLIN SMIRKS AT BULL LEA. Now, with Goldin gone, I stand behind the table at the front of the room and face the people sitting on folding chairs. Somewhere I lost the schedule sheet with the proper name of the club and the two leaders I'm supposed to acknowledge, so when one of the club leaders introduces me, I make believe I am saying his name and the name of the club. While I mumble, the night outside comes through the windows at my back. A humid night with the air so thick that if you are in it for a period of hours, you find your teeth continually grinding against a coating of grit. It is a loud night, too. Two fags are standing down on the sidewalk and screaming at each other through the roar of the diesel buses and the squeal of cars jumping away from a red light. And over it all is the main sound of the city of New York, the persistent *rump rump rump* that comes from somewhere and is turning us into a people with the most defective hearing in the nation. But the small noises get to me the most when I am tired and now I am soaked with sweat and I have to close my eyes when I try to think and somebody swivels around in a chair in the front row and the little noises send my shoulder blades at each other.

It is a girl standing up to ask a question. She is about twenty-five, with dark hair and wearing something gray. I can't tell much more than this. I'm looking only at her face and not even seeing that so well because I'm trying to concentrate on what she is saying. Anybody who says Norman Mailer and James Breslin are in this campaign so they can write books is ignorant of both our motives and of the technique of writing. When you are a candidate, your only interest is getting yourself and what you say across to people. You are not absorbing the little details that should flood through anything you write. At the end of some of the nights of this campaign I find myself unable to remember one place I have been since noon.

Now the girl in the front row of this club upstairs from the Chinese restaurant stands up and next to her a man shuffles some papers and I cringe, and the girl says, "Well, now, you were saying about this community control . . ."

There is a loud whine. It's a dog. I glance down. The girl in gray has a dog on a leash. Some kind of a black dog and he is twisting around on the leash and moaning.

The girl starts talking again. "Well, you see . . ."

The dog lets out a loud wail.

I'm waiting for the guy next to me, the club leader, to tell the girl to get the dog the hell out of the room. But he doesn't say anything. He stands there and the girl stands there and the freaking dog opens his mouth and lets out a long wolf howl.

I want to say something to this girl. I want to say something to her so badly that, to be sure I don't, I put my tongue between my teeth and clamp down on it.

Then I say, "Excuse me, miss, but before we go any further, does the dog have his shots?"

I swing my head around the room. Everybody is laughing. Very good. This puts it on a nice footing.

"Now, the question, miss?" I say.

"Yes, he has his shots," she says. She says it pointedly. "And now . . ."

The dog moans again. Nobody moves, and she just stands there until the dog stops moaning. *Beautiful,* I say to myself.

She keeps talking. She talks for two, maybe three straight minutes. The substance of what she is saying is simple. She is saying that I am a dope.

"Would you please ask a question instead of making a statement?" I say to her.

"Never mind," she says. She continues on with her attack. I look at the guy next to me, the club leader. Isn't he supposed to cut off somebody like this? He doesn't do it. I'm standing in front of this audience like a defendant and the girl is looking at me with a fire in her eyes. It is there really for some other guy, but she is directing it all at me and she won't stop talking and finally, in a shout, I say:

"Thank *you,* miss!"

That shuts her up and she sits down. I compliment myself. *Nice Jimmy, you didn't say a bad word to the girl.*

A small bald man gets up. "I saw you on the television and you said something about Puerto Ricans not wanting to be with blacks and you agreeing with that or something. Could you tell me just what you said?"

I jump at him. "I said this," I say. My eyes flick over the audience and I see a black woman in the last row. So I look at the man who asked me the question, but I'm really watching the black woman in the back. I want to see how she reacts to what I say. If there is anything I want to do, I want to say everything blunt and right about the color situation which has this town living in fear.

"Look," I say, "if there is one thing we have learned in this campaign it is this: every time a white newsman puts down 'blacks and Puerto Ricans' or 'Puerto Ricans and blacks,' the minute he gets to the 'and' the ones who know they are going to be mentioned next go into a burn. You see, we have found the divisions between blacks and Puerto Ricans are wider and deeper, if that's possible, than the divisions between blacks and whites."

The black woman in the back of the room is nodding vigorously. *Sure I'm right,* I say to myself.

"Look," I call out to the whole room, "any white man who comes here and tells you he has a special relationship with the black people is a liar. No white man has a relationship with the blacks any more. We've betrayed them too much. They don't believe us any more. Any Puerto Rican who comes in here and says he has a special relationship with the blacks is a liar. The race problem in this city is that bad. Let's get out in the open and talk about it. Maybe we can ventilate it. But don't let anybody come in here and lie."

The black woman is nodding. Very good. Hell, real good. The rest of them clap. The leader is up saying thank you and I shake hands with him and start up the aisle. I don't even look at the girl with the dog. I see Jim Scheuer. Forget him. He is in the process of spending more money for less votes than any candidate in the history of this city. And the crack about any Puerto Rican trying to say he has a special relationship with the blacks was aimed at Herman Badillo. I barely know Herman Badillo. He is nice when you meet him, but there is so much cold ambition it shows. And I remember when Tom Johnson and Adam Walinsky were around New York trying to do some sensible business for Bobby Kennedy. They always said, "Herman Badillo doesn't even have black people in his office in the Bronx. Forget him."

I come up the aisle with the eyes on the black woman and she is still nodding. Terrific, I say to myself. I come alongside her and I want to give her a big smile. The woman keeps nodding. She is nodding because she is sitting at a table and sewing the hem on a skirt.

Other times the little details around you in the campaign have been very clear. On a Sunday afternoon, the six of us running for City Council president stood behind these light brown lecterns in a CBS studio on West Fifty-seventh Street and took turns answering questions on a one-hour show which was billed as a television debate.

The answers hit the fifty-first-state idea right away. In any political meeting in this city, the first questions asked of all candidates is about the chances for the city of New York becoming a state. As none of these other politicians ever had the sense to advance what is a completely natural idea, they automatically must be against it. I defend the idea. I look into the camera, pretend I'm talking to two people in a living room somewhere, and point out that the idea is not only possible, but is inevitable. I tell them to look out for John Lindsay trying it in his campaign this fall.

Then I say, "Look, this idea isn't something Norman Mailer and James Breslin thought up just for a campaign. This is a solid idea. Why, the first man to speak of it in this state was Alfred E. Smith."

I was through. Out of the corner of my right eye I could see Frank Smith, who was next to me, finishing a scribbled note on a legal pad.

"Mr. Smith," Jim Jensen, the moderator, said.

"Well," Smith said, "Mr. Breslin mentioned Alfred E. Smith as a great leader of this city, and I think New York once again has another Smith who is providing leadership in the City Council."

"How the hell can he say a thing like that without laughing?" I said to myself. "Unless . . ." A black feeling ran through me. The feeling was verified later that night when I got home and I called a friend of mine, Louis Wallach, who is a judge in Queens. "Don't laugh," Lou said. "People like a thing like that. You see, you never can take anything for granted in this business. Look at me. When I ran for State Assembly, people used to vote for me because they thought I was from Wallach stores. Good clothes, he must be a nice guy. So I'll vote for him."

The next day, Sam Brown, who ran the student operation for Gene McCarthy, was telling me, "What place are you on the ballot? Third down? That's not too good. The first spot usually means 10 per cent more of the vote. People just pull the thing and get out. Unless you're in an area with people who are quite short, and maybe their first look won't be up that high."

I choked. It had been, by then, forty days since Norman Mailer and I started out on this time-chewing, money-burning, brain-chipping version of a political campaign. Forty days of ideas and trying to sell them, forty days of trying to speak the English language while the four words that would make the fine phrase slipped from mind and left you with drivel, forty days of pleading with people to please speak about the white fear of black crime and the black hatred of white ignorance and indifference, forty days of this; and now the experts tell you that what really is needed for you, third-spot-on-the-ballot Breslin, is an electorate made up of jockeys.

I think that was the hardest part of the whole campaign to accept: the fact that, yes, just as people always have said, politics is a business where imbeciles thrive because of the total indifference of people.

I could take anything else in this campaign. The hot Sunday afternoon at Gaelic Park, in the Bronx, for example. They had me scheduled to be there at 3:30, before the Irish hurling game was to start. There were to be six thousand Irishmen in the stands. Six thousand Irish-Americans who have read my very great pieces about the Irish in America.

"I don't think so," I said to Joe Flaherty.

"Oh, you got to be there," he said.

So we pull up at Gaelic Park and Frankie Durkin is standing at the gate. When he sees me, his face goes into mourning. "All right, James," he says, "if you feel you must."

He leads me inside.

"Scum!"

"Will you look at the fat bum!"

"Bring him over here so I can hit him!"

I look around. Hanging out the open windows of the packed Gaelic Park Bar is this solid row of flat, red-cheeked faces. All of them have short-cropped hair. The faces stick out of white shirts and business ties. They are my people and they are waiting for me. They are waiting to beat the hell out of me.

We go across the field and I hear these voices squalling at my back. "Somebody knock his brains out, if the poor bastard has any." At the gate leading to the special box for political celebrities, a short guy with dark glasses stepped up. He put a hand on Frankie Durkin's shoulder.

"They don't want him in, thank you."

Frankie looked at me. "I wanted to go home anyway," I said. I started back across the field. A big gray-haired priest looked at me and turned to the man with him and said. "Hmpf. He's wearin' a black suit. 'Twill take more than a black suit to save him."

Back outside, I got into the car and settled down for a long wait. One of the tires, of course, had been punctured while we were inside.

Norman Mailer and I were talking about this while we were walking along Fifth Avenue one hot afternoon. "How are you?" we kept saying to people and shaking their hands. Between people, Norman said, "I go into the synagogues and they look to destroy me. But they love you. So we'll switch. I'll play your people and you play mine."

I felt good. The idea could work, particularly in Queens. So I'm walking along, shaking hands, saying hello and being very careful of what I'm saying in front of the reporters with us. (Six months ago I was writing for the *Post* and the candidates had to watch what they said in front of *me*.) After much pain, Norman and I have found that Edward Katcher of the *Post* and Clayton Knowles and William Farrell of the *Times* are the only newsmen in New York who wrote of us and had the facts correct and in proper perspective. The rest of them are a pack of $240-a-week shipwrecks. Mayor Daley was right. Some of the bastards *do* belong in jail.

Well, I'm walking along like this and my chest is coming out and the "How are you?" is rolling off my tongue at the good people and here comes James Breslin, political candidate, and they all know me on the street and, hell, I may get elected.

"Mr. Breslin!"

A woman with sunglasses pushes through and holds out her hand to me.

"Oh, I'm so glad to meet you. I read your column in the paper every day. Are you covering a story here?"

SPEECH AT THE JOHN JAY COLLEGE OF CRIMINAL JUSTICE

NORMAN MAILER AND JIMMY BRESLIN

May 6, 1969

JIMMY BRESLIN

Good day to you. I'd like the record to state that I'm here without a lawyer. You know, once I was well liked by the police department, when the man who put this building together was Commissioner Mike Murphy. I wrote a column, and he had it reproduced and tacked on the wall in every precinct in the city. And then we got into periods following that where the traffic men would invite me to cross the street and then wave them on and step back and root for a fast Oldsmobile.

As for my credentials to be here, what can I tell you? I had a cousin who was killed on this job. I grew up in a house with an uncle who was first grade. He was nearly killed on the job too. You see, there was this girl friend he had, and he also had a wife who was suspicious. One day he left the house to go to Bergen Street in the car, and his suspicious wife followed him in another car. At Bergen Street the uncle picked up his girl friend. That was the extent of his duties at Bergen Street, and they were apparently heading for some sort of an outing at the Hotel St. George, when my uncle's wife came up behind them in the car and smashed into them. Her intent was to effect a thing known as homicide. My uncle jumped out and he screamed at her, "What are you, crazy? This broad's my informant."

Well, I come here to fight with the professor. I thought there would be a sergeant teaching the class—you got a guy with a beard. I don't come here as a genius; that's been well established early in my life. I think when the question period comes, I'll be able to learn something from you people, which is good, too, because you're going to get a lot of I-don't-knows from me. But I also have some views on policemen in this city which I'd like to express; but before I express them, I did look down and see that the chairs were bolted to the floor, and that's going to help. Because the way I see the city, and the way Mr. Mailer sees the city, when I'm mentioning what we're doing about it, is that that there will be no more New York Police Department as we now know it. Our idea is to have this city become a state, have the various sections of this city become cities right inside the state, and let them run their own police. Let's get the wisdom of the neighborhoods, give them the power, and let them run it. I say the plan is far better from a police viewpoint than the way we're going, because in my estimation policemen today are being used. The police get all the mistakes of all the people who are supposed to be more important and smarter than us. You've got all the mistakes—you're asked to go out and take care of them, patch up holes made in forty years of history by congressmen from New York who sat still while federal housing bills were being passed that didn't help us. They sat still while House Agricultural Committees forced a migration from the South into our cities. You're being asked to pay for the actions of union leaders who didn't do a thing for ghetto areas of this city and have kept people jobless, and when they're jobless, they look to do things. You're being asked to pay for a Board of Education which sat at 110 Livingston Street and kept everybody in the city illiterate, particularly in the areas you worry about most. And you're being asked to pay for the mistakes of white politicians who walked around and never even knew one black person and made the decisions which affected their lives and which caused an awful lot of the rancidness that's now in everyone's mouth over this situation. Now they created the problems. Now they turn to you, the policemen of the city of New York, and say "You go out and handle them." In my estimation, it's a disgrace. As usual, it comes down to us—give it to the fellow on the bottom, let him handle the problem.

They send people into Harlem and Bedford-Stuyvesant or Browns-

ville or East New York—white policemen. I think it's insanity, it's
an expression of enormous ignorance. Those days are gone where
white people can rule the black neighborhoods. I think that the
time also should be gone that we should ask a white person to
go in there. A fellow who is a cop with a wife and three children,
he comes into the city eight hours a day, and you send him into
an area where he's disliked and despised. It produces a volatile situation—I don't think that makes any sense at all. I think we're asking
too much of our fellows on that.

Now this city is in trouble, and the main thing is that we need
respect for law and its officers. But black people never again
will respect law under the present conditions. They just won't
respect this law, and they're not going to respect the people who
are instruments of it. That's been proven. Just walk around any
block, I mean you walk down Sumner Avenue in Brooklyn, you
hear what they say behind your backs. This is insanity if you let
it go on. And out of it you get the fear and you get the quick
reactions which shouldn't be there.

What we feel, and what I feel the problem is, people in these
neighborhoods, in all neighborhoods, have got to run their own
schools and their own police. You've got Boys High School, it's
four blocks from the 79th. I think Boys High School would make
an excellent feeder for the 79th Precinct. I don't think Massapequa,
Long Island, is a good feeder for the 79th Precinct. I think if you
had police cadet training starting in high school, instead of these
gym classes they have, they'd be able to find their own supply of
policemen for those areas, and they could run their own police departments. Certainly, I think the neighborhood would be in a lot
better shape law-wise than it is now.

Let me tell you what you're up against on figures. They tell you
to go in there and take care of this matter. You're ours, we love
you. There're candidates who come around, "God bless you, boys,
you're our line between us and doom." They don't tell you what
you're up against in figures. We'll take one high school in this city—
Benjamin Franklin High School. Next month 1000 high school tran-
scripts are going to be received there from kids supposed to come
into school in September. In September only 700 of these kids

show up. Right away, you got 300 kids out running on the streets. I don't have to tell you what that means. After four years, of these 700 who start in Benjamin Franklin, 75 of them wind up with academic diplomas. Three hundred graduate—they're given some certificate of attendance. A certificate of attendance at Benjamin Franklin High School normally entitles a kid to push junk—it has no meaning whatsoever. In other figures, in another way, 75 out of a thousand, out of an original list of a thousand, are at the end of four years hopefully citizens. This means 925 kids running around streets without an education, without any hope, with a very low reading level. Some don't speak English, and they wind up as your problem. But you're told go up there and handle it, and the Board of Education is sitting there every day creating criminals for you.

So I think we have to decentralize the situation. Let these neighborhoods run their own schools. They can do far better than we've done. You mean to tell me that in East Harlem, on 115th Street and Pleasant Avenue, which is where Benjamin Franklin High School is, that they can do any worse than graduate 75 out of a thousand? I don't see how that can be done.

You've got one other thing that we feel about police, which is why you're here, which is excellent. Too many times a fellow comes on this force and he does twenty years as a patrolman, and that's it. That means you've got a fellow who goes on with either no ambition, or he spends twenty years with flaunted ambition, and you see the results of this everywhere. You see it at Aqueduct Racetrack as a Pinkerton or, best of all, a mutuel clerk. You see it as a bank guard in Jamaica Savings Bank. I think it's a cruel, bitter way to end a career. I think there have got to be ways to open that up. I think this is primary right here—there must be college training, more of it. I think in a lot of areas, because of the civil service system we're now living under, we could hire police for shorter terms. They really don't want to stay twenty years. Four years—you could get kids who want to go to law school. You don't have to take on the pension requirements, because we need more police, we need many more police. We can't pay for them with the state pension hanging over you, over the situation. The only way to kill that is to bring people in for short periods, much more highly qualified than they have been, and we can use them to better extent.

We feel the situation in this city has to be ventilated. We talk about urban problems in the past. The urban problem now is a color problem. It starts in this city. We think the only way that this can be done is to send everybody to his own room and we'll talk in the morning, but we've got an awfully long night to go through first. And let's ventilate, let's separate, let's have people in control of their own destinies, control of their own police, control of their own education, make this city a state, and later on, somewhere along the line, we can start to mingle. But I see no way for this to continue. This is just insanity and it's going to lead to increased violence, and it's no help. The narcotics thing—you know narcotics, that's the whole game—do you think that these neighborhoods will allow as much narcotics to run rampant as the system now allows? I can't imagine it. I think the people are much better at controlling their own destiny.

With that I think I'm going to step down, except for one thing— you had a class about bookmaking in this room before we arrived; I could bring in a guest lecturer for that anytime you want.

NORMAN MAILER

Well, these are strange times aren't they? Now, I know that most of you feel that to the splendid introduction of me one more term could be added, which is "cop hater." I've had that reputation for years. Whenever it began to die, *Time* magazine would revive it. They would say, "Cop hater Norman Mailer said today that the grass in Prospect Park was not as green as it used to be." And in fact there were years of my life when I was a cop hater. There were years when I hated some of you guys so much it wasn't funny. As recently as three years ago when José Torres was fighting Wayne Thornton at Shea Stadium I was trying to get to his dressing room, and I will confess that I had had about eight drinks before I started, and I was intercepted by a cop in the alley under the stands, and I'm very proud of that day because it was the last time I ever went ape. I'm not really a very strong fellow, but that day I was so determined to get to José Torres' dressing room that ten cops were holding me and we were moving like a wave back and forth, back and forth. It was the only time in my life I've ever been strong enough to be on even terms with ten cops. Let me tell you, since I'm as yellow as any good cop, no punches were thrown by anyone; just a tremendous number of names went back and forth, mostly from me. New York's finest were finer that day than your humble visionary. Nonetheless, I have, and I admit this frankly, been obsessed as a novelist for years with the character of cops because it seems to me that the one thing nobody ever gives a cop credit for is that he's a very complicated guy, and a good cop is a fantastically complicated guy. In fact I've talked to little left-wing groups, students, student undergrounds, revolutionaries, Black Panthers, and I've argued with them about one thing—I've said to them that you've got to recognize that a good cop is a work of art, and that when you call cops pigs you're always hurting the best cops on the force because you are polarizing them down to the level of the worst cops on the force. The fact of the matter is that while I would not pretend that I consider myself in personality or temperament close to cops or their psychology, nonetheless the proof that I've been obsessed with what is the true nature of a cop is that I made a movie about the police force in a mythical city which was not named, although everybody seemed to think it was New York, a movie called *Beyond the Law.* And it's a pity that the police department never saw it because while there are many who think it was highly critical of the police department, I think it was the best movie ever made about cops, even though many of you may think it was unfair for one reason: which is that the cops in the picture (who were detectives) were as alive as the crooks, which is not something you can say for the average Hollywood film. In the average Hollywood film you guys are nothing but empty pillars of justice. In fact, you are shadowmen. In fact, it's hard I think that the average cop can recognize himself when he sees a cop movie. He says to himself, "Well, that's how those guys out in Los Angeles are, all those state troopers. We're not like that." At any rate, I'll go so far as to say that if there is curiosity in this place to see *Beyond the Law,* you're welcome to see it.

We'll have a showing here if I can talk my distributor into showing it for nothing, which is the basis of this promise.

All right. The introduction over, let me get to the point. Any man who is running for mayor by the fact of that declaration has also declared that he has to take the police seriously. A cop hater cannot be a mayor, a simple cop hater cannot be a mayor. A man who thinks that when a police force is less than its best is hurting every single thing in the city; he cannot conceivably be mayor. So what I've come here today to talk about is the platform we're running on that's going to make sense for practically everybody in this city, including the cops, because as you can gather from my running mate Jimmy Breslin's remarks, he feels, and I agree with him, that you guys have not been getting a fair deal either. We're running on a platform that's improbable: to begin with the fact that we're two amateurs, we have an amateur organization behind us, we have no money, we have been running right into the peak of a great big wave which is that we're running in fun. While I'm happy to talk here today because the one thing you guys know is that nobody who runs for office in this city is running for fun unless he's wearing a wig. I mean, you know, it's not particularly a funny way to spend sixteen hours a day, it's almost like having a double duty every day. But what we're running on are a set of ideas that we feel are good enough to give us an outside chance of winning. We're starting on the outside pole, the outside gate— you can see how much I know about the racetrack—we're starting on the outside gate and we're starting a pole back.

But we think that what we have running for us is not the beauty and the charm of our two splendid personalities, but ideas that are so sound and so sensible that they're going to appeal to everybody across the city. And the first thing we're running on is something that sounds so impossible when we first say it that people think we have to be running in fun because it makes no sense at all, which is to say that we're running on a coalition of the left and the right. And we are doing no less than asking large elements of the left and large elements of the right to each separately blow half their minds so that they can recognize that they have a common interest in the half of the mind that's left. We are running as left-conservatives. Not conservative radicals, not liberal leftists, not whatever you want to call it—we're running as left-conservatives. I won't speak for Breslin because he's never been a man on the left, but maybe he's running as a right-conservative; I don't know. But I, as a man on the left, I'm talking across the board to conservatives and saying that after all these years of thinking about political problems I've come to one conclusion, which is that you conservatives are right about one terribly important matter: that a man has to have control over his own life. He has to be able to shape his own life. He has to be able to work with his own future, and he has to know the immediate result of his work. People begin to get into trouble, people begin to get crazy ideas and go completely out of line when they can't see any product to their work day after day. In fact, there's nothing more frustrating in a man's life than to wake up in the morning with a bright idea and be forced to lose it by noon because he's run into a set of impossible systems that keep him from being able to express any of his dream. You take the worst drug addict in New York, he can wake up in the morning and say, "Hey, baby, I'm going to go to work, I'm going to work today." Of course by noon he's taken a shot because he's run down the steps very quickly. But you can take that obvious example and you can stretch it out over many more subtle examples and recognize that what is true about this city is that the city is less good than the people in it. The people in New York, whatever they are, right or left, are strong people, they're proud people, they're full of fight, full of ideas. Everybody in this city has more ideas than they can keep in their head. And there's no place for these ideas to go because the entire legislative thicket of this city, of the city charter, impedes every honest man, and in fact every dishonest man from making any kind of quick or interesting move. So neither the cops nor the crooks have a chance to get any better. And my idea is that a good society doesn't depend upon having a great police force or having a great criminal element in society, which certain revolutionaries would believe; but rather that a good society depends upon the cops and the crooks getting better. Think about it, it's an unusual notion, but the idea behind it is that if they both get better, everybody is doing more every day, which means you've got a richer society in terms of the real life that people are living.

Well, to go back to this point of the left and right coalition. What we believe is that this city is being run from outside by the federal government, by Albany, and that the major decisions that affect the most intimate matters of people's lives are decided without their will. That, for instance, people who live on Staten Island were handed the Verrazano Bridge without ever being given the opportunity to vote for it. When we were out at Wagner College we were told that there were polls that showed 90 per cent of the people in Staten Island didn't want that bridge. That's just a small example of what's been happening in this city. Over the last twenty years you've all seen how this city has gotten to look worse and worse and duller and duller because old neighborhoods were torn up, ripped apart, and had great big housing projects put in, which, believe me, do not begin to look nearly as attractive architecturally as the tombs. And these dull neighborhoods create more violence because—I don't have to tell you cops one thing, you know it—when a neighborhood that's a potentially violent neighborhood gets bored, it gets more violent. When violent people are interested in something, they tend to be less violent. And when they're bored, they're bad. And there's bad dull architecture going up all over the city without anybody having anything to say about it. It's all come in through government programs. There's been an idea that the problems of people can be solved from without and above by experts planning together and deciding that the way to save people is to lay out programs for them. I've come to believe in something which is a conservative belief which is that this cannot be done, because finally people have to have the feeling that they are working for themselves and saving themselves as well.

So this is the platform we're running on. We're running on three points which we think can turn this city around. We don't say that we can give you any guarantee that this city can be saved. We think that you can almost say that the question is not the shame of the cities but the ultimate crisis of the cities, a terminal deathbed condition of the cities. The cities are in terrible shape because nobody in the cities any longer has the ability to shape their own lives.

The common ordinary people can't do interesting things with their lives in the cities, and they're at the mercy of forces larger than themselves. So we're saying this, that the only way you can begin to attack this problem is to make certain very basic changes. And the first thing we're saying is that New York City has to become the fifty-first state of the Union, and we're saying that our candidacy makes that possible because if any of the others were to run on that, if Wagner would have run on that, or Procaccino, or Lindsay, it would be no more than a politician's promise. But if we get elected, improbably as that is, if we first win a primary, and then go from there against all the triple difficulties of having really major forces opposed to us—'cause now they're all laughing at us, and we like that—but once we win a primary we'd have to go on and win the mayoralty, that would be a tremendous uphill fight. If we could do both of those things as amateurs, what it would mean is that something fantastic had happened in the political history of this city and this country, and everybody would recognize that people all over wanted something new, some new way of approaching their problems. So we're saying that our candidacy embodies the idea of the fifty-first state, that if we're elected we are within a year of getting it because the alternatives would be too awful for the federal government to contemplate. They would give it to us. They would give it to us because they would recognize that this was the true will of the people. And we are saying that once we had that in the act of being elected, and I can tell you this, if we didn't get it in a clean election, in other words if we ever won the mayoralty in a three- or four-way race, we would throw it right back to the people and say vote on this, vote on whether you want this fifty-first state. So that we are assuming that we'd be able to move only if we get this mandate. If we got this mandate from the people we would then say that the City Charter has to be rewritten from top to bottom, and as a matter of fact it would, because we would not be a state. And we would set it up in such a way that there would be a constitutional convention and the notion on which we are running, the basic notion on which we are running, could be instituted, which is power to the neighborhoods.

Now notice, left-wing groups say power to the people. We are not saying that. We are saying power to the neighborhoods. And what we mean by that is that any neighborhood, of any quality or character—whether it's a historical neighborhood, a geographical neighborhood, or a neighborhood based on common economic problems—any kind of neighborhood, could constitute itself as a neighborhood, in other words, as a legal unit, a small town, a city, a village, whatever it wished to call itself, so long as the people in it voted to become a neighborhood. In other words we could not go around and say "You are a neighborhood." We would not do that because we think that's the beginning of the whole problem, since one of the problems of neighborhoods now is that they are confused with administrative districts. So what you get is half of one neighborhood and half of another neighborhood put together for administration. That's where all the trouble starts. And you all know more about that than I do. But what we say is wherever people would vote to constitute themselves into a neighborhood, they would become a neighborhood. And what that would mean is that they would get funded directly from the new city-state, and they would have the money to set up their own departments, their own police department first, if that was what was most important to them, their own board of education, their own fire department, their own sanitation department, their own parks. They'd be able to build themselves on any principle they wished. If they were a quiet, respectable neighborhood which wished security, they would be able to find it. If they were a poor neighborhood, with a long and bitter history of police relations, they might decide they wished to solve police problems their way. They might decide they wished to employ professional policemen because face to face suddenly with having a policing problem that they now had to solve by themselves as a neighborhood, they might decide that they wanted to keep some of the New York City police as presently constituted, hire them from the city. Or they might decide they want a brand-new system where they would police themselves. They would have votes among themselves to decide this problem. The point we are making is that we would not be telling people which way they had to administer their own community. Each community would be administering itself, each neighborhood which chose to become a neighborhood. Now mind you, in the beginning there might be very few neighborhoods that might wish to do this. Maybe only a third of the present population of New York City might wish to constitute itself into neighborhoods. The rest of the city would remain about as it is now, would be administered by the mayoralty as it is now.

So the basic program we're running on is the separation of the neighborhoods, the idea that people have the right to constitute themselves into the kinds of neighborhoods they want. That people have the right to control their own destiny. We even say, when we get funny, that we are running on everything from Free Huey Newton to End Fluoridation. We're running on the principle that neighborhoods can constitute themselves in such a way that they have everything from compulsory free love to compulsory church attendance. And with that let me say "thank you."

ON ACCEPTING THE PULITZER PRIZE

NORMAN MAILER

May 6, 1969

Is there anybody here from the New York *Post?* How about the *Daily News?* I see there's a gentleman from the *Times,* AP, UPI, we're all here. I'm gratified. It's customary for someone who wins the Pulitzer prize to express his profound gratitude and to admit that he is a humble man and not necessarily worthy of the honor. I would suggest to you that while this would be a fit set of remarks for working reporters to make, because the Pulitzer prize as far as I understand it is still a prize they regard with much pleasure when they receive it, in fact it is the goal of their lives. It would be false of me as a literary man to pretend that the literary value of the Pulitzer prize is what it once used to be. Occasionally very good books get the award. Last year, for instance, Mr. Styron's book *Nat Turner* won, and while I have not read it, I understand by a very good many that it is a most interesting novel. This year the trustees of Columbia University School of Journalism saw fit to choose *The Armies of the Night* in company with a book by Dr. Dubos. Now you can forgive me for having been around for so many years that I'm a touch cynical about such awards. It occurs to me that the Pulitzer prize people would possibly have been slightly embarrassed if they had not picked *The Armies of the Night* and that in fact it was finally you might say that the verdict was extracted from them and they showed the ill favor with which they bestowed the prize by enabling me to share it with Dr. Dubos. However, I am not full of sour grapes. Quite the contrary, I'm delighted, because now it enables me to address you guys and say something to you, which is that I have been honored by the highest prize in your profession. I don't mean the prize for non-fiction is the highest prize of the Pulitzer prizes, but that any man who gets the P.P. is a man who nominally should be respected at least for his professional ability by reporters. And I am saying to you that the treatment we have been given in our mayoralty campaign up to now has been close to scandalous. And I'm saying to you as a P.P. winner that if you continue to treat me this way, it's going to be a disgrace to your profession. Now I'm not just here to fulminate. I've got a series of items I want to point out to you. We have been keeping a book on the way we've been treated. I don't mean we're writing a book, I mean we're keeping a book of little clippings and comparisons and day by day this book gets richer and richer. This is just a few of the choice items that we have pulled for this press conference. Believe me there's more, there's much more. We are not getting a fair shake. Now let me just go through these points. We jotted them down quickly and they're not necessarily in chronological order, but I would like to point out to you something:

1. We've been campaigning harder than anyone else in this primary. We've been out as much as twelve to fourteen hours in a day. One day we got up at 5:30 in the morning and we didn't quit till midnight. There's been no day when we haven't been out there working all day. I think we've taken off something like two days in the last seventeen, and then we spent those days doing homework. I will say that in the days we were out not once did a reporter cover us from the beginning of the day to the end; and in fact most reporters who covered covered us talking at two colleges, let's say in a day, and called it a day on a day when we might have eight speeches, and we might have talked to three colleges, two neighborhood groups and three Democratic clubs at night, as well as going through several scull sessions with our staff. We have been working hard, there has not been a single mention of this in any of the papers. All they talk about is we are running in fun, we are two choice clowns, we are funnier than Wagner, Procaccino, and a couple of liberal fellows who are very nice guys. This has been the treatment we have been accorded by the New York news-

papers. I don't know about the out-of-town papers, but this is the treatment we have been accorded by the New York papers. No New York reporter has covered us through an entire day. Even my own paper, *The Village Voice,* wrote at having one nice story about us, the editor apparently felt that balance was necessary in these affairs, especially since Mr. James Wechsler of our opposing paper, the New York *Post,* had called Mr. Breslin and myself an odd couple and suggested *The Village Voice* was a house organ. In the next issue appeared an unfavorable story about us which spoke about one meeting at the end of a day. I had appeared at twelve meetings earlier that day. This described the one meeting and said that the air of political death hung over this meeting. Now you can see looking at me now that the air of political death is not quite upon this campaign yet.

All right, no reporter has yet followed us around for a whole day. Why don't you guys go out and do an honest day's work like we're doing and cover it and see what we're up to?

2. The *Times* still treats us as a joke, even when they recognize our ideas about becoming the fifty-first state. They say, well, of course the men who embody this are mavericks, clowns, they are not serious, the idea is serious. They had a small editorial about us on Saturday, May 3. The head of the editorial said "Mailer vs. Breslin." Jimmy and I may be two egomaniacs, but we have not butted heads yet. We have been working together as a team. And in fact the title "Mailer vs. Breslin" contradicted the meaning of the editorial which spoke about us as a team, which is terribly sloppy journalism for the *Times.* On April 10, going all the way back to April 10, at 2 in the morning a reporter named Jay Levin on the New York *Post* called up Jack Newfield, Peter Maas, and Gloria Steinem to ask about our running in the mayoralty campaign. This story was killed. After waking up three people at 2 in the morning on April 10, the story was killed. Two days later another reporter on the *Post* asked to cover us. Now we will not give you the lady's name, we will just say this, we will give it to you off the record, if you want it off the record, and you can check with her, two days later a reporter asked to cover us at the *Post* and she was told that a memorandum had been circulated that week by the

publisher, Mrs. Schiff, please, that means no one other than James Breslin, presumably because the *Post* has this fine principle Mr. Breslin will never receive a line of publicity during the entire mayoralty campaign. I call that precise and excellent reporting.

5. On Sunday, May 4, at 6 in the evening this last Sunday, Jack Newfield, who with Peter Maas heads up our press staff, personally brought a press release to the city room at the *Post,* and it stated that we were having a press conference in the morning. Nobody from the *Post* attended that press conference. The story yesterday about my winning the P.P., which I think might be of local interest to *Post* readers since I am Jewish and two thirds of their readers are Jewish—as we all know, the Jewish community loves a son who wins something—this story was buried in the drama page under a headline which gave credit to Mr. Sackler for his fine play *The Great White Hope.* I'm all for that. I was listed among the also wons. No mention that I was running for mayor. You might think they were two separate guys, maybe Arthur Miller is running for mayor and Norman Mailer happened to win the P.P. if they saw it. Now if we know one thing, we know that the *Post* respects the *Times*'s sense of news. The *Times* had the story on its front page. I was delighted to see it there on that front page because it's the first time I've ever been on the front page of the *Times.* And in fact on something like the thirty-eighth page was buried my comment. When the *Times* reporter asked me what I thought, I said I was delighted because the *Times* might now honor Mr. Breslin and myself with the same courteous treatment on the front page they had accorded Mrs. Guggenheimer the day before. Now when we announced our candidacy for mayor, the *Times* had that story on page 25. Two of us come out on the same day, we do not make the dullest press conferences in the world, we usually have something to say at our press conferences, that story was buried on page 25— a favorable story but buried on page 25. Mrs. Guggenheimer, who is running for the City Council was given two columns on the front page, even though, as Mr. Breslin pointed out later at a press conference, there are very few people in New York City who have heard of Mrs. Guggenheimer, and they probably think she belongs to the Guggenheim Foundation since she is so little known. I

do not wish to be ungracious to a lady, I merely wish to be ungracious to the *Times*. They are not covering the news.

Now the *Daily News,* to my knowledge, has attended one press conference, the press conference where we announced. I'm glad to see their man here today. Where is he? What are you doing back there? The first three rows are for the reporters. Did you think I'd throw a brick at you? Any man who runs for mayor is too tired to be violent. All right, this is the second time the *News* has covered us. Why don't you cover us for a whole day, just once? You'll see that we can walk farther than everybody with the possible exception of Mr. Murphy. And if it comes to it to win this mayoralty election we'll walk thirty-six miles in a day. At least, one of us or the other will walk thirty-six miles.

Now on the other hand the reason we are saying that this is a matter of improper if not outrageous treatment by the press is because it is obvious our candidacy is a story of great interest all over the country. We've been covered more by papers outside of New York than we have been covered by papers inside of New York with the exception of *The Wall Street Journal* and *The National Observer*. They have treated our campaign—I won't say they have treated it seriously—but they have treated us as having certain ongoing news interest. Finally, yesterday we released our first position paper. One gentleman appeared from the *Times*. That was the only coverage we had except for somebody from NBC who, incidentally, asked some excellent questions. Now in this position paper we had two enormous points, two points each much larger than any other candidate has brought out so far. One point was Sweet Sunday, which is that the condition of air pollution in this city is so hideous that people need a moment of peace once a month and that once a month everything should stop in this city. This ought to be of interest to *Daily News* readers. A lot of them complain about the noise. We're saying that we'd stop everything for one day, all cars, all vehicles, all airplanes, all electric motors except, obviously, for hospital generators and things like that, and let people have a day for quiet and reflection. It is a religious notion. The *Daily News* is supposedly a newspaper which caters to the religious principles of several million readers. It is ignoring the first religious notion that anybody who is running for politics in this municipality in this city has come up with in God knows how long, if you'll forgive me for taking the Lord's name in vain. The other point was even more important, which is that the only solution to air pollution is to stop all traffic in the island of Manhattan except for trucks, taxis, and buses, and we said that our next position paper on transportation was going to deal with these problems in detail.

Now, gentlemen, let me just end with this set of small thoughts, and I'm prepared for your questions. I've been given the honor of being given several literary awards this year, and I won't pretend that I'm displeased to receive them. I'm delighted to have received them, because if nothing else, it is the only way I can get hundreds of thousands, if not millions, of people to take me seriously. And I think that's for the good because for better or worse—and I've had a life which has had as much of one kind of thing in it as the other over these years—I think I've finally become a serious man, and I submit to you that in your heart of hearts you know that nobody like Breslin or myself could run unless we were serious. I will say that anybody who thinks we're running in fun has got a perverted notion of fun. This is too serious. If our candidacy gets laughed off the block, if we get shut out, if we don't get a fair chance, it's going to embitter some of the best and most interesting people of the left and the right in New York. I'm not threatening, I'm just saying it's going to embitter them, it's going to poison them, they're going to be more apathetic about politics afterward. They're going to say our lives are run by machines. On the other hand, if we lose and we lose fairly, being treated fairly, we won't have any complaints. We're going into this as amateurs, we know our inefficiencies, we know our inadequacies. But if we're treated unfairly, if the powers of this city, including the *Daily News* particularly, and the *Post,* are so afraid of us they won't give us fair treatment, and they're two of the three newspapers remaining in this great city, then we say that we will leave this election with the feeling that we have done our best but that what's coming on this city is worse than anyone knows. And when the time comes, and this city becomes the first Vietnam in America, you gentlemen will have the pleasure of having done your job properly. Thank you.

I'd like to ask why you think the Post *and the* News *are so afraid of your position that they—*

MAILER:

I'll tell you exactly why I think so, I can't substantiate this, this is just my opinion. I think that the *Post* is afraid of us because they're supporting Mr. Badillo and they sympathize with Mr. Scheuer and they think we're hurting Mr. Badillo and Mr. Scheuer. I think the *News* doesn't cover us because they know we will hurt Wagner and Procaccino more than those guys ever dreamed of. Now I think it is as simple as that.

Now seriously, how much money do you have in your campaign? How much will you make, where will you get it?

MAILER:

We've been running along on a few thousand dollars a week. We borrowed some money from someone with the promise we would pay them back just so soon as money came in. Our money comes in very little bits. We have no political machine that we're working with, and we do not get money from rich people because this money is not tax-free. And to the extent that we're treated as a joke, we certainly do not get money, because people don't throw their money around. We don't care. We're perfectly prepared to run without large advertising campaigns and without large television commercials. We'd rather run by getting out and seeing more people in the city before we're done than any other candidates and take our chances that way and meeting them in debates whenever we get the chance, and working on good position papers and just running the best campaign we can within our limits. In fact, we'd rather do it that way, we'd rather run and spend much less money than anyone else around because it will prove that much more if we ever do win.

With regard to the press coverage being unfair, I would like to ask that the reason for it may go a little beyond the fact that the Post *is going to support Badillo and the* Times *is going to support Wagner. It may have something to do with their attitude toward writing and the imagination . . .*

MAILER:

Well, I think you might be right on that, but I didn't want to go further than the immediate reasons because I can't substantiate any of this, it would just be my opinion. But, I will say that there is a basic attitude in this city that only experts can run its affairs, and that is precisely what we're running against. We're saying that people know more about running their own intimate government than experts do. And this is anathema to the liberal mentality. And we're running on a left-right coalition against precisely what I call the liberal-totalitarian mentality. I don't mean the liberals put people in concentration camps, for they certainly don't. But they do think that anyone who does not subscribe to their ideas is seriously deranged. And they have been treating Breslin and me as if we were deranged. And we frankly can't enjoy that very much.

If you have no more questions, I have one final comment, and then that's it. I was talking yesterday to some kids who represent the high school underground press, and, as you know, I believe the center is dominating our lives so that nobody has any power over his own life any longer, and that's why I'm calling for this coalition of left and right. And these kids said to me, "Mailer, you are kidding yourself." They are very tough kids, they said, "You are kidding yourself, you are nothing but an agent of the establishment." And I said "You kids don't begin to know what the establishment is, you don't begin to know how complex it is, you don't begin to understand. . . ." I didn't even get to the point of being able to say this to them because they were talking with the strength of ten.

But I started to say that the establishment consists of people, too. It is not an ironbound machine; it is in fact called the establishment because it has a certain velvety quality to it: It does things subtly, smoothly, comfortably, where it can. But the establishment is also capable and has been all through history capable of making startling changes, of recognizing extreme and serious situations and adapting to them. And I am running on the notion that the wounds of this city can still be put together. But I had to say to those kids at the end: "I don't know, let's see, let's see who's right," and they said, "You are an agent of the establishment, we may yet have to work against you." And I said, "Who knows, let's see. Just follow it. Give me a fair chance to see if there's anything going here." Now that's what I want to ask of everyone in this city—that we be given a fair chance to run our campaign. To the extent that we're running for fun, we'll be so exposed if you give us a fair chance, it won't be funny. We'll have to leave this city under the cover of darkness—and that just shows how hard I've been running, if the P.P. winner has to use a cliché like that to finish a sentence . . . Let me quit while I'm one millimeter ahead. Thank you.

AT THE VILLAGE GATE

NORMAN MAILER

May 7, 1969

Now, look, let me talk, because it's my evening and you know it. I listened to you a long time, and I'll tell you why I listened to you. I'll tell you why there are no black people here tonight—it's a simple reason. It's because Adam Clayton Powell has not decided whether he's going to declare yet or not, and the black people know they would be foolish to declare for a maverick candidate until Adam Clayton Powell has made up his mind. It's as simple as that.

All right, now look, let me have your attention, really. Let me try something. Can you hear me without the mike? All right now, let's get into a couple of very simple small bags, which is—one, we're in the Village Gate, which has the worst psychedelic acoustics in the whole world. The acoustics in this place are hooked, *(yea, fuck you,) are hooked out of Art D'Lugoff's beard. And I love Art, 'cause he is an ogre just like me, and Art decided a long time ago that he was expendable, but he said to the whole world and New York, "To hell with you; shove it up your screw. I'm here, I'm running the Village Gate. You cannot stop me unless you come in here and wipe me out." And they never came in, and Art created a neighborhood.

Now the reason I hate talking into this mike is because it sets up a hypnotic trance which is full of the weaker bullshit in our continuing relationship. Now get away from me, everybody. Now look, look, let's be sensible for a little while. You're just nothing but a bunch

* Parentheses are response to audience heckling.

of spoiled pigs—and there ain't a cop in the house! And yesterday, I went up to the Police Academy and talked not to the cops first, but to the students at the John Jay Criminal Justice Academy or whatever it is called. *(Please get away from me, and stop all this dull bullshit. I'm onto it—I'm onto it. Don't interrupt me when I'm talking, I'll be interrupted soon enough.)

(From audience: Norman, talk about the fifty-first state, you're among friends.) Hey, I'll tell you something. Shut up. You're not my friend if you interrupt me when I'm talking 'cause it just breaks into the mood in my mind. So fuck you, boo. All right, I said you're all a bunch of spoiled pigs. You're more spoiled than the cops. I'll tell you that, I'll tell you that. You've been sittin' around jerkin' off, havin' your jokes for twenty-two years. Yeah! And more than that—more than that. You all want to work for us? You get in there, and you do your discipline, and you do your devotion. You get in there, and you do some dull work. Don't come in there and help us because "we're gonna give Norm a little help." Fuck you! You help us or don't come near us. I'll tell you why—'cause we can win this thing. We can win it, if we're very good. We can win it with all of you angels and devils. But we can't win it, we can't win it if you come in here with your dull little vanities. The cops I talked to yesterday were a more impressive group of people than all of you. I'll tell you that.

Now is there anybody here who is not familiar with our program by now? No one? All right, then this I say to you. This I say to you. You are all gonna go through a tremendous hour of horror, panic, and vomit if you start to work seriously for us, because you know I'm not the only nearsighted crazy man in America, and some of you could get hit. Get it straight. If you're gonna come in and work for us then work, but leave your ego at the door. If you think I'm in this for fun, then I feel sorry for you, 'cause I might have to pass on you after I have gone through. Got it? Got it? All right. Then fuck you. Got it? If you're gonna help me, then help me. But I don't want any of those dull mother-tired ego trips. Work.

Now, to prove to you how good this mayoralty is gonna be . . . I didn't quit while I was ahead, I'm about to reinvest my winnings and see if I can capture some of the more delicate spirits in the house. The point to what we're up to is that we are either running in fun or not. Since the neighborhood assembled here has only one thing in common, which is that they have a ticklish little liver and anus on the notion of who is putting who on, they think, they think that we are running in fun. Some of our own people put out campaign buttons like "Mailer-Breslin Seriously." Let me point out to you one quick little notion. Anybody who is runnin' in fun in the mayoralty election in New York deserves to run in fun.

Now I wanna finish with a small story, which you can shove down your throats. Years ago, I went out with the distinguished novelist, Mr. Ralph Ellison, to Iowa for a schlock magazine called *Esquire* run by a martinet and tyrant named Harold Hayes, who wouldn't know a good piece of writing until the Pulitzer prize kicks him in the back of the ear. One of my dearest friends! And we went out there. A little fellow named Mark Harris—he's a little Jewish fellow with a big cigar which he blew in everyone's face, he's a tiny version of Groucho Marx, and Dwight MacDonald looking as though he was gonna die of asthma and apoplexy twenty-two years ago, and Ellison, and myself. And we went out there to Iowa and we said—this is back in 1959—over and over again that the country is in a terrible time. It is full of the worst disease. You don't begin to know how bad this country has become. You people in Iowa have to recognize this is a marvelous state, Iowa, but it really doesn't begin to know how awful things are outside. And we got this marvelous applause, and we kept saying people in Iowa—we didn't know the word "turned on"—we kept saying people in Iowa are marvelous, until we found out they all were graduate students from Michigan and, ah, places like, ah, Philadelphia. So when it was over, like a high school team that fought a very good game and finally lost in the last quarter, I turned to Ellison in the dressing room—we were having some drinks with some marvelous-looking Republican women—and I said, "Ralph, what the hell do we do it for? Why do we work so hard?" And he said, "Well, we're expendable."

So get that into your head. There's a very simple little notion going on, which is, we're all going to run and we're gonna do our best, and we'll go on for eighty-two years or more. But the notion to get through your heads is to get over your silly little ego-tired trips. If you have a lot of money and that's the way that you turn on to workin' for us, then thank you very much. We can use that money if you give it to us, and you can give it to us any way you want— publicly, privately, quietly, at large or small. If you have other ways of working for us, work for us.

What we really want is to get out into the neighborhoods. I want to go out and talk in every neighborhood before I'm done. I'll talk in the sweetest neighborhoods and the worst neighborhoods. But I'm running on the notion that New York can't begin to become the incredibly absolute and magnificent city that it is until there is power to the neighborhoods. Two weeks ago at the end of a long evening of campaigning, speaking at a marvelous, to me, Irish Club in Park Slope—overcome with happiness, I said, "I am running on everything from Black Power to Irish Self-Righteousness," and the good Irishmen in that place laughed and applauded, and I thought I had a victory until I read in *The Village Voice* that the smell of political death was upon us. I know what the fellow was up to. He was saying—"Get out of this campaign. You're just a little Jewish fellow from Brooklyn, and you don't know what's up." Well, let me tell you something. I know what's up because the greatest Jewish paper in New York, the despicable New York *Post,* won't print a word of what we're up to. And let me tell you what that means—let me tell you this—I am proud of my people. Very few people understand the Jews, but I do, 'cause I'm one of them. Fuck you, Let me talk. The Jews are an incredible people at their best. At their worst they are swine. Like every WASP I ever met, at their worst they are awful. All people are awful at their worst. Some are worse than others. But the Jews are sensational at their best, which is rare enough, given Miami and a fur coat. No, don't laugh, because you don't know what you're laughing at. Think about it. Whenever a people loses its highest race, there's nothing funnier going on in the world.

What we're running on is this: that this town has come to the point where this town, that many of us grew up in, the greatest city in the history of the world conceivably, is now some sort of paralytic victim in an orphan asylum. This city must be saved by vigorous activity by everybody within it, and I'm not just talking in my cups. But as the people of New York turn on and become fantastic, which we all are because I've met more interesting people in New York, per capita, than anywhere else in the world . . . Come on, let's not spend any time on applause, let's get to the point. The point is simple. Unless this city turns on and becomes fantastic, it'll become the first victim of the technological society— you know what that means? That means that the smog, the dead, dull air of oppression will be upon us first, and we will destroy each other first, because we all have too much within us to be able to bear the unendurable dullness of our days in New York when we all know we're capable of so much more.

So this I say to you. If we don't save our city, our city will become that little ward, that ward of eight million. There'll be a fifty-mile bypass around us, and they'll say, "We understand there are three divisions of Marines in there to keep the populace down." *(No, keep quiet! Let me finish 'cause I'm talkin' very hard. Look—don't come here to be entertained), we're into somethin' that's deep. Don't kid yourself on this. We're running on the notion of power to the neighborhoods. What we're saying is very simple. We're saying— Shut up and fuck you! Let me talk.—we're here on something very simple, which is that nobody knows any longer which idea has more validity than another, because there's no ground, there's no content, there's no situation for an idea. We're running on one notion—let the left and the right have their neighborhoods. Let them each see what kind of society they can create and then decide on the basis of a thousand contests and a hundred bloody encounters which particular neighborhood, or style, or conception of life is more interesting than another. Let people at least be ready to begin to put their notion of existence behind themselves, in front of themselves, within themselves. Let them begin to work for something they believe in. Nobody in this city can begin to work for anything they believe in, 'cause it just isn't there, it just doesn't exist.

This city is controlled from without. That's why everybody is going crazy in this city, because they have no objection correlative, which I remind you literary people is a remark first coined in twentieth century cultural history by Mr. T. S. Eliot, of all people. There is no objective correlative in this city, but we say power to the neighborhoods would give an objective correlative that would give a notion of where everybody is. We are running on one profound notion. Free Huey Newton, end fluoridation. We're running on another profound notion—compulsory free love in those neighborhoods which vote for it along with compulsory church attendance on Sunday for those neighborhoods who vote for that. What we are running on is one basic, simple notion—which is that till people see where their ideas lead they know nothing; and that, my fine friends, is why I am running. I want to see where my own ideas lead. Thank you very much.

A SPEECH TO THE TIME-LIFE STAFF

NORMAN MAILER

June 3, 1969

If I win the primary on June 17, I am—as Breslin always says—in trouble. I'm in terrible trouble. I will then have to go on and work in the mayoralty campaign all summer and earn not a sou. And after that point, if I win, I'll be in the paltry position of entering the mayoralty a tremendous number of bucks in debt. How will I ever keep from becoming corrupt? So you have to assume my candidacy is a prima facie case of seriousness. No man runs to win in such a way as to pauperize himself, unless he is either the victim of a *grande idée* or paying his debt to society. I submit that I'm paying my debt to society, and that is why I'm running for mayor.

Since I have brought the mood of this audience down to zero, in my feisty little way, let me present the simple campaign notions upon which we're running. They are several. One, that New York has become a city so sick, so wracked with pain, so torporous, feverish, edemic, pandemic, and miserable that, as my running mate, James Breslin, says: "To run frivolously in a city as mortally ill as New York would be a sin." The city is suffering from every disease that sets upon America, including the disease of bad reportage. None of us, by now, has an accurate notion of what is going on anywhere at all. We have the most extraordinary network of communications in the history of western civilization, and we have less sense of where reality resides than perhaps at any time in our history. And the reason is that we are a divided nation. But we are a nation divided within the soul of each man and woman alive in the country because we are racing forward, on the one hand, at a great rate toward the most extraordinary adventures in the history of man, and on the other hand, we find ourselves each year, each season, virtually each month, more and more unable to solve our most fundamental social problems. And in New York the diseases of America settle, and develop, and fester, and finally begin to burn and suggest that eventually they may even explode. We live in a city which has an enormous welfare roll. We have more than a million people on welfare in this city. The figure is actually one million two hundred thousand people. The money that we spend for welfare are over a billion and a half dollars a year now—they're larger than the amount we spend for education. Yet that welfare roll we support in this city—not through direct payments—although more than directly we support it, as I will try to suggest a little later, that welfare roll is not even of our own creation.

There have been extraordinary developments made by the kind of corporations who produce farm machinery. They have discovered ways to mine the bottom lands of great cotton states like Mississippi. And in the course of that, whole hordes of tenant farms who'd been liveried in a miserable existence but nonetheless a cultivated one, because they at least partook of a culture down South, were uprooted and came here to the North, where they immediately were drawn by the fact that New York was a city with a mildly liberal tradition, a city which sought to pay people on welfare a little more than people were being paid in other cities. So a disproportionate number of dispossessed farm workers came to New York, and our welfare rolls began to grow, and grew at a huge rate.

We had, at the same time, a series of powerful unions in this city, who would not let black or Puerto Rican people into those unions. So the people who came here went on welfare and stayed on welfare, and their condition deepened until it became a way of life. And as it became a way of life, so it became a way of criminal life; and criminality became attached to the edges of welfare, so that many a hard-working woman lived on her welfare check and brought up her children, legitimate or illegitimate, and the young boys who grew up in this environment began to look more and more for purposes in crime. Because crime, for a man who is poor and landless and disenfranchised and living on a government dole, is finally a witty activity. It is the one way in which he may express himself.

So the crisis of the city deepened. It was like a boat waterlogged with welfare. On the other hand, all sorts—to use the worst word for crime—all sorts of rats were feeding on the cargo. This ship has been staggering along and getting into worse condition year after year after year, until now there's grave question whether it can really be saved, short of a federal takeover of the economic necessities of this city. Now in this situation, any man who runs for mayor has good cause to examine his motives, if he's interested in attacking the problem on the old basis. To wit, running for mayor in such a way that he would be elected: making the old deals in the old ways, coming into power with an administration and a bureaucracy and a set of municipal unions who are all waterlogged themselves, all corrupt themselves, all full of crime themselves. Trying to work and accomplish anything in such a city—no matter how brave or honorable or worthwhile or even noble he may be in his own mind and to others—his hands are tied, he is manacled to the oppression of his condition because he too is oppressed. He has to deal with an administrative system which is impenetrable. So, at that point, he may be a man as well-intentioned as our honorable John V. Lindsay and still fail. He can work like a Trojan for four years and go down to abysmal defeat after defeat. The difficulty in the situation is that there is no way to solve the problems of New York, because the most fundamental problems of New York are not only aggravated by the farm machinery, but by the legislative morass of the North in Albany.

So over the last year, as must have been suggested to a thousand men in this city, many people came to me time and again to say, "Well, why don't you run for mayor. If Bill Buckley could run for mayor, you certainly can run for mayor." And I kept saying it was impossible. It was hopeless. One would not even begin to think of running for mayor. It is too terrible a job to contemplate if you ever won.

Until that marvelous day, and I blush to admit this, when a magazine editor talking to me said: "Norman, have you ever thought of the fifty-first state, of New York becoming a separate state?" And at that moment I said, "Good Lord, I've now found a way to pay my enormous account to you. I can work, I can campaign, I can serve. I can run on a notion that makes sense to me, which is that if New York can become the fifty-first state, it can begin to attack its incredible problems. Because if I run, and win a primary, and go on from there to win a mayoralty election against the extraordinary opposition of forces by stealing a primary election, then indeed a small miracle would have happened in this city; and the people of this city would have voted for a set of ideas which would be unheralded in previous political history. To wit, they would not have voted for their immediate security, but for setting out on an adventure whose end could not be foreseen. Because at that moment when the people would vote to become the fifty-first state, which as I say would be embodied in our candidacy, at that moment the city would have declared that it had lost faith in the old ways of solving political problems, that it wished to embark on a new conception for politics.

Now this new conception would revolve around the second point in our platform, which is power to the neighborhoods. And what indeed could that possibly mean? It means something unheralded in American politics. It means that, because a state had been declared by majority vote of the citizens of this city and I can say in parenthesis that if the mayoralty election were won in a three- to four-cornered race, and one did not have a majority, there would be no recourse but to throw the city open to a referendum, where the people of the city would vote on whether they wished to have a fifty-first state or not, because one could not begin to proceed without a majority of the people in the city voting to become the fifty-first state—one could not steal or trick such an election. At that point, having won such a majority, one could then call into being a constitutional convention, which might be one of the most remarkable moments in the history of this city or of any city, because the talent and the dedication and the hard consciousness of people in this city is remarkable. There's more talent waiting on line in this city, there's more energy bottled up and pent waiting to express itself in this city than perhaps in any city in America— and that's possibly a way of saying any city in the world. The people in this city have been disenfranchised from any kind of power, any kind of approach to the problems before them which could have political issue for twenty years. It is impossible for any man, even a man of power, to get anything done in this city, and it has been impossible for many, many years. So, at this moment, we might assume that an extraordinary amount of intelligence and experience might collect to write a constitution which would be a remarkable document, because it would have to contend with the age-old problems—no, the two centuries old problems of the constitution. It would have to deal with checks and balances, the proportion of power. It would have to contend primarily with the notion, upon the one hand of power to the neighborhoods, and on the other hand that power which is due in respect to the Constitution of the United States, to the Supreme Court, the decisions of the Supreme Court, and to the power of the new state. Under the umbrellas of the Constitution of the United States, the Supreme Court, and the powers allocated to the new state, power to the neighborhoods could have its expression. It would begin by neighborhoods' voting themselves into existence in the new state, declaring that they wish to become neighborhoods incorporated, small towns, small cities, hamlets, villages—whatever. These neighborhoods would have powers to deal with their own immediate problems in a way they cannot deal with them now. And so a great variety of neighborhoods would soon begin to flourish, one might hope, in this city. At the very least, if the acrimony, if the sense of combat and strife in these neighborhoods was fierce, people living in these neighborhoods would have a sense of whether they adhered to the principles of the neighborhood, or if they really, literally, wished to move out and move on. But the one virtue of this, it seems to me, is that the energies of the people of New York, which at present have no purchase or power—no purchase on their own natural wit or intelligence—no purchase other than to watch with a certain grim humor, a gallows humor, the progressive deterioration of this city, those energies could now be attached to working for their deepest and most private and most passionate ideas about the nature of government, the nature of politics, the nature of man's relation to his own immediate society. And it's possible that out of this interaction of these neighborhoods—which would be like small towns only in one sense, which is that they be small—these people might produce extraordinary results. So I present to you this notion: that we might begin to discover the nature of our reality as men and women in this seventh decade of the twentieth century. We might begin to discover which political ideas had validity, the power to continue themselves and nourish themselves, and those ideas which, finally, were surrealistic, nihilistic, excessive and destructive to the ultimate aims of society, which finally is to find some balance in the lives of men and women.

Now, on this notion, I would like to throw some time open to you for questions and I will do my best to answer them, and then proceed with a peroration, if that still remains within our possibility. Thank you.

What makes you think you could get the fifty-first state?

MAILER:

I would ask you to use your imagination. We are not talking about the city as it exists today. We're talking about the city after Mailer and Breslin, forgive me for talking like a conventional politician, after Mailer and Breslin succeed in stealing a primary election in the Democratic Party from Meade Esposito, Mario Procaccino and a few other people. Now, at that point, that is an extraordinary moment in the history of the city, nothing less. If we then go on, but I would submit that is easier to do than win the mayoralty election, because at that point the time is so surrealistic that people might just say, "Oh, the hell with everyone. Let's just vote them in. Vote them in, so we'll have some amusement." Well, at that point, we then have four months to run through a hot summer through September and October, working under the long shadow of John Lindsay, who will seem more viable to leftists, liberals, conservatives, and reactionaries alike each day that they come face to face with the fact that if they vote for us, they are voting for an embarkation upon an unknown journey, which may end with the city of New York being cut loose from the mainland of America and being shipped out to sea. So I say to you, at that point, when we win the mayoralty election, this city will have gone through a transformation so extraordinary that the questions with which we engage ourselves today are not likely to be nearly so alive and pressing.

If you were mayor or governor of New York would you be able to continue writing?

MAILER:

I think, since I pay great attention to my betters, that would be a small sacrifice to make. I would merely have confirmed the fond opinion that *Time* magazine has of me, which is "this fella better stop writing or none of us will benefit." Seriously, I would not be able to continue writing, dear lady.

What are the legal steps necessary to achieve statehood?

MAILER:

There are three steps. A constitutional convention would have to be called; it would doubtless take months for a constitution to be written. At that point, it would be submitted to the state legislature in Albany for ratification; once Albany had ratified it, it would go to the Congress of the United States for ratification, and on that happy day we would be a state. Now, if you say how is that possible, how would Albany ever begin to pass it, let me point out to you, sir, that something like 42 or 43 per cent of the legislators, I think it's actually more than that, 44 per cent of the legislators in Albany come from New York City. And one would assume that the large majority of those men and women would be prepared to vote for statehood about the time we had gotten in, for that would be the shock from which no one could recover. It would mean that people who felt they really understood the political game would have to recognize they didn't understand it at all, and so they would be inclined to go along with the winner. Politicians keep that as their last resort. If you can't figure out what else to do, go along with the winner. I think we could find another 5 or 10 or 15 per cent in the upstaters who are proud and feel that we in New York City have been dragging them down for 182 years. On top of that, I think that President Nixon might go to the phone and talk to Rockefeller and say, "Now look, there's not much else you can do. Are you going to put on your tin hat? Are you going to go at the head of the State Militia and cross at Yonkers?" He'll be worse than that; he'll say, "Will you defile through the hills of the Bronx? Cross the Harlem River? Move south? You will never reach Central Park!"

Do you have political ambitions beyond becoming the mayor of New York City?

MAILER:

It's precisely because I have the stature I have that my ambitions are limited. I wish to be mayor of New York. Lindsay, who's a tall fellow, looks further.

You've put forward a very provocative idea, the fifty-first state. Do you feel anyone is listening to this at all?

Mailer:

When we go down the street, we find that more people have heard of this idea than have heard of us, when we get out in the neighborhoods. They say, "Oh yeah, you're the fellows who are running with the ah—what is it—the fifty-first state." And I get the feeling, maybe, that I have nothing but candidatitis; but I also get the feeling that people are particularly excited by this idea. Of course, I have an interest in thinking that way.

Why did you support the dual admissions policy for CCNY?

MAILER:

Well, I was the only candidate who supported the dual admissions plan, and I was pleased to find myself in such a position because it meant that I was living well, since it's almost impossible in a mayoral primary in which you have five men running in one election and two in another to find yourself on one side of an issue . . . well, you're all very serious about CCNY, aren't you? All right, I'll talk particularly straight about CCNY. It gives no one any pleasure, who has grown up in this city as I have, in Brooklyn, to enjoy seeing the pearl of the free higher educational system in New York having its standards adulterated. But the fact of the matter is simply this: we really don't know. One, we have no idea at all what's going to happen after two or three years; in other words, the students who succeed in being admitted without academic standards to CCNY will have much more life experience, presumably, than the students whose marks are a little better, because they've grown up in an environment which is near criminal for many of them. So I would just suggest that a great many of the people—among them the candidates who have been bleating about law and order and getting the crime off the streets—are acting like unconscionable hypocrites. Would they rather have those young people out on the streets, unemployed, living on welfare and looking for extraordinary varieties of mischief or would they rather have some of them going through the Draconian steps of trying to reorient themselves into an educational system, and conceivably some of them even wrestling with books at night to catch up? So to begin with, what was marvelous about the dual admissions system is that it would have opened the system to the kids who are presently wrecking and sacking the high schools and running through them with only one sort of expertise, which is, whoever is most adept at disrupting the educational system in the high school because there is no future past these high schools. They know their marks are so poor that they can't begin to contemplate getting into a university. Having them now being able to contemplate the fact that, yes, they can get into universities, they will feel that first moment of fear—of what happens if I go to a university and I'm completely ill-equipped? Some of them might even begin to start studying in high school, which opens up the possibility that the high schools may be seeded by this first seeding and may begin to improve a little bit, so that the morale of the teachers may begin to improve at that point also. Now, all these matters, I think, are more substantial than the fact that the educational standards at CCNY may be lowered for a period. It's my optimism and my hope that black and Puerto Rican students who enter CCNY will end up being fine students, and the academic standards of CCNY, after a few years, will become as high as they are now or even higher. But even if that does not happen, we have to recognize that we are merely paying our dues, because the history of the treatment of black people in this city is not an honorable history or an agreeable one. They've been kept from getting into any of the powerful unions of this city, so they have not been able to enter the working class and the middle class in any numbers. And now that they've been shut out from all other opportunities, now that they are pushing into the colleges, we bleat when we discover that white boys who are qualified are not going to get into these colleges. Well, I say fine, because that's the point when you're going to begin to have community colleges in this city built to fulfill precisely that need. The moment white boys can't get a free education, then you're going to get the community colleges, not before. So long as black boys can't get it, you're going to keep having the same buck-passing and the same complaining about expenses, and so that was why I supported the dual admissions system.

Wouldn't communities set up along geographical lines tend to freeze in present racial and economic distinctions very poor cities or very poor mini-cities that couldn't afford the police, the sanitation, and the fire departments that they would need . . . ?

MAILER:

I think you'd have to begin with the notion that the fifty-first state would be able to command more moneys than New York City. We've had people working on it, and they can't come up with any figure that's really sufficiently satisfactory to present to a technical audience or even a critical audience, because there are too many fluctuations in too many of the figures. We estimate that, immediately, it would be worth between two and three billion dollars more a year to New York City, if it were a state. For instance, there are all sorts of taxes that we would be able to collect directly, like the cigarette tax, the gasoline tax, the tax on registered automobiles, the take on parimutuels—and if off-track betting were legalized, there would be a tremendous amount of money there. There would be any number of funds available that we don't have now, so we would have more money to deal with immediately. It seems to me that you would have to make some sort of estimate of the funds that are going into each neighborhood now. For example, when you take poor neighborhoods you would have to estimate how much of the money that goes into those poor neighborhoods is spent on police. After the neighborhoods were constituted block to block, you could figure out what the administration of those neighborhoods had cost in the past, and these moneys would be passed over to the neighborhoods so they could elaborate their own forms of administration. They might wish to save money on one service or another in order to have more money available for other purposes. But on top of that, this could be any place in the city, and this is why I call myself a left-conservative. We would have to recognize that the history of these communities is not a fair nor an equitable history, and they are not capable of solving their problems through their own human agency nearly so well as we are in more fortunate communities. And so a majority of the new moneys in the new state would have to go toward economic funding in these communities. Now the difference between that and federal funding, which is going to happen anyway, is a great one, I think—because these particular poor neighborhoods would now be administering the funds themselves. So when people working in these programs began to cheat and swindle the programs they'd be cheating and swindling their own people rather than the federal government, and that I think would make a noticeable difference. I don't mean that all crime and all corruption and all embezzlement would stop; but I do think that it would make a big difference, because not only would they be cheating their own people, which might give great pause, but also they would have to face their own people, which might give even greater pause. So I think that would make for a more lively basis for economic funding for economic self-development in the poor communities.

Even more than financial problems you might have the freezing of racial enclaves and the polarization of communities which I think we've got to try to correct in New York.

MAILER:

Well, I think what you'd find is that you'd have a certain freezing into racial enclaves, as you put it, although I would suggest that that's exactly what we have today in the city, because there are few white people, for instance, who are going to just travel on the loose through Harlem after dark—just as a small example. So, as a practical matter, Harlem and the rest of Manhattan are more separated, I'd say, than East Berlin and West Berlin. But apart from that, what you also could recognize is to the extent that certain neighborhoods declared themselves for this sort of separation, other people who had been rather tolerant, fairly noncommittal liberals up to that point might say, "This is a disgrace, now we've really got to work for integration because we're about to really lose it." They might recognize that integration is something that has been given to us from above, and if they really wish to work for it, they now have to work for it directly. So I think you would have communities that would form themselves on principles of integration and collaboration and tolerance. And on top of that, you've also got to recognize that New York is a particularly curious city, and there are any number of blocks in this city and small neighborhoods in this city where you have a mix of six, eight, ten minority groups, and they all get along together reasonably well. Sometimes there's a historic tradition for it. There's one neighborhood, Park Slope in Brooklyn, that's marvelous, and I think one of the reasons for it is that architecturally it's a superb neighborhood. So even though people live there who are rich, poor, of all minority groups and races, the architecture—the character of the neighborhood—is lovely. So there's a certain possibility for getting and living together.

Are you worried about hurting Badillo's chances in the primary?

MAILER:

Let's take it head-on. One, I don't think Herman Badillo has the chance of a snowball in hell of winning the primary, whether I'm in it or not. That's because I don't think he's a winner. I think he's a congressman, and I'm prepared to support him for Congress on that happy day he runs. Two, if Herman Badillo ever did win the primary he would hurt Mr. Lindsay's chances, because you would then have Lindsay running against Badillo, and you could be certain that you would have Marchi or Procaccino running on some other ticket. In fact, you certainly would have Marchi running against them, and you would have two liberals running against a conservative at that point. You would have an unhappy situation for yourself if you were a liberal. So I don't think I'm hurting anyone's chances because, since I'm running as a left-conservative, I'm to the left and right of every man in the race.

If elected to the Harvard Board of Overseers, would you undermine Nathan Pusey's position as president?

MAILER:

I think Nathan Pusey undermined his position on the campus many years ago when he put up that building on Mount Alban Street, that Medical Health Center which is fourteen stories high and expresses a style in architecture known as brutalism, which is unfinished gray concrete. That building is one of the six ugliest buildings in the United States. And the campus at Harvard, no matter what you might have said about it in the past, was not a disagreeable campus, and Mount Alban Street was one of the pleasanter streets in our vast vanishing western world. I think on that day that Dr. Pusey permitted that building to be put in, one could read the future. He would do something precisely so idiotic as calling up the Cambridge cops to get the kids out of University

Hall. So whether I'm elected to the Board of Overseers or not, I can't say that I have a high opinion of the ongoing potentialities of Dr. Pusey's presidency.

Primary odds?

MAILER:

Breslin figures he's an odds-on 2 to 3 favorite. I think I'm running as a 20 to 1 shot. But in the handicap, the mayoral handicap we set up the other day at Aqueduct, we did say that while I was by Amateur out of Statehood and it was my first start, I was out of a good barn. So the handicapper put stars after my entry and said "Best Bet." Of course, the handicapper was my campaign manager. Would you like to hear the rest of the handicapping? Well, it was the mayoral handicap, and in post position one was Wagner, a twelve-year-old gelding by Meade Esposito out of Machine. The handicapper's comment on him was "Knows the track." The odds were 8 to 5. In the second post position was Procaccino, a Bronx ridgling. Now a ridgling, for the ladies I must say to you, is a horse of evil disposition. In fact, the Italian word *vellano* is the only way to describe the disposition of a horse—what you do with a horse or a man who's *vellano*—I'll leave the man out of it—but in any case what you do with a horse who's *vellano* is you're obliged to perform a curious testicular operation—ah—which leaves the fellow with one nut. A ridgling. There was Procaccino, a Bronx ridgling. This is the one argument I had with my handicapper, who wrote this particular sheet. He had "By Fear out of Law and Order." I said to him after, "You should have had 'By Prunes out of Law and Order'." Anyway, the comment on him was "Moves up on a sloppy track." Then there was Badillo and Scheuer. They were an entry. They were both "By Liberal out of Loser," 11 to 1. And finally there was our own entry. "Best Bet."

So the notion that we're running on, finally, is that everybody in this city suffers from the same disease that everyone in America suffers from—that we suffer from it doubly, triply, and in exaggerated form, which is, we do not have a proper sense of our own identity. So, we argue that statehood, the quality of statehood, once achieved would perform several wonders for this city. Not because we would get more money, although I think we would, and I think that money would be terribly necessary, but because the citizens of this city would have embarked upon an adventure in voting for that statehood particularly since we're the candidates, at the moment, who embodied that desire. So to get to statehood at that point, they would have to vote for us, which means they would be voting for amateurs, which means they would be deserting their belief in expertise because we run on one notion over and over again, which is that the experts have driven this city right into the ground. And we run on the notion, finally, that politics is philosophy and that one cannot begin to solve the problems of a city without engaging in philosophical arguments with oneself and with one's neighbor.

And the particular small continuing event which gives me most pleasure since I've been campaigning is I find that I can give my speeches at the level at which I wish to give them, I never try to talk down, I say what I wish to say to an audience, trying to pick up the mood of that audience, talking at my best to reach that audience, and I find that the philosophical density of the argument never bothers them one bit. I've talked to left-wing audiences, to right-wing audiences, to all sorts of audiences, and they all listen. The right-wing audiences listen even more carefully than the left-wing audiences because, perhaps, our words are fresher to them. At any rate, the powerful notion in it, which I think is appealing to all people in degree, is that if each group of people, each interest, each force in this city can begin to think in terms of neighborhoods, then it can begin to think in terms of discovering whether its own ideas and one's own ideas have validity, have savor, give energy to others, give energy to oneself or don't.

The tragedy of this city and the tragedy of this country is that we all live in a situation where none of us know what the reality is, and we explore for it and we explore for it—we spend our lives exploring for it—and we never find an objective ground where we can begin to locate whether some pet idea of ours or some profound idea of ours is partially true or partially untrue.

To talk about the situation, even briefly, people on the right wing feel that the black people are lazy, spoiled, ungrateful, and incapable of managing their own society. Black people feel, I would guess on the one hand, that they have extraordinary possibilities and that they are great people. On the other hand, they have to feel that they can't possibly know, because they never had an opportunity to express that desire. So, if nothing else, black communities working with their own power in their own neighborhoods could show to other neighborhoods one of two things, which is either that black people were right about their potentiality for the future or that they were wrong and that, finally, they are incapable of making those extraordinary steps. And so that even right-wing people would have, at the end of that time, the confidence of knowing that they were seriously right or seriously wrong about some extraordinary matter. In turn, right-wing neighborhoods would discover in living with their principles whether their principles were nourishing and could maintain a society against all of the nihilistic tides of the twentieth century, or whether, finally, their principles were not sufficiently flexible to meet the extraordinary quality of the age. And on top of that, we would have the marvelous, if somewhat comic, alternatives of considering all those magical LSD communities where you would have children living on LSD for five years. At the end of that time they would either be creating castles, or they might be two-thirds dead of liver disease.

The notion that we're running on, then, is that until we begin to know a little more about each other—not through the old-fashioned New Deal governmental methods of tolerance—but through the quality of human experience in societies, small societies and somewhat larger societies, founded upon various principles—philosophical, spiritual, economic, geographical, territorial, historical, or whatever—we know nothing at all. And that's why I feel a certain optimism about this candidacy. Because what I think it offers to all the people of the city of New York is a chance to turn this city around and make it what it once was—the leader of the world. Thank you.

MAYORAL CANDIDATES DEBATE

NORMAN MAILER AND OTHERS

WPIX, May 15, 1969

The Community Affairs Dept. of WPIX-TV Presents the Democratic Mayoral Candidates Debate. Here is your host and moderator, Lee Nelson.

LEE NELSON

Good evening. They say that being mayor of New York is the toughest job in the land. They say the nation's largest city is ungovernable. There are even some who say being mayor of New York is the end of the road politically, and yet this year a record number of candidates is running in the Democratic primary. Perhaps in light of this we should be grateful for at least two things: for the confidence the candidates display, and for voting machines to tally the vote.

Tonight all candidates are participating in this debate, and it's now my pleasure to introduce them. First, Congressman James Scheuer, Mr. John Cedar, author Norman Mailer, City Controller Mario A. Procaccino, former Mayor Robert F. Wagner, and Bronx Borough President Herman Badillo. Now I'd like to welcome the candidates and briefly review the ground rules for the debate as established by representatives of candidates themselves. Each candidate will have two minutes for an opening statement, with the order of appearance already determined by a drawing by the candidates. Then each candidate will receive one and a half minutes for a statement on the topic of his choice. A period of rebuttal will follow each statement. Rebuttal will be limited to one minute, and each candidate will be limited to three rebuttals during the entire debate period. Finally, each candidate will have two minutes for a closing rebuttal or statement, with the order of appearance the reverse of that established by the drawing. So gentlemen, then shall we begin, and first with Mr. Scheuer.

JAMES SCHEUER

This is a very difficult time for the voters of New York in selecting their candidate for mayor, and it's particularly difficult for the liberal voters because there's been such a failure, such a crisis in liberal leadership. And so therefore I would like to address myself to the progressive mainstream of the Democratic Party, those of you who are deeply concerned about the state of our city. Now we do have real and difficult and tough problems in our city, problems of crime, problems of welfare, problems of an escaping, fleeing middle class. And these problems are real, but they are not going to be licked by repression or reaction on the one hand, nor by the re-tired programs and the wearied leadership of bygone years. They will only be licked, they will only be faced by tough, effective, modern programs. Now I have been an achiever, a shirtsleeves worker, both in business, in law, and as a member of Congress. When I went to Congress four years ago when we began to worry about welfare, I didn't just sit around and bemoan the problem, I put together a job program that has worked across the country in getting people off of welfare and into jobs. I can do that in New York. When we became concerned about crime, I studied the situa-tion, I became an expert in crime, and I sponsored a bill along with Senator Ted Kennedy that for the first time put the government, the federal government, squarely into the business of helping cities fight crime. My anti-crime activities can help in New York. I know with this forward-looking, effective shirtsleeves working leadership I can be a successful mayor of New York City.

Thank you, Mr. Scheuer. And now we'll turn to you, Mr. Cedar.

JOHN CEDAR

Good evening. Some weeks ago we saw pictures in the papers of families dressed in rags living in miserable shacks, children with distended bellies. Some of these pictures were from Biafra, some of these pictures were from South Carolina. And we New Yorkers thought, well, South Carolina, what can you expect from a backward place like that. I suggest to you that hunger is closer to home than you may realize. This summer, in New York City, there will be hunger and malnutrition as a result of the welfare cuts enacted in Albany last month. Think about what that means. Think about a mother trying to explain to a crying two-year-old that there is no milk and there is no food, and the next check is three days away. Think about that most magnificent of all the works of almighty God, the human brain, stunted and dwarfed, its full growth stopped by protein insufficiency in the early years of life. This brain damage is permanent, it can never be corrected. And this will happen this summer in this city, this greatest city of this wealthiest and most powerful nation in the world, a nation that calls itself civilized. I entered this campaign with these five good men, each with his own special talents and abilities and experience, because I didn't feel that I heard from them the sense of urgency about the enormous crisis that faces this city. And if they have solutions . . .

Thank you, Mr. Cedar. And now we will turn to Mr. Mailer.

NORMAN MAILER

Good evening. Mr. Cedar's words were quite moving, and I agree with him that there's going to be enormous hunger in the city this summer. There's also going to be a continuing sense of another kind of hunger, which is a spiritual hunger. The people of this city are separated a great distance from any sense of who they are, or what they belong to, they've lost their sense of pride as New Yorkers. We're a city that sits on the edge of a sense of disaster. That is why my running mate, Jimmy Breslin, and myself are running. We're running as amateurs, not only to dramatize the fact that this city suffers from almost insurmountable problems of welfare, a lost year in school, problems of law and order, problems of what the experts sometimes call alienation and anomie. But more than that this city suffers from the fact that it no longer has faith in its experts and for good cause, because the politicians of this city have ridden this city right down into the ground. This city suffers from the fact that it has lost any sense of how it can go forward and solve its problems. People are beginning to think of how they can get out of New York rather than how they can stay in this city and work for it. And so we run as amateurs precisely because we think we have an outside chance of winning on just that notion. Because we have a program for this city that we believe can save it, and if we win with our program, then we can show you people of New York, and we can show the world how extraordinary the possibility still remains for us. This program is built upon one basic notion which is that New York City cannot begin to solve its problems until it becomes the fifty-first state of the Union. Now any one of these other candidates, with the possible exception of Mr. Cedar, could run with that promise and it would not mean a thing. If Mr. Wagner, Mr. Procaccino, Mr. Badillo, Mr. Scheuer were to be elected because they were advocating a fifty-first state, everyone would know that it would mean that easily twenty-two years would go by. But if Jimmy Breslin and myself can win the primary and then go on to win the mayoralty election, our candidacy being embodied in the notion that we're running to become the fifty-first state, New York City would become the fifty-first state of the Union . . .

Thank you, Mr. Mailer. And now, Mr. Procaccino.

MARIO PROCACCINO

Good evening, ladies and gentlemen. We face one of the most critical periods in this city's history. We have gone from a city in crisis to a city in chaos. We have gone from procrastination to confusion. There's no question in my mind who is the best qualified to save the city of New York. Most of the candidates here tonight offer you campaign promises and even some record of performance. Frankly, I'm glad it's not my record. One candidate wants a fourth chance as mayor, after leaving our city in crisis. I ask for only one chance as mayor. I will serve with courage, energy, dedication, and tremendous experience. I will continue to fight for better schools, housing, transportation, and libraries, to fight for equal rights and opportunity, for the finest museums, parks, and other improvements. They belong to all of us, but we must enjoy them without fear. Twenty-five years ago, Fiorello LaGuardia started me in public life. He believed in dedicated action, not committees, and so do I. Look me over. You're looking at a man who has been an assistant corporation council, chief law assistant of the Supreme Court, administrator of the city's middle income housing program, deputy controller, judge, member of the faculties of City College and Fordham University for over twenty-one years, and now the controller who has fought for the rule of law and respect for the rights of others. Our town will be what we want it to be when we have peace in our daily lives, harmony among all people, understanding of mutual problems, security in all our homes, and safety in the streets. I have the courage and qualifications to make this a safe city, a clean city, and the greatest city.

Thank you, Mr. Procaccino. And now we'll turn to Mr. Wagner.

ROBERT WAGNER

Good evening, ladies and gentlemen. A number of months ago I certainly didn't feel that I would be running for mayor again in the city of New York. But so many people in all walks of life, in the streets, in the subways, in the shops, came to me and said, would you please come back and try to help us in this crisis. I had a vacation. I suppose it's good for mayors to have a vacation. I think the present mayor should get a vacation. And therefore I'm back again because I feel I can supply that leadership, that leadership to bring about peace among our people through conciliation, the ability to bring people together, to work together for a common

cause, a better and finer New York. I believe, too, that I have
the qualifications through experience to manage the city properly.
We've seen the services of the city depreciate to such an extent
that for instance in the Sanitation Department never have the
streets been so filthy in the entire history of our city, as far as I know.
We know that we need leadership to run those departments, and we
know that we also have to have experience on the part of people
who are able to innovate, to bring in new methods to solve new
problems, and we can't just rely on the old methods. I supplied that
innovation during my term of office for twelve years, and I can
supply it again. And I know that we have to work together to have
a safe city, a city where people can walk on the streets, whether
it be on Park Avenue or in the greatest slums of our city, a city
that has order and social justice for all of our people so that we
can move ahead to a better day.

Thank you, Mr. Wagner. And now to Mr. Badillo.

HERMAN BADILLO

Thank you. I'm a candidate for mayor because I believe I have
the education, the experience, the energy, and the determination
to be a good mayor of the city. I was born in Puerto Rico, but
I'm a graduate of the City College of New York and of Brooklyn
Law School. I'm a lawyer and a certified public accountant. I have
been a city commissioner in the Department of Relocation for four
years, and now I am the Borough President of the Bronx where
I have been for three and a half years. In the Bronx we have
a microcosm of the city of New York. We have low-income people,
and middle-income people, and high-income people. We have Jews
and Italians and Irish and blacks and Puerto Ricans. We have
people who live in tenement houses and in middle-income apartments and in one- and two-family homes. I have shown what the
office of the Borough President can be. I have shown how a man
in the city of New York can work with all of the local community
groups. For years we have been talking about improvements in the
Bronx. In the past three and a half years I brought over $1

billion in capital projects to the Bronx. I have brought a library to Throgs Neck, a vest-pocket park to Riverdale, the benches along Pelham Parkway have been fixed, I brought a new community college to the South Bronx, and a new health center for Soundview. And it is no accident that when the fourth platoon went into effect it went into effect in the Bronx because the mayor knew that the Borough President of the Bronx was on top of the situation and would be calling and has been calling for additional police. But most importantly, during the past three and a half years we have had people from the Bronx, from all areas of the Bronx, come to City Hall to testify, and never has one group spoken against the other. We have all worked together in the Bronx, and I think that we can all work together throughout the city, and that is what I would like to do and that's the reason I'm running for mayor.

Thank you, Mr. Badillo. Well, that concludes our opening round of opening statements, so now we get to the main body of the debate. Once again I will remind the candidates that in this round they are entitled to one and a half minutes each, and those who wish to rebut at any time may do so by signaling with this sign. Again we'll begin with you, Mr. Scheuer.

SCHEUER

Most New Yorkers are chiefly concerned about violent crime, about attacks against their person and their property. That's what they fear the most. Now there are things we can do about crime. First, we can get more police on the streets. Second, we can deploy them more effectively. And third we can bring science and technology to our police system. First of all, I would get all police out of non-crime fighting functions. We have at the present time about a thousand police officers who are assigned to gambling work and to supervising the private morals of consenting adults. I would reassign those police to getting after the criminals who are terrorizing our city: the rapists, the muggers, the dope peddlers. And then I would make sure that police who are now involved in ticketing, in towing, and typing in the police precinct headquarters are assigned to crime fighting. I would create a police reserve, patterned after our army reserve, to supplement the police forces, and I would urge a city-state-federal strike force to wage all out war on the dope addiction that has placed our city in peril. Crime is the number one problem, but we can do something about it.

Thank you. Next to you, Mr. Cedar.

CEDAR

The cost of welfare and Medicaid in New York State is now running at the rate of $2,700,000,000 a year. The federal government is paying a little under 40 per cent of this. Now practically every editorial writer, every study group, every governor, every mayor, state legislature that has looked into this question has come up with the same conclusion—that the federal government must assume a larger part of the financial cost of welfare. But all of these speeches, studies, and reports put together will get us a ride on the subway if we have twenty cents. On May 7 Congressman Edward R. Roybal of Los Angeles introduced a bill in the House, H.R. 11044 which would set minimum national standards for welfare payments which would be followed by all of the states and would increase the federal reimbursement to the states for welfare from 50 per cent, which it is now in New York, to 90 per cent, which it is for the interstate highway program throughout the country. Ninety per cent for poor people, 90 per cent for highways. This bill would bring an additional $1 billion to the state of New York, and about half of that would be passed along to the city. If this bill were passed it would be possible for the governor to call a special session of the legislature to restore all of the cuts in welfare, education, libraries, and most of the cuts in state aid and still roll the sales tax back from six cents to five cents.

Thank you, Mr. Cedar. There are no requests for rebuttal, so we'll move on to Mr. Mailer.

MAILER

With the exception of Mr. Cedar, who announced in the *Times* he is not running so much for election as to educate the people about the problems of welfare, the other candidates and myself are all quite serious, we are all running to win. Now you've heard the others. They all talk about this city as if it is a manageable proposition. They talk about it as if when they get in they're going to fix this and they're going to fix that, they're going to get a thousand more police here, or they're going to get five hundred more dollars there, and they're going to make this city work. Well, this city is designed to run on gasoline and there's nothing to run it now but water. In other words, these men are talking about an antiquated political machine which they helped to create themselves. They helped to put New York in the fix it is now, and they cannot solve the problems of New York because they are the very engineers and mechanics who created the mess in which we find ourselves today. So I propose to you that the real problem of this city is not to save a few dollars here or there, but to find a way to make people care about this city again, work for this city again, love New York again. And they're not going to do that until they find themselves in some relation to the intimate power of government. And so Breslin and myself are running on a powerful notion, which is once we become the fifty-first state, we are going to give the power to the neighborhoods. And what that means is that we will not sit there in our office and draw a map of the city and say this will become a neighborhood, and that will become a decentralized zone. What we will do instead is that we will give the power to the people to vote and declare themselves as neighborhoods, where the particular philosophy of people who live in different neighborhoods can be expressed, whether it be a philosophy of the left, center, or the right. And once people have that philosophy they can begin to work on their own kinds of schools, their own kind of policing, and the rest.

Thank you, Mr. Mailer. And now to Mr. Procaccino.

PROCACCINO

Thank you. Let me say just one word about our college problem. As I pointed out I taught in two of them for over twenty-one years. I fought to keep City College free of tuition, and I fought to keep the Baruch School open, I fought to admit 2300 students to City College, and I won every one of these fights. I agree the students have the right to dissent, the right to object, the right to be heard. But this does not give to them the right to riot.

MAILER

Yes. Mr. Procaccino's ideas for making this city work seem to consist of a massive application of law and order. The fact of the matter is that the more law and order you bring to a problem, very often the worse government you have. When you bring in more police, very often it means nothing more than your government is so poor that you need more police to maintain the same bad government in office and in service. Mayor Lindsay has increased the police force by five thousand policemen. It has merely made things worse, not because the policemen are inefficient but because when you have a deteriorating situation, when you have a city in crisis, bringing in more police does not solve anything. If we have a massive application of law and order, as Mr. Procaccino is promising, what we will get in turn is a Vietnam in New York, because people are living lives that are so intolerable not only economically but spiritually that they cannot put up with the thought of being deprived any longer.

Thank you, Mr. Mailer. We have one further request for rebuttal, Mr. Badillo.

BADILLO

Yes. I was a delegate to the State Constitutional Convention in 1966, and I voted at that time to have free tuition in the state of New York, not just in the City College but in the state universities, because I believe that one of the things that we must do is to give the first priority to education. We keep talking about the cycle of poverty, about housing, and jobs, and education. But it seems to me that unless we insure that our young people are able to get a college education, we're not going to truly be able to break into that cycle. If our young people can get an education, they will be able to get a job and they'll be able to provide housing for themselves. And one of the things that has not been done is that the mayor has not made a clear commitment that education would receive the first priority. This I would do.

All right. We'll continue now with our statements, and Mr. Wagner.

WAGNER

Well, we've heard a good deal of discussion about bills and votes. As a matter of fact I'm sure Herman Badillo realizes that I was a delegate too and voted for that same proposition that didn't go through finally. It was changed. But it's interesting to note when you talk about what you want to do, you have to match it with what has been done. And I'm very proud of the fact that when I was mayor we, I was the first one that opened up the opportunities for the deprived youngsters who didn't quite have the marks that you had to have to get into our city colleges so that they could go into the colleges, and I was very proud of the fact that on the recommendation of their principals and their high schools they went in and they did very well. And this was the first start in this direction. In other words, what you have to realize is that you are going to have a lot of talk about things, but experience certainly is a qualification. These days it seems to me that anyone with experience in city government seems to operate under a handicap, and I just think this is not so. I think that a person with experience has the ability to move ahead to innovate new programs, and we innovated more new programs during my time than during the history of this city, and appointed some of the best people to office in the history of this city, and I have two of them I appointed on each side of me right here.

Thank you, Mr. Wagner. We have a request for rebuttal, first from Mr. Scheuer.

SCHEUER

Both Mr. Procaccino and Mr. Wagner have discussed their experience, but I think that the experience of both of these men proves that they don't have the qualities to do the job that the mayor must do in this city. Mr. Procaccino has talked about security, he has talked about law and order, but he wasn't able to provide security and law and order for those city dollars that went all the way to Switzerland, he wasn't able to provide security and law and order for his own financial consultant in his own office who was indicted for taking bribes, he wasn't able to provide security and law and order for the gross waste and the incompetence and the graft and corruption in the HRA and the Poverty Programs where the taxpayers of our city paid the bill. And Mr. Wagner too wasn't able to provide that forward leadership. He left this city in turmoil, our schools were a disgrace; just as he left our financial rating went down the drain. So experience only proves worthwhile if it is backed up by success and accomplishment.

Thank you. Mr. Mailer.

MAILER

Mayor Wagner talks of his experience but in fact his administration was a limp and complacent administration. The city was left upon his departure with a quarter of a billion dollar deficit in the budget. We've balanced the budget in the last three years, we will have to balance that budget over and over again, we'll be paying for that debt long after Mr. Wagner and his administration has been forgotten. He was on vacation in 1964 when the Harlem riots broke loose. He did not come back from that vacation. There was a considerable loss of life, there was enormous property damage. Mr. Wagner remained on vacation. When he left office, half of the sanitation trucks were inoperative. I think that this is merely a symptom of the general air of lethargy and confrontation beneath the table which went on during the Wagner administration.

Thank you, Mr. Mailer. Continuing rebuttal, Mr. Procaccino.

PROCACCINO

I always thought that Mr. Scheuer was at least a man of character, and I think that it's very vicious, cheap, and desperate political maneuver which he just tried to pull here this evening. I think it's utterly irresponsible. You see, if you're ignorant of the facts, then admit it. You've been a congressman for four years, and that's all you know how to do, you don't know the first thing about city government. Let me point something out to you, Mr. Scheuer. We have a portfolio of $5.4 billion, the yield under my stewardship has been the highest in the history of this city . . . Just a moment, just a moment, please, equal time. Let me tell you there hasn't been a penny lost of the city money, for your information, again showing what you don't know about it. And I have achieved the finest operation that this city has ever seen in a controller's office. I think you better stop hitting below the belt, sir, and let's get on with the facts here, let's get on with the issues rather than smears.

Thank you very much gentlemen. Next in line with a request for rebuttal is Mr. Wagner.

WAGNER

I don't know if Mr. Mailer is really serious about running for mayor or not; he's getting a good deal of publicity on it, but I would just like to straighten out a few facts. First of all, the riot he's talking about was in 1965. I was away. I flew back immediately, went up there, there was no loss of life in that riot, as a matter of fact we've had some happenings since where we've had loss of life, loss of lives, rather, but they've been called happenings, not riots, here in the city of New York. Now you can't leave the budget out of balance, Mr. Mailer. It always has to be balanced, as I'm sure the controller will agree. There was borrowing done with the approval of the state legislature, with the understanding that we had hoped that the off-track betting bill would be approved. If that bill wasn't to be approved then we would have to find a substitute tax that next year. Now there was a great deal of discussion as to whether that was right or not, but there was no deficit in the budget. Mr. Lindsay never changed that position.

If there are no more requests for rebuttal, we'll move on to our final statement, Mr. Badillo.

BADILLO

I think it is important while we talk about the past and the future that we also speak about the present, and I would like to ask the support of my five competitors here in connection with a very important matter that is happening today. The legislature passed a school decentralization bill which gave the five borough presidents the power to appoint the members of the local school board. I have set up in the Bronx a screening committee made up of eleven citizens who are now interviewing candidates for the position and who will recommend five, they will recommend five people for me to make a selection. I have asked the other four borough presidents to join with me in discussing what kind of board we're going to appoint to make sure that the people who will be appointed will be able to work together and will make the bill that was passed by the legislature workable and will insure that we will not have another year of chaos. I have not been able to get the support in this proposal of Borough President Abe Stark. I would like Mayor Wagner to see how he can use his influence so that we don't have Mr. Esposito being a screening committee for candidates. I have not been able to get the support of Borough President Levis, and I would like Controller Procaccino to see how he can use his influence. Now I would like the other candidates to join with me in calling upon all of the borough presidents to work together to insure that we will have a school board that will avoid next year the kind of chaos we have had this year.

Thank you, Mr. Badillo. And now for rebuttal, Mr. Procaccino.

PROCACCINO

I'd like to just emphasize the manner in which I stated at the outset we needed action and not words. Before the borough president did anything about it I issued a release this morning covering this very subject. That's before he spoke. And I called upon the boss of Brooklyn, Mr. Meade Esposito, to stop interfering with the educational system in interviewing candidates for membership on the Board of Education. I called on former Mayor Robert F. Wagner to intercede with this political boss and tell him what Mr. Wagner has been telling us all the time, that politics has no place in the selection of our school members. And I think that Mr. Meade Esposito should cut out the old-time machine philosophy that every job in his borough must pass through the county leader, and I certainly don't want our school board members to go hat in hand to him in order to be qualified, in order to get an appointment. That's degrading to the city of New York.

Thank you, Mr. Procaccino. I believe Mr. Wagner wants to rebut.

WAGNER

Clarify the record, I've never discussed this matter with Borough President Stark or anybody else. As a matter of fact, I've been very critical of that phase of the decentralization bill that calls for the appointment of the board, temporary board, on the part of the borough presidents and the election of the board members. I still think the old system of having the mayor appoint from a screening committee is the best way to get the best people. I think you do get involved in politics, and I certainly join with anybody and

with everybody I'm sure in the city to make sure that we keep
politics out of any selection of anybody, whether it's in the temporary
board or the permanent board.

Thank you, Mr. Wagner. Any further rebuttal. Mr. Scheuer, you
have a minute remaining.

SCHEUER

The war in New York City that you've heard discussed tonight
must come to an end. Our city is in turmoil, where mistrust, and
suspicion and tension is the order of the day. Each citizen feels
that he personally is being taken advantage of by inadequate city
services, that he is being picked on when the schools close, when
the garbage isn't collected, when there isn't a policeman in sight
when he most needs one. And the fact is that this tension, this
turmoil is going to continue until we get a city administration that
can produce adequate city services for all of us so that this city
can work for all of us. But that will never happen until we get
effective, tough, strong-minded leadership team in this city, and
Vincent Broderick for controller, Charles Rangle for assembly can
provide that. We have known nothing but success in the past, and
we will accept nothing but that kind of success in the future.

All right. I will remind all of the candidates that there are additional periods, minute periods, for rebuttal if they wish to use them.
So I will move on to Mr. Cedar, would you care to avail yourself
of the opportunity of three minutes to rebuttal time? This is not
the closing statement. We haven't . . .

CEDAR

Three minutes? I have suggested a program that I think will have
a dramatic effect on the budget. Ambassador Wagner has indicated
that his experience has been considerable, and I think he was
probably misquoted in Sunday's *Times* when he was asked about
the budget and he said, I haven't studied it yet. So I'd like to

yield the rest of my time to him to hear his proposals for the city budget problems.

MAILER

Oh, I object to that. I think that's not proper under the arrangement. There was nothing stated that one could yield his time to another candidate. Is Mr. Cedar running for Mr. Wagner or for himself?

Mr. Mailer, you are now speaking in rebuttal? Have you concluded your rebuttal?

MAILER

No sir, I have not begun it. Mr. Wagner was right about the date of that riot, it was '65, not '64. About very little else is he correct. The fact of the matter is that the city got into the dreadful shape it is in while he was administering it. During those twelve years all of the programs that we needed to be done weren't done. The relation of the people to the city became more and more estranged, and further and further apart. The difficulty in which we find ourselves now is as much a product of Mr. Wagner's administration as Mr. Lindsay's. In fact, my running mate, Mr. Breslin, said that Mr. Wagner is so much in touch with the local situation that when he came back from Spain the first thing he did was to call up Cardinal Spellman.

Thank you, Mr. Mailer. Mr. Procaccino you have a minute remaining in rebuttal time.

PROCACCINO

I'd be happy to say a few words, particularly to what Mr. Cedar said. I agree with you, as a matter of fact I carry it even further. I think the federal government should foot all of the bill insofar as welfare is concerned in the city of New York. I've advocated this, I've said it openly, I make no secret about it, it's not a campaign issue. I said this three years ago, I keep saying it. And I want to point out that insofar as welfare is concerned in this city, it's frightening to see that it's spiraling that one in three people working is on welfare. One is not, and three are working. I think this is frightening. I think it's due to the failure, and I agree with you, Mr. Cedar that there should be some federal standard established not to invite people from Alabama or Mississippi to come to New York. I believe that that is of paramount importance, and I commend you for coming out at this time, and as a candidate maybe you do have an issue.

Thank you, Mr. Procaccino. Mr. Wagner, you have one rebuttal period remaining if you care to use it.

WAGNER

Well, I would say that anyone running for mayor or who would seek to be mayor would be delighted to have the federal government take over the costs of welfare. As a matter of fact, again referring to the state constitutional convention, we adopted a proposal there that, calling for the state to take over the welfare costs. Welfare costs have become very staggering, and therefore I am sure every candidate would be more than delighted to have that happen. I'm not so sure that it's going to happen, and that's why I said at the outset that one of the problems, one of the very serious problems that a mayor faces in the next four years is to be able to manage within the amount of money available to the city, and it isn't going to be in the great amounts we hope, because Congress has not moved that fast in the past, and I don't see it moving that fast in the immediate future, although we hope so. Therefore it will call for a great deal of ingenuity and ability and innovation.

Thank you, Mr. Wagner. Mr. Badillo, you have two minutes remaining of rebuttal time if you care to use it, but following that, in the event you do, or either way, then we will begin the closing statements with you.

BADILLO

Fine. I'd like to analyze a little more deeply the issue raised by Mr. Cedar, because basically I think what the nature of the problem is is that we have to have a basic change in the institutions of this country. We've gone through similar periods in our history, in the 1930s, when for example the farm problem was regarded as a local problem and then books were written about the plight of the farmers, and the nation began to realize that although the farm problem comprised only a small section of the economy that it should be looked upon as a national program, and a national movement took place under which the federal government took responsibility for the plight of people on the farms. This is what has to be done now with respect to welfare. It has to be recognized that the problem of poverty is not a problem only of New York City but it includes Puerto Rico, Mississippi, and every part of this country. But the answer is to form a true national coalition which will begin to address itself to that problem. And what I am trying to do in this mayoralty campaign is to begin the formation of that national coalition here in the city of New York. If that national coalition, that new Democratic Party, can be started on June 17, then we'll be in a position to carry it out in every major city throughout the country. And that's the reason why I've said that Mrs. Eleanor Guggenheimer who is my candidate for City Council president will be assigned as the coordinator in Washington and in every city throughout the country of this program in order to insure that we will be able to put the kind of pressure upon the President and the Congress which is necessary to accomplish the program which Mr. Cedar has been speaking of.

Thank you, Mr. Badillo. I believe that all of the candidates with the exception of Mr. Cedar have availed themselves of the opportunity of three minutes of rebuttal time. Mr. Cedar, you have used only one of your one-minute periods.

CEDAR

Well, I gave it away. I don't think it's fair to give it back to me.

All right, fine. Then we shall move on to our closing statements, and may I remind each of you that these are two minutes in length, and we're reversing the order of appearance here, and this time we'll begin with Mr. Badillo.

BADILLO

Thank you very much. I think that the most serious problem, and of course we can talk about police and housing and welfare and all the other problems of the city, but the most serious and the most urgent problem is to insure that the people of our city begin to work together. And I think that one of the difficulties has been that the people of the city elected a liberal mayor when they elected John Lindsay in 1965, and I think that they still want a liberal mayor, but at the same time I think the people of New York City want a mayor who will be an effective administrator, who will understand that we want to maintain New York City as a city of opportunity for the new groups who are coming, but at the same time will insure that every citizen receives his fair share of city services. It is my intention to make sure that New York City continues to be a city of opportunity. It is my intention that insofar as it can be done by the mayor of the city of New York to change the institutions of our city so that there can be full opportunity for all. But it is also my intention to insure that every citizen feels that he is getting his fair share of the city's services. And that is why I have said that if elected mayor, I would by executive order give the borough presidents, the local councilmen, and the local community planning boards full power to prepare, to develop and carry out local neighborhood budgets so that it would be clear that it would not under my administration we would not be having a Manhattan-oriented administration, that every area of the city would be receiving his fair share of city services, that every citizen whether he is low income or middle income or upper income would be receiving his fair share and in that way we would begin the process of the people of our city understanding each other and trusting each other so we could move on to carry the fight to Albany and to Washington where the fight could really be made.

Thank you, Mr. Badillo. Next, Mr. Wagner.

WAGNER

Well, I certainly appreciate this opportunity to participate with my fellow candidates here this evening. I feel though that we get back to a couple of very crucial points. Number one, who can best lead this city in the next four years. I admit that the last three and a half years have just not been three and a half years but been rather crucial years in this city and this country and in the world, too. But things haven't changed that much so that you have to discard everything just for the sake of change. What you have to do is hold onto those things that are good and then improvise and innovate new programs. And that's why I feel that I have the experience, the ability, the energy, and the disposition to be able to lead through conciliation, bring people together, and I just don't talk about this as a hope or a dream, but as a reality because for the years I was mayor I was able to do that, bring people together, work together, whether it be a labor problem, whether it be a problem of race, whether it's a problem of groups working for the same cause and working towards a general direction for a better day. I feel too that we have to have a mayor who has the ability to govern with experience and also with ingenuity to be able to carry on the day-to-day programs of the city and at the same time be able to think ahead and to see what programs are needed and to lead people in the goal and the quest for those programs. I also feel that a person who is the mayor must be able to lead in the fight to make our city safe, not through Hitler tactics but with police free of politics and out there to do their jobs responsible for what they do but there to do the job for everyone in our city regardless of where they live.

Thank you, Mr. Wagner. And now to Mr. Procaccino.

PROCACCINO

I am sure that all New Yorkers realize that this city needs a man of courage, experience, achievement, sincerity, and understanding to lead it out of chaos. It certainly, and I must disagree with former Mayor Wagner, it certainly does not need one who procrastinates, who abandoned the city during a threatened transit strike, who has already had three chances as mayor, and who caused a loss of the city's credit rating through his borrow-now-pay-later plan which cost the taxpayers millions of dollars extra in taxes. It does not want one who has made and is still making political deals with bosses and politicians and who really wants to run for the U. S. Senate next year again leaving our city in crisis. I want just one chance to serve the city which has done so much for me, and as always I will fight for all issues affecting the well-being of our people. Above all, I want this to be a safe city, a clean city, a great city with equal justice for everyone. When you elect me mayor of New York City, and when you elect Frank Smith, my running mate, as president of the council, and Abe Beame as controller, the man we have endorsed for that position, we promise one thing, we will in this city, whether you're black, white, Jew, Gentile, rich or poor, I ask you just one question: Are you a good guy or a bad guy? Thank you very much, it was a pleasure to be here.

Thank you, Mr. Prococcino. And now to Mr. Mailer.

MAILER

Mr. Procaccino ends always by saying I only care about one thing, are you a good guy or a bad guy. What I would say in answer to him, it doesn't matter any more whether you're a good guy or a bad guy. This city is in such bad shape that it's going to take more than being a good guy to help it run. This city has the worst air of any city in the United States. It has the worst traffic, it has functional illiteracy in the schools, it has 800,000 units of substandard housing, it has racism, it has the paranoia of every political group in the city, the left, the right, and the center. Each are afraid they are going to be destroyed by the others. It's the situation which is approaching crisis. And these men that you see over here, these gentlemen over here on the left, are all fine men, no doubt, but they all look alike, and they've all worked together in this city for years, they all talk the same way, they think the same way, they argue about tiny little things, they pick at nits while the city is burning. So I say to you this, the only thing that can save this city, in our opinion, is a thoroughgoing rehaul of the basis on which it is constituted. We've got to become a state, the fifty-first state of the Union, in order to solve our financial problems. At the present time we spend $14 billion a year in taxes, we get back $3 billion a year from Albany and Washington. So if we became a state we could begin to have more money immediately to attack our problems. Beyond that, we would be able to give the power to the neighborhoods. Once New York City became a state, every neighborhood that wished to in this city could vote to declare itself an incorporated city or small town, and that would mean that people in their own neighborhood would be able to have a real say in the way they ran their schools, the way they ran their police department, they would be able to have police who live in their neighborhood, they would have intimate relation with their police instead of having the police come in from out of town. At the present time half of the police who work for the police department live out of New York City limits. They come in as paid mercenaries. It's as bad as that. He can't begin—the policeman has a hard job, but he can't begin to do his job properly unless he bears an intimate relationship with his community. They don't have that now. On top of that, they would be able to create a work for a style of life, a philosophy of life that might have meaning for them. Each neighborhood could be different. Each neighborhood could live with the others.

Thank you, Mr. Mailer, Mr. Cedar.

CEDAR

I think it's a tragedy that the congressmen who represent the urban centers of this country have not formed a bloc to pursue and push and promote the interests of the cities the way the farm bloc has, the way the trucking associations have, the oil companies, and so on. There are twenty-one congressmen that represent New York City, I believe, and forty-one who represent New York State, and they pay the sales tax upstate the same way they do here. There are twenty-seven congressmen in Pennsylvania where the entire legislature and governor will be thrown out next year because they're putting in an income tax. They're putting in an income tax in Illinois for the first time and the governor has proposed a 45 per cent increase in the budget. Imagine that—45 per cent in one year. These problems of constantly rising state and local taxes are not New York's, they are New York, Philadelphia, Baltimore, Cleveland, St. Louis, Los Angeles, they are Michigan, Massachusetts, Illinois, California, Missouri. And the congressmen who represent these states constitute a mathematical majority in the House of Representatives. All it takes is somebody to get them together and stick together. The measure that I have proposed is an interim measure to shift the financial cost of welfare to the federal government where it belongs during the three- or four-year period that it will take for a complete overhaul of the welfare system, which is certainly necessary but will take a lot of study and a lot of national discussion. My program is very simple, it's not my face, it's right here, it's H.R. 11044, and I urge all of these candidates and Governor Rockefeller and you to get behind it.

Thank you, Mr. Cedar. And now to Mr. Scheuer.

SCHEUER

I applaud Mr. Cedar's ideas and I want Mr. Cedar to know that the liberal congressmen, the urban congressmen, have gotten together. We are members of a Democratic study group which is the

Urban Liberal Congressmen, banded together in unity of purpose. And it was as chairman of the Full Employment Subcommittee of that Democratic study group that I devised the new careers program that has changed our idea nationally about what we can do for the long-term hard-core unemployed. And across this country hundreds of thousands of people, Mr. Cedar, are working in meaningful jobs who were on welfare. And this we can do and this we must do in New York. Now, Mr. Procaccino has talked about the good guys and the bad guys in his typically simplistic fashion. But the difference between the good answers and the bad answers and the good programs and the bad programs is a very much more sophisticated and perplexing difference, and Mr. Procaccino hasn't been able to come up with that difference in his own office, either as to the personnel, the men, or the programs to protect city funds and to make sure that we get full benefit for every taxpayer's dollar that is spent. Now we've heard a great deal about welfare. Neither Mr. Procaccino as the watchdog of city dollars nor Mr. Wagner as our former three-term mayor ever did the minimum to connect people looking for jobs with jobs looking for people. There are 125,000 jobs in this city now looking for people, but welfare has never been job-related, success-related, pride- and self-esteem-related. And that's what we can do if we make New York City a model new careers city that will connect people with jobs. Only in this way will we get out of the ever escalating welfare burden. Only in this way will we be a city that hangs together that is relevant to everyone, where we can build bridges of reconciliation.

Thank you very much, Mr. Scheuer. Now if I may, ladies and gentlemen, in conclusion reintroduce all six Democratic candidates participating in tonight's debate: First, Congressman James Scheuer; then Mr. John W. Cedar; author Norman Mailer; City Controller Mario A. Procaccino; former Mayor Robert F. Wagner; and Bronx Borough President Herman Badillo.

This has been the Democratic Mayoral Candidates Debate. WPIX-TV has also extended an invitation to the Republican candidates for a debate. The time and date will be announced. Thanks for joining us, and good evening.

PART TWO

Some Choice Clippings

AN ODD COUPLE

JAMES A. WECHSLER

New York Post, April 25, 1969

Suddenly, at a few moments after midnight yesterday, the truth was inescapable: Norman Mailer is taking himself seriously as a prospective candidate for mayor. Others may be putting *him* on, but he is viewing his incipient campaign with deadly solemnity, nay, even sobriety.

The revelation came on Johnny Carson's show where, after a brief appearance by lovely Senta Berger, Mailer took the stage. But this was not the Mailer of local folklore, garrulous, disheveled, rambling, and profane. This was The Candidate, his demeanor sedately and sedatively reminiscent of Robert F. Wagner.

Consider his response to Carson's question about the seriousness of his political intentions. In unmistakably Wagnerian tones, Mailer responded that he would officially declare his availability "only if the support is there."

His voice had the ancient sound of a cautious politico nervously awaiting the results of a secret Lou Harris poll.

There is a certain discrepancy between Mailer's televised tentativeness and a full-page ad in the current issue of his Greenwich Village house organ. That manifesto, adorned by photographs of Mailer and Jimmy Breslin, his designated running mate for president of the City Council in the Democratic primary, proclaims, "We're on the March and We Need the Troops" and, in the usual fashion, indicates an address to which fiscal nutrition can be addressed. There is no indication that impetuous investors will get a refund if the trial balloon floats away.

So perhaps the decision is truly made, and Mailer is only shrewdly seeking to evoke quick pledges of commitment by the veiled threat that he will abstain unless there is an instant, spontaneous outpouring of dough and devotion. Unhappily, I have no authoritative sources in his camp.

Nevertheless, apart from some ambiguities in the Mailer program —again comparable to Mr. Wagner's delay in issuing position papers—it is not too late to air other questions.

For example, the word is out that his liaison with Breslin reflects a canny appreciation of the latter's appeal to the disaffected working-class vote. Breslin has long exhibited a vaudevillian tendency to impersonate what is vulgarly called the common man. But Mailer and his backroom advisers are surely suffering from an acute loss of memory.

For Breslin's last involvement in the affairs of the working class occurred in June 1966, in a time of labor travail on local newspapers. At that juncture Breslin emerged as spokesman for an odd ensemble of journalists who gathered at Gallagher's Steak House to announce that they were fed up with proletarian domination of the Newspaper Guild (by typists, clerks, and other lower forms of toiler); he proposed to establish a union restricted to the elite of "creative" personnel.

When someone noted that this issue had been fought in the 1930s and Heywood Broun's battle for an industrial union had prevailed, Breslin commented, "We know nothing of the past," a disclaimer that seemed superfluous.

While Breslin's anti-common-labor stand will inevitably haunt the projected ticket, hostile researchers will also find him painfully vulnerable among many intellectuals to whom Mailer is presumably addressing himself. It was in September of the same year that Breslin obtained an audience with John Roche, then Lyndon Johnson's serious-thinker in residence. In his subsequent report Breslin enthusiastically quoted Roche's attack on the "alienated intellectuals" who were questioning our involvement in Vietnam, then volunteered his own vitriol against the "West Side intellectuals" who "send out a flow of words against the war in Vietnam and against Lyndon Johnson."

It is true that Breslin belatedly gained consciousness and abandoned Roche's holy war, but politics is a cruel sport and no adversary is likely to overlook the earlier warmongering of anti-warrior Mailer's second man.

Mailerites may protest that I am evading the true issue by ignoring extended discussion of his qualifications for the top post and devoting so much attention to his partner. A swift answer would be that I cannot imagine any qualifications to discuss. Mailer is a major writer whose achievements have been justly heralded by those whose opinions matter far more than mine. He also has as much claim to the mayoralty of New York as would a college graduate (myself), who once flunked his written exam in basic training, to the post of Secretary of Defense. (In 1952, a frenetic local columnist warned that Adlai Stevenson was grooming me for that role.)

It will be said that Mailer could bring as much to City Hall— when he visited it—as Bill Buckley would have done if he had won in 1965. But Buckley at least had the grace to say that he would demand a recount in the hour of victory.

What worries me is that Mailer wasn't smiling or reckless on the Carson show, and some nice kids may be beguiled by his advertisements for himself. Moreover, the place of controller remains mysteriously open; the addition of Truman Capote to the ticket could overshadow exposure of Breslin's record. Or is a deal with Abe Beame in the making?

OBSERVER: CHEERS FOR POLITERATES

RUSSELL BAKER

New York Times, May 6, 1969

WASHINGTON, May 5—The idea of a literate man holding public office is so outrageous these days that when one announces he would like to try, everybody suspects him of joking.

Thus, Norman Mailer's candidacy for mayor of New York produces no cheers from the press, but only speculation whether he can possibly be serious. And from this we are invited to draw the conclusion that if he is, then he must surely be a fool.

William F. Buckley, Jr., another man of letters, faced the same handicap in his mayoralty campaign four years ago. Adlai Stevenson's ability to compose a literate paragraph without cant may not have cost him the presidency, but it gave many a voter an easy excuse to justify his emotional preference for General Eisenhower.

POLITICAL LITERATES

Mailer's candidacy should be an occasion for cheers instead of jokes. As long as politics can still attract a man of artistic sensibility, there is still hope. Jefferson, Madison, Hamilton, Lincoln, and Theodore Roosevelt were all highly literate men as well as capable politicians. Why do we automatically assume nowadays that a candidate who can write his own speeches must be playing games with the voters?

The fact is that Mailer has already produced one of the few original and exciting ideas for dealing with what is tediously called the urban problem. He proposes to make New York City the fifty-first state.

Amusing? Not at all. The big cities everywhere are stepchildren of state legislatures, which are usually run by alfalfa growers with a vested interest in detouring the federal gravy into cow country.

EQUALIZING THE LEVERAGE

By freeing the fifteen or twenty biggest cities from the tyranny of the backwoods and giving them the prerogatives of states, millions of city dwellers would finally have the same political leverage in Washington now accorded to sheepherders in Nevada and oil lords in Oklahoma.

With the population headed for four hundred million, the old state boundaries make less and less sense anyhow. Even at present population levels, it is hard to see what Chicago has in common with Little Egypt, Los Angeles, and Eureka, or Atlanta with Tobacco Road.

Mailer has a good idea. Or an idea, at least. This is more than can be said about any of the other candidates for mayor so far. (It should be noted that from Mailer's viewpoint it is a particularly good idea. If elected, he will be Mayor Mailer. This is not quite as bad as being Major Major, but it is still the kind of handicap that needlers find easy to exploit. Governor Mailer, on the other hand, sounds just right. In fact, it sounds so good that one is tempted to try—just for sound of course—President Mailer.)

Having ideas is the work habit of the literate man. It is essential to his calling. Without ideas, he can command no audience. He is not like the lawyer, who can sway masses with pure sound; nor like the businessman, who can move them with money; nor like the electronic-age politician, who can charm them with teeth and a hair styling.

Our modern politics is often accused of intellectual shabbiness. If true, this is not hard to explain. It is a politics of lawyers, business-men, and entertainers, based on the power of sound, money, teeth, and hair styles.

The man whose habit is having ideas has been rare in the business for too long. The occasional literate man pressed into politics as ghost writer commonly finds that he must break his natural habit of having ideas and acquire the new one of writing about ideas. His employer does not want a speech with ideas, which might start somebody to thinking, but a speech without ideas, which will keep the audience anesthetized while sound, money, and good dentistry do their dependable work.

ENCOURAGING PROSPECT

Mailer should not be joked about, but praised. With respectful treatment, his candidacy may encourage other literate men to take up politics. After Governor Mailer of the state of New York City, we might go on to Governor Buckley of the state of Upstate New York.

This might encourage John Hersey to become governor of Suburban Connecticut, which might encourage Ogden Nash to become governor of Baltimore, which might even persuade S. J. Perelman to become senator from Pennsylvania. There is no telling where it might end, but it would be an improvement on sound, money, and teeth. *Ave,* Norman!

MAILER PLAYS A NIGHT CLUB DATE IN MAYORAL QUEST
He Alternately Harangues and Entertains Crowd at The Village Gate

SIDNEY E. ZION

New York Times, May 9, 1969

An overflow crowd at the Village Gate was alternately entertained and harangued by Norman Mailer in the early hours of the morning yesterday at a "party" for the mayoral candidate and his running mate, Jimmy Breslin.

Mr. Mailer, a glass of whisky in hand and a slight southern accent on his tongue, told the audience that he was not interested in their "ego trips" and that he did not want their help unless they were willing to do "the drudge work."

"We're with you, Norman," said one man in a front row of the Bleecker Street night club.

"If you were with me you wouldn't interrupt me," Mr. Mailer shot back, beginning the sentence with a familiar expletive that he was to repeat throughout the half-hour address.

It was Mr. Mailer's first campaign trip into the four-letter world. Until yesterday he had carefully avoided his usual profanity, apparently out of a desire to overcome what his backers refer to as "the credibility gap."

By this they mean that the press and public are not likely to take Mr. Mailer and Mr. Breslin, a candidate for Council president, seriously.

When Mr. Mailer, who on Monday won the Pulitzer prize for his book *Armies of the Night,* took the stage shortly after 1 A.M.

yesterday, it was clear to many in the audience that much of the careful work was about to be overcome.

THE EROSION BEGINS

"If you're in the campaign for fun, you're in it for fun," Mr. Mailer said as he attacked the notion that his candidacy was less than serious.

"Profound," someone yelled from the back of the room.

"Norman, play me 'Melancholy Baby,'" somebody else said for the first of eighteen times.

"Shut up," Mr. Mailer responded, preceding the command with the same familiar expletive.

Being, in his own term, "a very cute fighter," Mr. Mailer turned the audience on and off during the speech.

"I'm running on a platform of 'Free Huey Newton and end fluoridation,'" he said. "We'll have compulsory free love in those neighborhoods that vote for it, and compulsory attendance at church on Sunday in those that vote for that."

At the conclusion of Mr. Mailer's speech, Mr. Breslin was nowhere in sight, rumors started that he had fled.

"I deny it," Mr. Breslin said yesterday afternoon while dressing for a black-tie dinner. "I was upstairs trying to get a prominent Republican senator's wife into the joint, which I couldn't even do, she was dressed too nice. I did that because I am a gentleman politician, which is something new in this town."

Was Mr. Breslin somehow trying to disassociate himself from Mr. Mailer by the "gentleman" crack?

"No," he said, and then added:

"That's the trouble with this thing, you learn to lie right away."

$ MILLION FOR MAILER'S NEXT

New York Post, May 13, 1969

Norman Mailer today had one thing that none of the other candidates for mayor can claim: Nearly $1 million in advance royalties for a book of which he's not yet written a word.

The Pulitzer prize-National Book award-winning author may have as much as $1.5 million in hand once the film rights are sold for his book on the first manned moon landing, expected to be published early next year.

His American publisher, Little, Brown, paid $150,000, New American Library matched that for the paperback rights and *Life* magazine paid $100,000 for serial rights. Foreign publishers are supplying a good deal of the rest.

For walking around money, Mailer has a $20,000 advance for a book to be done for Doubleday with some of his associates in his race for the Democratic mayoral nomination. Mailer said he would use this money in the campaign.

MILLION ADVANCE FOR MAILER SEEN
Book on 1st Moon Landing Will Be Started in July

HENRY RAYMONT

New York Times, May 13, 1969

A book Norman Mailer plans to start in July, dealing with man's first landing on the moon already has drawn close to $1 million in advance royalties, his literary agent reported yesterday.

Scott Meredith, the agent, said he was "quite positive" that the total publishing rights would exceed that figure by the time the book is published in January or February by Little, Brown & Company of Boston.

If film rights are sold, the agent estimated the total for Mr. Mailer, a mayoral candidate in New York City, could approach the $1.5 million paid for the memoirs of former President Lyndon B. Johnson.

In writing the book on the moon landing, the author will use the same reportorial techniques that characterized his last two books, *The Armies of the Night* and *Miami and the Siege of Chicago*. He plans to visit Cape Kennedy during the launching of Apollo 11 interviewing the astronauts and describing the drama of the space center. He also plans a chapter on the philosophical and technological implications of the moon landing.

HIGH FIGURES COMPARED

In the publishing world, the unusually high figure for the still-to-be-written story of the Apollo 11 moon shot is being compared to the sum paid last year for *Twenty Letters to a Friend,* by Svetlana

Alliluyeva, Stalin's daughter. The book is reported to have brought in more than $2.5 million through book rights and newspaper and magazine serialization here and abroad.

In American book rights alone, however, the Mailer work has received $150,000 from Little, Brown—about three times the advance that Harper & Row paid for Mrs. Alliluyeva's book. Also, New American Library paid it $150,000 for the paperback rights and *Life* magazine has paid $100,000 for magazine serialization.

"We were not surprised over the interest of the American publishers," Mr. Meredith said. "But what did amaze us was the phenomenal competition among foreign publishers for book and magazine rights. There is no doubt that Mailer has become the most sought-after author in America today." In Germany, the Droemersche Verlagsanstalt of Munich paid $50,000 for the German-language book rights, an unusually high figure there. Other prominent European publishers who acquired the book included Weidenfold & Nicolson of London and Robert Lafont of Paris.

Life magazine plans to run the first of at least three excerpts of the book about two weeks after the Apollo 11 launching expected about July 20.

WRITING FOR CAMPAIGN

Mr. Mailer, who earlier this year won the National Book award and the Pulitzer prize in non-fiction for his account of a peace march in Washington, said last night that he would not allow the Apollo project to interfere with his campaign for the Democratic nomination for mayor.

"I am devoting all my time to my candidacy for mayor," he insisted. "The only writing I'm doing at this time has to do with the campaign."

The forty-six-year-old novelist-reporter has just completed a six-thousand-word article on the campaign for *The New York Times Magazine*.

The article will be incorporated in a book he and some of his campaign workers have been asked to write for Doubleday & Company. They include Jimmy Breslin, Mr. Mailer's running mate for

City Council president; Jack Newfield, author of *A Prophetic Minority*; Gloria Steinem of *New York* magazine, and Peter Maas, author of *The Valachi Papers*.

Kenneth D. McCormick, senior editor of Doubleday, said the book, *Running Against the Machine,* would appear in August, simultaneously in hardcover and paperback editions. Mr. Mailer said the $20,000 Doubleday had paid on the book would go entirely to help pay his campaign expenses.

TALKING TACTICS

MARY MCGRORY

New York Post, May 19, 1969

Last Friday noon in the Russian Tea Room on West Fifty-seventh Street, the Mailer-Breslin ticket, like so many other things here in New York, was threatening to fall apart.

Jimmy Breslin, the former columnist who is running for City Council president, came barreling in, looking for Norman Mailer, the Pulitzer prize-winning candidate for mayor, to tell him he was pulling out.

His beef: "The campaign is getting serious and we'll end up making fools of ourselves."

Mailer, who wears a dark blue pinstripe suit and a solemn expression these days, agreed they had strayed from the path of "responsible blitheness." He meekly accepted Breslin's critique of his appearance on an all-candidate TV debate the night before— "You stunk"—and promised to get back on the track.

"What were you doing yelling at Wagner, like some two-cent politician?" fumed Breslin. "What was I doing thinking you were right? We ought to be out there being evil, scaring the hell out of them. Somebody's got to scream at them about what's wrong."

He swung off to make a round of calls to his Brain Trust, which includes such high-powered talent as President Kennedy's brother-in-law, Stephen Smith, and Mayor Lindsay's old trainer, Robert Price.

He returned and told Mailer he had reconsidered. The slate re-assembled, Mailer went off to Brooklyn and Breslin sat down to brood over his own guilt in the professionalism that had begun to taint New York's most literate political adventure.

"My ego was getting into it," he said. "You can't say I was sniffing glue. The glue was shoved under my nose. Some guy told me I could win, I have a recognition factor of 34 per cent, stuff like that."

The regular Democrats of New York, bored by the other candidates, are curious about Mailer and wistful about Breslin. Breslin is bulky, blunt, and black-haired. He talks about social justice and reform out of the side of his mouth. The New Left likes the words. The man in the street likes the diction. In the station houses, the cops are remembering the good things he said about them in the old days.

He goes into white neighborhoods and tells them the only trouble in the city is black-and-white trouble. "Don't think you can move out to the suburbs and get away from it all. It will come under the door like flood water."

He goes to Harlem and says, "White people have lost the right to tell you what to say."

He is serious about the solution he and Mailer advocate—neighborhood rule, with money and control given directly to each locality.

Mailer is known euphemistically as an uneven campaigner, says press secretary Jack Newfield, one of several *Village Voice* dropouts staffing the effort. "He'd like to be Brendan Behan." Mailer succeeded in emulating the brawling Irish writer one night to remember. At a fund-raiser at the Village Gate he reviled his benefactors with four-letter words. Breslin called up Newfield at four the morning after and wailed, "I'm running with Ezra Pound."

"We might take Madison Square Garden for a rally to fill it up with disgruntled people," says Breslin. "We could do it. You know how many people would show up just in hopes Norman would flip."

Mailer is now embarking on a serial assault on the synagogues, where he will tell his fellow Jews to repent and rid themselves of the obsession with black anti-Semitism.

"He'll scream at them," said Breslin, eyes snapping with pleasure. "They'll come in with his books for him to sign and they'll go out crying. He'll tell them they're letting Hitler run their lives from the grave."

Breslin will concentrate on TV to tell New Yorkers to repent of their racism. The unlikely missionary pair hope to take votes from former Mayor Wagner and Mario Procaccino. If they help Lindsay in the process, they don't mind.

Mailer, who has developed new respect and contempt for politicians—for their stamina and ideas respectively—hopes to be "more fantastic than I've ever been in my life in the next two weeks." This indicates he continues to dream, but Breslin thinks the danger of their even thinking they might win has passed and they can go back where they belong, "kicking, fighting, and spitting."

THE BORE BUSTER

WILLIAM REEL

Sunday News, June 1, 1969

On a recent sunny, sky-blue afternoon, to the accompaniment of blaring sound trucks, Bob Wagner, on East Forty-second Street, endorsed tolerance; Mario Procaccino, on the Grand Concourse, opposed crime; Jim Scheuer, in Queens, denounced drug addiction, and Herman Badillo, in the South Bronx, favored substantial housing, quality education, higher incomes, and a better life for all the people.

Banality would surely have carried the day had not Norman Mailer, author, enemy of orthodoxy, and the fifth candidate for the Democratic nomination for mayor of New York, preached people power to three Negro housewives minding their children in a quiet park in the Red Hook section of Brooklyn.

With a diffidence that belied his reputation as a roisterer—a reputation thoroughly deserved, but acquired as a result of lapses in deportment induced by whisky late at night—Mailer introduced himself to the women and asked them if they would be so kind as to consider voting for him in the June 17 primary.

"Why?" one of them asked, smiling shyly. "What will you do?"

Mailer had just toured the area and had seen the mounds of uncollected garbage and heard again and again complaints about the scarcity of police. He explained how his platform would uplift run-down Red Hook.

"I would make New York the fifty-first state, and give power to the neighborhoods," he said. "Individual neighborhoods, like Red Hook and Highbridge and Forest Hills, could incorporate themselves as towns and thrash out, at the grass-roots level, their own solutions to their particular problems of police, sanitation, schools, and so on.

"Right now, New York is administered from above and without—from Washington, from Albany, from the superagencies at City Hall. We must save ourselves from the inside out. Red Hook could forge neighborhood government responsive to the people's needs and demands."

"It sure sounds good," one of the women said, "but I'm not registered to vote."

Everyone laughed, including the candidate, at this polite way of telling him he had been wasting his time. Mailer told the women he was pleased to have met them—it appeared that he really was—made a couple of gracious remarks, and left.

During two hours in Red Hook, Mailer met perhaps fifteen people. A few of them knew there was a Democratic primary coming up, and a couple showed vague signs of recognition when he introduced himself. Although Mailer is thought by many to be one of the finest writers in America today, literary personalities ring few bells in these precincts. Brentano's has no Red Hook outlet.

"Why bother with Red Hook?" Mailer was asked as he rode into Manhattan.

"I'm talking about the neighborhoods and making an appeal to the sense of neighborhood identity, so I want to be familiar with them," he said, brushing back his mop of silver-black curls. "I want to be on firm ground. I want to really know firsthand what's going on."

Mailer has anxiety about being thought a phony. He takes pains to squash the notion that his campaign is an ego trip. He is, he points out, a Brooklyn boy himself, having grown up poor in the streets of Crown Heights. His rhetoric in describing the temper of his city—"Heavy, sullen, dangerous as a wad of oil-soaked rags waiting for conflagration"—rings with passionate sincerity.

Is he running to get material for a book?

"I've proved that I can write books without working this hard," he said.

Is he sure he's serious about this mayoral project?

"I knew I was serious the minute I announced," he said, "because I double-crossed my friend, Herman Badillo."

Mailer likes Badillo, but deplores his doctrinaire liberalism. He calls himself a "left-conservative," and explains how this is not a contradiction in terms.

"I believe, like the conservatives, that man must save himself by his own actions," he said. "The government can't save him. But I'm a man of the left in that I believe the conservatives have exploited society. Government must see that the poor get the necessary resources to help themselves."

In Mayor Mailer's city-state of New York, the overflow taxes of the people of Forest Hills would be the wherewithal for the people of Brownsville to lift themselves out of the mire. But the people of Brownsville, hammering out their destinies in bitter debate, would do the lifting themselves.

How would Mailer keep the neighborhoods from warring?

"I'd grow in stature," he said, laughing heartily.

Mailer has seen enough of the other candidates to form some opinions. He is impressed by Wagner's demeanor, but balked at going so far as to describe it as elegant. He thinks Scheuer is a stiff. His one meeting with Procaccino was not, he said, memorable.

"Did you ever visit a small town and have your picture taken with the local mayor?" Mailer asked, conjuring up the Procaccino image. "In those pictures there's always a third person, someone who likes to hold the mayor's coat and be photographed with his arm around the mayor's shoulder. That's Procaccino."

Mailer was sure that Procaccino would not resent this description of himself. "After all," he said, "it will get him the votes of all the people to whom that image appeals."

Mailer dropped into The Phoenix, a successful East Harlem narcotics rehabilitation center, to form some insights into the addict mentality. He would use the information in an upcoming position paper on the subject. Then he donned coat and tie, and headed for a cocktail party at the Americana Hotel.

This was Mailer country, and the guests, getting effusive with booze, fawned upon him. With a bourbon highball in his hand and a glint in his eye, Mailer is the quintessence of animal energy. The women were coming on strong.

"How do you manage to get along with Jimmy Breslin?" a matronly Park Avenue type wondered. She was obviously sold on Mailer, but skeptical about his running mate. Oh-so-liberal WASPs just can't be sure that Jimmy, who is, after all, Irish, and who does, you know, come from lower-middle-class Queens people, could really have enlightened attitudes about, well, *black* people.

Mailer mumbled something about not having any differences with Breslin, although he allowed that there may have been occasional clashes in their campaign styles.

"As a campaigner, Jimmy is the greatest in-and-outer I've ever met," he said happily. "You can never predict his form off his previous day's performance."

Mailer had several bourbons, his first drinks of the day. "I seldom drink in the afternoon," he said, "because then I have nothing to look forward to at night." Then he was off to Sunnyside, to address the West Queens Independent Democratic Club.

The meeting was in a church basement. Perhaps two hundred people, including several urchins and a handful of grandparents, greeted Mailer with warm enthusiasm. Hunched over, his right hand in his pocket and his left jabbing out front like Willie Pep, Mailer discussed ills and cures.

"Alienation is the disease of our time," he said. "None of us have any power. The ideas in our minds have no relation to reality. To stay sane, people have to discover the results of their actions.

"I propose a few powerful ideas in an amateur candidacy. Remember, the experts, the geniuses of mediocrity, the technicians, have run this city into the ground."

Mailer explained that the approval of Albany and Washington was necessary for New York City to become the fifty-first state.

"The miracle of the election of Mailer and Breslin would mandate the fifty-first state," he said. "It would serve notice that our city is awake and electrified. Washington wouldn't fight us. It would be too disagreeable. They would have to occupy us as Russia occupied Prague."

This heady analogy moved the crowd. Mailer beamed.

"Politics is property, and we have none," he said, driving home the clincher. "Washington and Albany own us."

Mailer called for questions. "Riddle me if you can," he said.

A red-haired ten-year-old asked Mailer what could be done about school strikes.

"Each neighborhood would create its own school system," he said. "So you would still have strikes, but not all at one time. You would have many small strikes all the time."

Would he legalize abortion, a girl wondered?

"Only if you would let me outlaw the birth-control pill," he said. "The pill is part of the slime that overlays civilization."

How about legalizing marijuana?

"No, because the cigaret companies would take it over and put vitamins in the pot," he explained.

Someone suggested that the Mailer program was theoretically attractive, but that it was visionary and romantic.

"I don't suggest it as a panacea," he said. "The problem would be knotty. Society would still be corrupt. But there's a difference between a corrupt society that is on the verge of burning up. It's the difference between hell and purgatory."

Mailer got a rousing hand. The red-haired kid followed him to his car and asked for a Mailer-Breslin lapel button. "I want the one that says 'Vote the Rascals In'" the kid said. The only variety Mailer had with him was the recently discarded "No More Bull ——," which he has stopped handing out because it enrages middle-class voters, to whom he is trying to appeal.

The candidate thought it over, and decided to give the kid the button anyway. "Tell your parents you stole it," he suggested.

A couple of days later, Mailer attended a peace rally near his Brooklyn Heights home. With him was his wife, Beverley, a vivacious and charming woman, and three of his six children.

"Even if you blow the election, you can be father of the year," suggested campaign manager Joe Flaherty. Flaherty spent ten years as a longshoreman before embarking on a successful writing career that has been interrupted by the exigencies of electing Mailer and Breslin. He was asked how he thought Mailer, a Harvard man and a literary intellectual, was getting across to the rank-and-file voter.

"The way Wagner and Procaccino pulled out of the TV debates helped Mailer," he said. "The average guy hates punk, and he senses the punk in Wagner and Procaccino. Let's face it, they're scared witless of Mailer. People hate dog, in prize fighters or politicians."

Congressman Ed Koch, who represents Greenwich Village, observed to a reporter that although he was supporting Badillo, he was glad Mailer was in the race because "He'll keep the other candidates intellectually honest." So why is Koch supporting Badillo? "Experience," he said. "Herman has the necessary experience in political life to handle the job."

"Experience, my rear end!" boomed Jimmy Breslin, the uncouth curmudgeon, when apprised the next morning of Koch's remark. Jimmy was furiously scribbling notes for a TV debate against his opponents for the nomination for president of the City Council.

"What kind of experience has Badillo had?" he asked loudly. It was a rhetorical question. "He was Commissioner of Relocation under Wagner. That's like bein' the lookout on the Titanic."

Jimmy Breslin throws those lines away with such apparent ease that it annoys the hell out of a lot of people who wish they could do it. But they can't, and Breslin can, and the knack enabled him to parlay a brilliantly offbeat column in the late *Herald Tribune* into nationwide celebrity status as an elfin eccentric.

Breslin's talents developed unaided by formal education.

"In fact, it took me five years to get out of John Adams High School in Queens," he said proudly. "I was class of '47. That class produced fifteen firemen, fifteen police, thirty-two prominent felons and seventy-five body-and-fender mechanics."

Before bailing out for good with a best seller about the first year of the Mets called *Can't Anybody Here Play This Game?*, Breslin worked for a number of New York papers as a sportswriter. Among these was the late *Journal-American,* which he left under a dark cloud.

"I went around to Mutchie's saloon one day and got drunk,"

Jimmy explained, "and then I called up the publisher, Joseph Kingsbury Smith, and I said to him, 'Joseph, go ——— yourself.' It wasn't a formal resignation."

Breslin got his campaign rolling by pledging, after announcing his candidacy: "If elected, I will go to Queens." On the same occasion he dismissed Mayor Wagner's candidacy: "Wagner is so far behind the times that when he first considered running this year he called Cardinal Spellman to tell him."

Breslin chatted with Hugh Carey, a personal friend and the Council president candidate on the Wagner ticket, before they went on camera at NBC. "Hughie Carey is great, I would be supporting him if he was running for mayor." Breslin said later, "But he ain't. What do I think of the other guys in the race? I think they're all bums."

Breslin comported himself well on TV. He made his points about the desirability of the fifty-first state lucidly and with gusto, and without—much to the relief of his campaign followers—lapsing into the saloon argot with which he is most comfortable. This was a live show—in other words, the technicians couldn't blip out reversions to the vernacular—and Jimmy might easily have blown the entire Catholic vote with one slip of his favorite adjective.

Breslin is pungent when decrying the slave-master relationship that obtains between New York City and the state legislature in Albany.

"It's insanity that we let a lobster fisherman from Montauk and a bunch of jerks from Niagara Falls tell us how to run our schools," he told the TV audience. "Those dairy farmers in the legislature think Ocean Hill-Brownsville is a new breed of cow."

On race relations: "There's one problem in this city and that's the problem of black and white. Unless we give the ghettos a chance to work out their own problems, we're going to have a situation where you'll see shotguns on Park Avenue."

On campus disorders: "A $25 gun knocked out Bobby Kennedy. A bunch of old labor leaders beat McCarthy. There were 450 boys killed in Vietnam last week. The question is, why is there so little campus strife?"

On crime: "Another five thousand cops can't control the crimes committed by the thousands of kids who flunk out of our inferior high schools every year. We're wasting our only product, which is people. We don't have oil wells and crops in New York. We produce people, and we're spilling our treasure across the floors of the criminal courts buildings."

On the condition of New York: "This city is a cancer patient."

After the debate, Breslin repaired to Hurley's, a saloon near Rockefeller Center, where aides assured him that he had won in a walk.

"Ah, it's tough for you to say," he said. "You can't be objective, you're a rooter. I'm gonna call my old lady and ask her how I done."

Breslin went to a phone booth, placed a call, and came back looking sour.

"She says I was last," he said.

Both Mailer and Breslin concede it would be a miracle if they were elected. But win or lose, they have succeeded in fulfilling the third objective of their campaign. Their three-part platform reads:

"The Fifty-first State"

"Power to the Neighborhoods"

"Kiss Off the Boredom of the Democratic Machine"

IN THE NATION: MAILER WITH HIS HAIR COMBED

TOM WICKER

New York Times, June 12, 1969

A lapel button for Norman Mailer and Jimmy Breslin reads: "The other guys are the joke." This is wry rebuttal from the two writers-turned-candidates of the belief of numerous New Yorkers that the Mailer-Breslin ticket is either a joke or a publicity stunt. But in another sense, the slogan tartly expresses the basic Mailer-Breslin position that politics and politicians "as usual" have nothing further to offer a city they fear is dying.

Indeed, history may show that the other guys *are* the joke in New York City's municipal campaign. At best, they are offering more or less of the same, while Mailer argues that it is impossible "to change this city for the better without creating a new political basis." He believes Mayor Lindsay, for instance, "is the proof of this because he worked manfully in the old tradition, tried to wed a new tradition to it, and failed."

The "new political basis" Mailer and Breslin are offering is to make New York City the fifty-first state; but it is not that specific idea so much (nor others, like prohibiting private automobiles in Manhattan), nor even the fact that the Mailer-Breslin campaign has managed to struggle out of the joke category, that makes it so interesting.

It is rather that for the first time the fundamental reorganization of a great American political entity has been made the central theme of a campaign for major office.

Mailer, shy handshaker but a hard worker, is serious, all right.

He is as assertive on behalf of the fifty-first-state idea as he is in his books; greeting voters yesterday morning at Montague and Court streets in Brooklyn, he encountered one scoffer who insisted the only solution for New York was "millions of dollars from Washington."

"I couldn't disagree more," Mailer said. "There's got to be a structure to pour the money into. Otherwise it's like pouring concrete on the ground."

WHAT THE CITY NEEDS

In the afternoon, before an audience of old folks in the breezy courtyard of the Menorah Home and Hospital on Bushwick Avenue, the Pulitzer prize winner ("He reads well," a lady said of him in Albee Square; "Maybe he'll do well.") insisted that the city needed a "new beginning," just as had the immigrants who came here from Europe—not physically, in the case of the city, "but in its laws."

And when one, Abraham Frank, took the microphone to tell Mailer that it appeared to him that a New York City mayor had to have "the power of an elephant and the brains of an Einstein," the candidate, rocking a little in his punchy boxer's stance and with his hands thrust in his pockets, replied bluntly that if New York did have such a mayor "it still wouldn't work because the city won't work."

No doubt there are flaws in the fifty-first-state idea and it certainly would not be easy to achieve, although Mailer insists, as he did to one voter while walking on Fulton Street, that "if I can get elected, that would be sufficiently shocking to everybody that I think we could do the rest of it. It wouldn't be a political situation then but a historical situation that they couldn't resist."

What Mailer and Breslin have done is to dramatize a fundamental issue, not only for New York but for all America, in demanding "a new beginning." For the fact is that the most powerful nation in the world, with its population shifting inexorably into vast city-states that are little more than political vassals of the fifty historical accidents of the federal system, with both these jurisdictions further subdivided into mazes of overlapping, inefficient, and jealous units, with a central government that absorbs a lion's share of all the revenues available and thus is responsible for delivering a lion's share of all public services, for most of which it has little aptitude and less understanding—even the most powerful nation in the world, in such circumstances, is simply not organized to do what its ingenuity and resources would otherwise permit.

LIKE CITY, LIKE NATION

The point Norman Mailer and Jimmy Breslin are making about New York City, therefore, is one that sooner or later someone is going to have to make about the nation, if it is not—as Mailer already fears for New York—"to come to the end of its time." And when someone does make that point, it is altogether likely that he will be as new as Mailer and Breslin are to politics—at least to campaigning. It is even likelier that he, too, will be looked upon as something of a joke.

Everybody talks about new ideas and fresh thinking in this country but few do anything about it. A lady on Montague Street, who hesitated to shake hands with the once-flamboyant Mailer, told him this morning: "I didn't recognize you with your hair combed so nicely." That ought to make another lapel button.

VICTORY IN DEFEAT

JAMES A. WECHSLER

New York Post, June 19, 1969

Do not be misled by headlines; John Lindsay won much more than he lost in Tuesday's primary. His name will not appear on the Republican line. But the setback he suffered (by a very narrow margin) at the hands of the listless local GOP will produce many big dividends in the form of support from men and groups who traditionally support Democratic nominees and would have found it difficult to back Lindsay if he wore the Republican label.

In important measure, of course, his gains are a result of what happened in the Democratic primary while he was being rejected by his Republican brethren. If Wagner or Badillo had been designated by the Democrats, Lindsay's trouble would have been almost insurmountable. But the Marchi and Procaccino triumphs are an invitation and incitement for wholesale defection among liberal and Reform Democrats to the Lindsay banner. Discussion about the timing and structure of such efforts had already quietly begun in many places yesterday.

It had been indicated in advance that there would be an independent line on the ballot to supplement Lindsay's earlier Liberal Party endorsement if he lost the GOP contest. Now, in the light of Procaccino's success, that independent bloc will enlist far wider support than it could have if any of the Democratic liberals had prevailed on Primary Day.

On the morning after, one man who must have felt peculiarly foolish and frustrated was Norman Mailer. Surely nearly all of the

41,136 votes Mailer polled would have gone to Herman Badillo if he had pulled out; they would have been sufficient to carry the night for the Bronx insurgent.

Thus, in a perverse way, John Lindsay is once again indebted to a member of the writing fraternity who allowed dreams of glory to befuddle his senses.

In the 1965 mayoralty race Bill Buckley's candidacy—bitterly aimed at Lindsay—backfired when he drew more votes away from Democrat Abe Beame than from Lindsay. In the current circumstance Mailer's motives were quite different, but the final posture was equally grotesque; by remaining in the race, he prevented the Badillo miracle and opened the door to Procaccino.

Mailer may now intimate that he was really for Lindsay all along and rendered him the ultimate service by eliminating his most formidable liberal adversary. But this could only be charitably described as an afterthought to a venture that embodied appallingly little thought. In fact, what is most memorable about Mailer's effort is not only that he took himself with such ponderous seriousness as the campaign progressed but that a number of intellectuals professed to detect a deep message in his muddled manifestos of conservative leftism (or was it leftist conservatism?).

There are many victims of Tuesday's fall out. Poor Louis Stulberg of the ILGWU, who seems hopelessly accident-prone in politics, invested his union's funds in a widely publicized long-distance phone call to Bob Wagner in Madrid, beseeching him to agree to salvage New York (and incidentally abet Stulberg's private war against the leaders of the Liberal Party). And poor Wagner heeded the summons. New York's AFL-CIO chief, Harry Van Arsdale, usually a prudent man, gave his public all for Wagner and thereby succeeded only in proving once again that there is no monolithic "labor vote." It's hard to believe that Van Arsdale will dig himself into deeper futility by trying to shift his non-supporters to Procaccino.

Amid such sufferings the Liberal Party's Alex Rose—often described by his long-time colleague and friend Dave Dubinsky as "a lucky genius"—was again quietly triumphant. At a time when the

Liberal Party's endorsement of Lindsay was in some doubt (there were some who favored opening that party's primary to Wagner and others), Rose warned that Lindsay's survival could hinge on whether he had sole access to the Liberal line. If Lindsay wins in November, that decision may prove to have been the most crucial one in New York's battle of 1969.

Lindsay still faces a long, rough fight. But many of us who remained up to watch his "concession speech" at 2:45 A.M. were persuaded that his GOP defeat—and the prospect of competing with Marchi and Procaccino—had given him new spirit and strength. He had lost a skirmish and found the real dimension of his cause.

There were a few murmurings yesterday about the possible emergence of a liberal Democrat as a late starter in the mayoralty contest. But such talk will subside swiftly. The only men who could give even small validity to such a dead-end enterprise— Badillo and Paul O'Dwyer—are against it. Badillo's strong showing guarantees his own political future; he is too intelligent—and responsible—to discredit his achievement; O'Dwyer does not believe in the politics of desperation and confusion. The odds are high that such men will be in Lindsay's corner before many days have passed. Who said Lindsay "lost?" Spiritually and politically, he is in better shape than ever.

BE MY GUEST, NORMAN MAILER

JAMES A. WECHSLER

New York Post, July 1, 1969

I yield today to the gentleman and Pulitzer prize winner from New York, Norman Mailer.

—J. A. W.

"Surely nearly all of the 41,136 votes Mailer polled would have gone to Herman Badillo if he had pulled out . . ."
—James A. Wechsler, *The Post, June 19, 1969*.

It will soon be a liberal canon, cemented in concrete, that we ruined Herman Badillo's chances of winning the mayoralty primary and plunged New York into a right-wing era. Well, let us consider the possibility that Badillo did better because we ran. Points: (1) We enlivened the race and so helped to bring attention to him. (2) We stimulated people to vote who would otherwise not have voted. Badillo was then able to capture them—we lost half of our estimated vote in the last week. (3) We attacked Wagner severely and consistently. We chipped votes loose from him. If we did not succeed in getting them for ourselves, we managed apparently to drift them to Badillo.

There are ironies within the ironies of this election, however. If Wechsler is correct, and our race actually hurt Badillo more than it helped him, then consider what would have happened if we dropped out. Badillo and, conceivably, Carey would not be running against Lindsay, whereas Procaccino voters would be moving over to Marchi.

As for Badillo, it is hard to feel sorry for him. He ran a professional race, marred only by his lack of fire in three debates, and an unseemly rush to safety in the dual-admissions imbroglio at CCNY (where I would remind Wechsler *I* was the only mayoral candidate to speak out on the side of the blacks and Puerto Ricans). But Herman is hardly in bad shape. He is now the leader of the liberal wing of the Democratic Party, a luminary in this city and leading candidate for many a big office in politics next year. In fact, I might even support him in his next race if the New York *Post* will stop kicking us in the back long enough to give our ideas a hearing.

Since we never succeeded in getting the *Post* to treat us seriously, readers of this newspaper might not know that we had a few ideas—a few ideas more, in fact, than the other candidates—and so cannot feel sorry that Badillo is not in contention because our fundamental tenet is that New York City will not begin to be able to even attack its problems, no matter who is mayor, until it becomes the fifty-first state, and succeeds in getting power out to the neighborhoods, out to the people in the street who are beginning to go mad now, mad because they have no power, and no participation in democracy.

We ran as left-conservatives, we ran to the left and to the right of Badillo, we were saying altogether different things. While I thought he was the least undistinguished of four not very monumental candidates, I could not pretend in my own mind or heart that he would make a real difference. That is why I did not support him in the first place.

In our minds, we were running the only serious campaign, serious enough to offer a few exciting solutions. But there was no dialogue. We were never treated seriously by the liberal media, certainly not by the *Post,* and so there was nobody in liberal circles to come to us at the end and ask that we withdraw. Not a soul. The liberals had given us no party workers, no money, nothing but a whispering campaign—begun by a column of Wechsler's—that we were The Odd Couple. One doesn't work for one's manhood for forty-six years in order to have it sneered over by a liberal columnist writing in his cubicle. Since little but distortion had been printed about us, why should we have been ready to believe the word of liberals that Badillo had a real chance.

Besides, you speak too quickly of how we should have conceded. Did you ever consider our ideas? Did you ever ponder the possibility that Badillo could fail no less than Lindsay, Marchi, or Carey, or Procaccino with matters as they are? With the city impoverished, the ghettos and the universities in rebellion, traffic and smog our booming products, and crime our first creation, drug addiction our benevolent milk? Shame, Wechsler, for burying the real issue in this campaign—Breslin and I had a program, a detailed program with much new thought in it. Badillo had a liberal machine— the same liberal machine which contributed to spoiling the city in the first place.

Jimmy, stop moldering like a potato in a plastic box and come out. Meet the people. Get hip. We are not on an ego trip. We are not running in fun. Nobody runs for fun in New York any more. There's too much talent and trouble waiting on line. Or haven't you heard?

—Norman Mailer

PART THREE

The Position Papers

I. AIR POLLUTION

PETER MANSO

The Department of Health, Education, and Welfare tells us that New York has the worst air in the country. Dirt, garbage, gases, and noise infest our atmosphere. Waste products remain with us, on our streets, our window ledges, our bodies, and in our lungs. It could be said, biblically, that these wastes do not return to the earth from which they came. So our pollution problem is a contradiction of nature, an artifact of technocracy. Its cure must therefore involve Draconian steps. But let us first look to a few key figures on the indices of air pollution.

One pollutant is sulfur dioxide, an invisible, pungent gas released by the burning of coal and heating oils. Reacting to the flesh of the lungs, it destroys the lacework of lung tissue and creates respiratory difficulties, often fatal for the aged or the middle aged afflicted with heart and lung disease, asthma, or related ills. More familiar is carbon monoxide, a near-to-exclusive product of automobiles. Odorless, colorless, carbon monoxide displaces oxygen from the red blood cells. Levels of even 50 to 100 parts per million cause headache, dizziness, nausea, and collapse, not to count psychological and physical impairment and an increased susceptibility to pneumonia infection. Yet such levels, 50 to 100 ppm, are average in New York's traffic jams and tunnels. While men are obviously not comparable to dogs, nonetheless the results of experiments in which dogs were exposed to such levels of carbon monoxide for an eleven-week period showed on autopsy—pity the poor dogs!—severe heart and brain damage. While no official figures have been released, premature heart attacks are not uncommon among those working in the city's tunnels who from day to day are exposed to 100 ppm of the gas.

Still another family of pollutants are the oxides of nitrogen, which compound in the lungs to nitric acid and cause emphysema, a debilitating respiratory disease which kills some two thousand people yearly in New York alone, about 3 per cent of our annual death rate. Some figures are considerably worse. London in 1952 experienced an inversion, which is to say a period of pollution so severe as to leave four thousand dead in a week. The death rate was up over 300 per cent that week. Another thousand Londoners died during pollution episodes in 1956 and 1962. Several hundred died here during pollution "alerts"—as in 1953, 1957, 1963, and, most dramatically, over the Thanksgiving period in 1966 when sulfur dioxide levels increased three to four times and killed 168 persons, escalating the death rate by 10 per cent, and sent an incalculable number of asthmatics to emergency clinics in the five boroughs. During London's 1952 catastrophe the weather was stagnant for five days; here, in 1966, for three days, a holiday period of exceptional warmth which kept the operation of both cars and furnaces at an unusual low. How many additional New Yorkers would have died, one speculates, had conditions been different?

Over the past four years New York has made but a single major step toward reducing its pollution: It has forced Con Ed to lower its sulfur dioxide emissions by one half, thus decreasing the total amount of the gas in the city's air by a fourth. However, this still keeps the city's sulfur dioxide pollution greater by four times than what federal health standards advise. The problem of sulfur dioxide will only be solved when low-content sulfur fuels, as are presently used in the LA area, become widely available in New York.

Our solutions? One could begin by suggesting a series of specific and practical steps but it is better to recognize that air pollution is the tangible concomitant of a spiritual disease—greed and the excessive pursuit of logical technical processes which prove eventually illogical. So in recognition of the essential despoliation of nature implicit in New York's multitudinous pollutions, it would be desirable to have a day set aside, perhaps the last Sunday of the

month, when nothing would move or operate in the city, no vehicles, no ships, no trains, no planes, and no electric power but for
places of dire emergency. So a silence might come upon the city,
a short period of rest not only for air and the lungs, but for
the ears and the nerves, a brief period of restoration for the citizens.
Sweet Sunday would be a symbolic as well as actual event—the
assumption is that symbols nourish the heart more than statistics.
So it might serve to underline the gravity of our situation, our bad
air, which makes every other problem in New York function more
imperfectly.

That peace granted, we might find it easier to suggest the
severities of the following brief but clear-cut program.

1. A search for means to expedite the installation of traps to
catch sulfur dioxide in the smokestacks of factories, where the gas
could be converted to sulfuric acid and marketed. This idea, underlined by Jane Jacobs in her book, *The Economy of Cities,*
suggests the possibility of the fifty-first state offering encouragement
if not direct aid to new businesses prepared to design and install
such traps in stacks from which they could subsequently proceed
to market the sulfuric acid at a profit. To quote Miss Jacobs:
"The test had a delivered market price of $8.00 to $10 a ton. The
cost of capturing and converting it costs $7.00 a ton. In effect,
the process amounts to a new way of mining sulfur for sulfuric
acid."

2. Carbon monoxide and nitrous oxide are the product of automobiles. Since traffic moves at an average rate of six miles an hour
from noon till evening in the island of Manhattan, the pollution from
idling motors is multiplied many times. There is no solution to this
problem other than terminating the bulk of traffic. The election of
this candidacy would be followed by a referendum giving the mayor
power to abolish all gasoline-consuming vehicles on Manhattan, but
for buses, taxis, and trucks. The buses and taxis could additionally
be required to carry crankcase emission devices which could be
checked periodically for inspection since such devices are sensitive
and break down easily.

It is now obvious that we have reached the boundaries of our next position paper which will deal in more detailed fashion with problems and possible solutions to this step and the incidental development of new systems of transportation. We will present this material next week, on Thursday, May 8.

II. TRANSPORTATION

PETER MANSO

No one living or working in New York is unaffected by the city's traffic and transportation ills. It is estimated that more than half the people using our subways lose twenty to forty days yearly in excess commuting time to inadequate and frustrating trains, while taxis, private cars, trucks, and buses inch along at an average speed of six miles per hour. These three million gasoline vehicles attack our ears with their din, clog our streets, befoul our air, damage our lungs and hearts. Each day 9,600,000 pounds of carbon monoxide are deposited onto the streets by cars alone.

The future is even gloomier. According to the Federal Power Commission, vehicle registration will be doubled by 1985. Midtown will be forced to receive, if possible, not the present 750,000, but 1,500,000 daily commuter cars. At that point our average rate of progress through the streets is likely to be reduced to six-tenths of a mile per hour.

It is therefore obvious that New York must have a public transit system. The improvement of existing services must be combined with the creation of thoroughgoing new facilities. This is no longer an option but a necessity. Therefore we propose a feasible plan: that the city finance and build a system of high-speed monorails and free, connecting jitney buses. Supplementing subway and bus facilities, such a system would not only serve the two million people working in the Midtown area, but obviate the need for private automobiles in Manhattan.

During the period of the monorail's construction, however, New York must take more immediate steps to relieve its traffic and transportation crisis. Interim improvements are many and inexpensive. We suggest the following.

Improve subway service. All experts agree that the rapid transit system must run at speeds of at least thirty miles per hour and, yet, the present subway barely manages twenty miles per hour—and at an annual financial loss of $85.5 million. An improved schedule of one- and two-car, air-conditioned trains could be instituted. These smaller high-speed cars will come through stations every ninety seconds and eliminate long waits in lonely stations. The cars can be insulated against noise and, where station facilities permit, be equipped with separate doors for entrance and exit.

Present rush-hour schedules can be retained, but a system of graduated starts should be introduced so that more trains will run between heavily used stops and better serve concentrated areas. The city's buses have used this plan successfully, and if adopted by the subways would reduce the number of cars traveling to the end of the line, nearly empty at both ends of the run.

The smaller, high-speed trains and graduated rush-hour schedule would save both time and money. Presently 85 per cent of our subway cars are inoperative six or seven hours a day, while five rush hours daily account for 55 per cent of total subway use.

Subway directions must be improved. Stations and lines should be color-keyed for easier use. Complete, consistent, and intelligible maps must be prepared and each subway car should display a map showing the routes and stops for that particular train. Subway cars themselves should be color-keyed. A central passenger information service for all methods of public transportation must also be established. A combination of the Paris-Metro system, where an electronic board lights up a color-keyed route when a destination button is pushed and the telephone-request system used in London should also be adopted.

We must also expand bus service, especially on cross-town routes. Express buses, like those which run into central Manhattan from Riverdale and Bayside, now save thousands of people an hour or more daily. An increase of these commuter buses at various central points throughout the five boroughs would drastically reduce the 75,000 commuter cars entering Midtown every day.

Individual neighborhoods should be encouraged to establish extra transportation to meet their particular needs. These Neighborhood Auxiliary Transportation Systems (NATS) could link up with the centralized municipal system and benefit both individual areas and the city as a whole. Such systems have been tested in Harlem and proved successful. They should be encouraged, perhaps with financial aid or loans from the city.

Yet ultimately New York's transportation problem can only be solved through major if not radical moves. We must ban all private cars from the island of Manhattan. Their convenience is a sad myth. Midtown is nearly impenetrable from midday to dusk and each single breakdown ties up hundreds of thousands at bridges, tunnels, and expressways. The noise and congestion of our streets, as well as the pollution of our air—we have the worst air pollution of any city in America—all dictate the measure. Ambulances, fire-fighting equipment, taxis, and buses would remain, their engines and eshausts regularly inspected to minimize pollution of the atmosphere. Doubtless, the loss of private cars would work a hardship on some, but surely it would benefit the many. Even so, such legislation could not be put into effect without an alternate and superior means of transport at hand, and so we come to the heart of our proposal: a high-speed monorail skirting Manhattan, with spur lines to the other boroughs terminating at vast city-sponsored parking areas. Co-ordinated in Midtown with a supplementary network of jitney buses and improved subway and bus services, such a system would not only be efficient—which is to say fast and comfortable and allowing for the elimination of all private cars on Manhattan—but inexpensive as well. Clearly it is the way New York must go . . . But first a look at the specifics.

Running at speeds up to seventy miles an hour, the two-way, double-laned monorail would run some thirty feet above the West Side and East Side drives, circling the Battery and 155th Street. Making eight stops at Manhattan, Queensboro, and Triborough bridges, at Broadway and mid-155th Street, and along the West Side at 125th, 96th, 42nd, and Chambers streets, the monorail trains would circle the island of Manhattan, a twenty-six and a half mile route, in less than thirty minutes. Going around Manhattan twice every hour, each twenty-four car train, capable of seating 576 people, could carry 2304 passengers an hour. The entire system, calculated at forty-two trains, could move 96,768 additional people every hour during peak rush-hour periods, or thereby supplement the five-hour rush period by a half million extra passengers.

Lightweight, low-roofed cars measuring thirty feet in length and six in height would seat twenty-four passengers and permit no standing. Everyone traveling would be assured a seat. Rapid entrance and exit would be through transparent gull-wing doors swinging upward on both sides of the car, exposing parallel rows of individual bucket seats into which passengers would slide. Seats themselves would be separated by Plexiglas partitions to assure comfort and create, in effect, a private compartment for every traveler. Each of these would naturally be heated and air conditioned. The trains themselves would run suspended from monorails raised on stanchions, mainly along Manhattan's river drives. Electrically powered, they would require but a single conductor manning the lead car. The entire system would be computerized so as to insure the steady progress of each train and to avoid the tie-ups and delays characteristic of our present subway system.

Spur lines serving such central and accessible areas as Port Morris or Hunts Point in the South Bronx, the Maspeth Creek basin in Queens, and Brooklyn's Navy Yard, would complement the main system and merge with the Manhattan line at the appropriate bridge terminals. Each of these areas is chosen for its proximity to existing subway and highway arteries and could easily accommodate massive new parking facilities for commuters approaching the city by car. Each spur would consist of a continuous monorail loop. The Queens link, the longest of the three, would run eight miles round trip, and its six trains, each doing the route in less than eight minutes, would carry 55,296 passengers an hour. Ultimately an extension would be added to the then-existing Queens line which would run seventeen and a half miles along the Long Island and Brooklyn-Queens expressways to La Guardia Airport and then on along the Grand Central Parkway to Van Wyck Expressway and Kennedy Airport and Aqueduct, finally circling back to the Maspeth Creek parking area and main spur into Manhattan. Both JFK and La Guardia airports could share the expense of this spur as it would serve their customers and facilitate service. Brooklyn and Bronx loops, circling five and three miles respectively, would each run five trains and have an approximate capacity of 43,000 passengers during peak rush hours. The over-all system would, in effect, be a system—simple, efficient, practical, and serving not only those living in Manhattan but the millions who work in the city's main borough.

Compared to the Metropolitan Commuter Transportation Authority's Phase I subway-expansion costs of $37.5 million per mile, our proposed monorail would be relatively cheap. It would require no excavation, no rerouting of electrical, sewage, or gas mains. It would run on city-owned rights of way. It would require no land purchase. Running fifty-eight trains, or 1393 cars, over its forty-two and a half mile route, it would cost, it is estimated, no more than $5 million a mile for planning, construction, and equipment, with the system as a whole coming in at a round $250 million with extra cars, emergency equipment, and repair facilities.

Throughout Manhattan's Midtown area a system of electric jitney buses, linking with both monorail and existing train terminals, would supplement the improved rapid transit system. These jitneys would eventually phase out our present buses in Midtown. On carefully chosen routes—indicated in the accompanying chart—these would run circularly, doing seven cross-town and four up-town-downtown loops within the 32nd–59th Street, First–Ninth Avenue area. Their block-by-block coverage would be maximum, unlike any present bus or subway system. Pedestrians would have to walk no further than two or three streets to reach either direct or transfer jitneys, and since they would be far more numerous than our present buses, and the traffic almost non-existent, waits would never exceed two or three minutes.

The jitneys themselves would be smaller and more maneuverable than conventional city buses. Like San Francisco cable cars, or the caravans designed by city-planner Mary Hommann, they would be

open on both sides, with large running-board aprons for standing.
During bad weather their accordion sides would be closed. Each
would seat thirty-eight and stand upwards of twenty-five. They
would stop every other block, and their open sides would permit
rapid entrance and exit. They would afford unparalleled and actually
pleasurable transportation to our city's busiest and most populous
area.

Economically, our system is more than feasible, it's practical.
Funds for constructing and operating the monorail and jitney systems could be raised through an increase in both gasoline taxes and
car-registration fees. A modest raise of 50 per cent in gas taxes—
six to seven cents per gallon—and a similar increase in vehicle-
license fees—from the present average of $35 to $45 yearly—would
bring the city an additional $58 million every year, one-fifth the
cost of the entire monorail network. Further revenue could come
in the form of parking fees collected at municipal garages. At a
daily rate of $2.00 per car, these parking facilities would gross
$2.5 million every week, or $124 million yearly, one half the cost
of a six-tiered garage for 75,000 automobiles. Then, too, the twenty-
cent monorail fare would constitute a source of further revenue,
especially significant because it would come from previously car-
driving commuters. With daily commuter traffic of 500,000 vehicles into Midtown Manhattan alone, this additional money could
easily amount to $35 million per year. The electric jitneys, es-
timated at $25,000 each, would replace our worn-out, $35,000 city
buses as the occasion arose, and so would partially compensate
for their lack of fare revenue. Incalculable would be their savings
in terms of time and cleanliness.

It is therefore obvious that not only must New York have a new
transit system but that such a system is possible in every respect.
A combined program of improving present facilities and creating
new ones—the monorail and jitney network—as well as eliminating automobiles from Manhattan can both solve the city's transportation dilemma and make it a far better place in which to work
and live. Such a program is no longer an option. In our time it is a
necessity.

NEW YORK MONORAIL COSTS
(Computed at $5,000,000 per mile including planning, construction, and equipment)

Manhattan: 26.5 miles (155th Street Crosstown, West Side Drive, Battery Park, East River Drive; eight stops at Manhattan, Queensboro, and Triborough bridges, Broadway on 155th Street, along the West Side Drive at 125th, 96th, 42nd, and Chambers streets)—$132,500,000

Queens: 8-mile spur loop (Queensboro Bridge, Vernon Boulevard, Long Island Expressway, Hill Boulevard, Maspeth Creek parking area; two stops at Queensboro Bridge and parking area)—$40,000,000

17.5-mile supplemental system (Maspeth Creek parking area, Long Island Expressway, Brooklyn-Queens Expressway, La Guardia Airport, Grand Central Parkway, Van Wyck Expressway, John F. Kennedy Airport, Southern Parkway loop to Aqueduct, Queens Boulevard, Grand Avenue, Maspeth Creek parking area)—$87,500,000

Brooklyn: 5-mile spur loop (Manhattan Bridge, Flatbush Avenue to L.I.R.R. Station, with link to Navy Yard parking area; two stops)—$25,000,000

Bronx: 3 miles (Triborough Bridge to Port Morris parking area; 2 stops)—$15,000,000

Total Mileage: 42.5 miles (60 miles with supplementary airport link)

Total Cost: $250,000,000 (with extra cars and repair facilities)

RAPID TRANSIT 1968—SUBWAY

	Subway	Total (Plus Bus)
City Operating Cost/Yr.	$ 369,345,944	$ 481,344,956
Net Income/Yr.	283,866,388	379,991,260
Loss from Operation	86,471,556	101,345,696
No. of People Using Transit/Yr. (1968)	1,303,465,841	1,738,372,297
No. of Route Miles (Total Track Mileage)	966 miles	1522 transit miles

Cost of Recently Acquired Subway Cars: $107,000—$137,600 (Depends on specifications)

Total No. of Cars Purchased since 1953: 4060 regular cars

400 low alloy, high tensile steel with stainless steel exteriors and aluminum roofs

(contracted for) 400 similar to above, plus air conditioning

TOTAL 4860

SURFACE TRANSPORTATION 1968—BUS

	Bus	Total (Plus RT)
City Operating Cost/Yr.	$111,999,012	$ 481,344,956
Net Income/Yr.	96,124,872	379,991,260
Loss from Operations	14,874,140	101,345,696
No. of People Using Bus/Yr. (1968)	434,906,456	1,738,372,297
Bus Route Mileage	556 miles	1522 transit miles
Revenue from Bus Fares	$ 91,338,829	

Source: Transit Record, vol. XLIX, No. 3, March 1969.

RAPID TRANSIT—SUBWAY
BREAKDOWN of REVENUES and EXPENSES for YEAR of 1968

	Amount	Per Cent of Operating Revenue
Revenues		
Passenger Revenue	$ 276,040,980	97.51%
Advertising	6,036,684	2.14
Other (Building Rental, Prop. Equip., Misc.)	788,724	.27
TOTAL	$ 282,866,388	99.2%
Expenses		
Maintenance of Ways and Structures	$ 59,430,228	21.01%
Maintenance of Equipment	62,937,771	22.25
Operation of Cars	164,741,384	58.24
Power	43,221,984	15.28
General and Miscellaneous (Incl. rentals)	84,358,057	29.70
TOTAL	$ 414,689,424	146.48%
Credit from City for Transit Police	$ —45,343,580	16.03%
TOTAL Operating Expenses and Rentals	$ 369,345,844	130.45%
NET LOSS	$ 86,471,556	30.45%

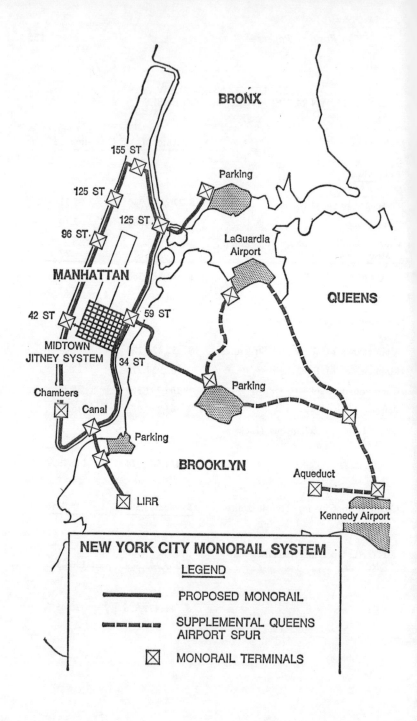

BRONX

155 ST

125 ST

125 ST

96 ST

Parking

LaGuardia Airport

MANHATTAN

QUEENS

42 ST

59 ST

MIDTOWN JITNEY SYSTEM

34 ST

Chambers

Parking

Canal

Parking

BROOKLYN

Aqueduct

LIRR

Kennedy Airport

NEW YORK CITY MONORAIL SYSTEM

LEGEND

────── PROPOSED MONORAIL

━ ━ ━ ━ SUPPLEMENTAL QUEENS AIRPORT SPUR

⊠ MONORAIL TERMINALS

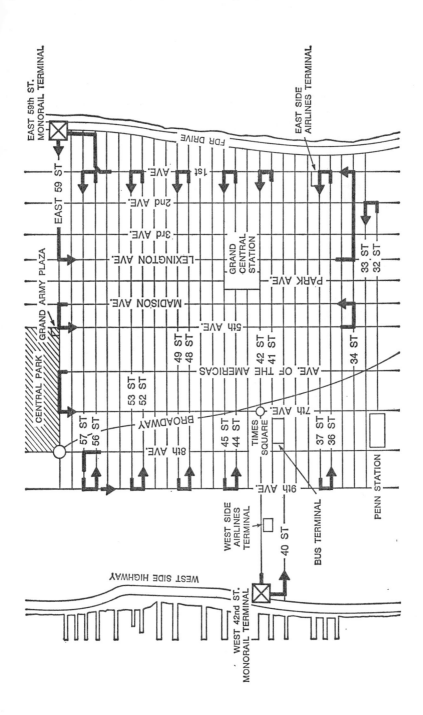

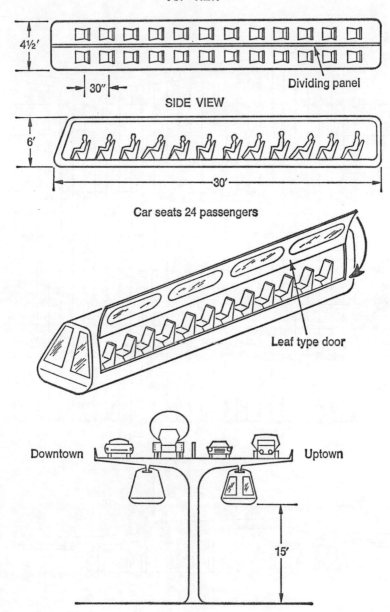

TOP VIEW

4½'

30"

Dividing panel

SIDE VIEW

6'

30'

Car seats 24 passengers

Leaf type door

Downtown

Uptown

15'

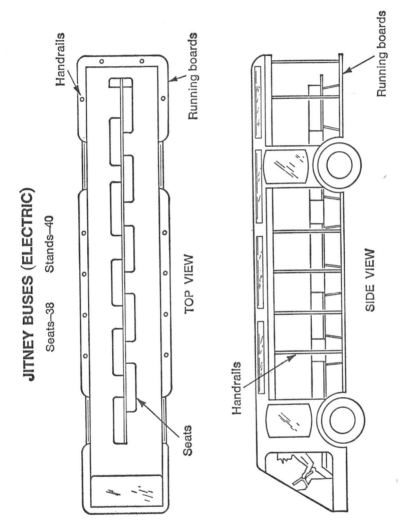

JITNEY BUSES (ELECTRIC)

Seats—38   Stands—40

Handrails

Running boards

TOP VIEW

Seats

Handrails

Running boards

SIDE VIEW

III. HOUSING

JOE FERRIS

We are losing the battle to provide decent housing in our city. A combination of forces—bureaucracies, governmental arrangements, lack of capital, archaic rules, and municipal codes all combine to accelerate the deterioration of housing in the neighborhoods of our city.

The centralized governmental approach is bankrupt. It has failed repeatedly either to stop urban decay or to provide a break-through for additional housing.

We believe there will never be any solution to the serious housing needs of New York City until people in their own neighborhoods, as citizens, obtain the administrative and financial power to purchase their homes or apartments, improve them, and participate in planning for neighborhood life.

Our answer to slums, deteriorating housing, and rent control is the establishment of Neighborhood Housing Authorities and Neighborhood Housing Banks.

Slums, housing shortages, low-income, middle-income, Title I, Mitchell-Lama, HUD, Model Cities, NYCHDA. A litany of words and initials employed by public officials, bureaucrats, media commentators, and urban planners revolves around the figures of countless studies, reports, pronouncements, and legislative thickets.

800,000 deteriorated substandard units

150,000 dwelling units demolished between 1955–65

Three quarters of 400,000 new units constructed between 1955–65 were high rental

15,000 abandoned buildings

The figures go on and on into the handbooks of agencies, department reports, the newspaper clippings of last year, the last decade. Statistics which continue in an unending repetitiousness.

The citizens of New York know without any special reading of statistical data that centralized governmental direction is rapidly debasing all housing to an abysmal level of quality and quantity.

In the Brownsvilles, South Bronxes, South Jamaicas of our town is to be found the reality of New York City's housing decline. Peeling paint full of lead poison, broken plaster, rat droppings, the smell of soil lines oozing into walls; the gray, broken concrete of treeless, flowerless streets overflowing with uncollected garbage— hopelessness, ugliness, madness fester in this interminable hell. That's housing in New York City—it's not just the statistics which everyone in the official world drones on about.

Of course, housing funds have constantly increased both from federal and state sources. But New York City is still unable to maintain the level of its housing, let alone increase it. The number of dwelling units which become substandard or abandoned on an annual basis has rapidly accelerated.

A short analysis vividly illustrates this acceleration. During 1968, 1841 buildings were demolished, accounting for a total of approximately 10,000 units lost—practically all low-income. Three years ago only 2400 dwelling units were destroyed. It is estimated that there are presently 15,000 more abandoned buildings containing some 90,000 units which are awaiting the wrecker's ball.

Present construction of low-income housing is running at 2000 units per year, down nearly 500 per cent from a decade ago—with abandonment, this makes an annual net loss of 8000 low-income units. If suddenly deterioration was to halt, it would require, under the existing pace, forty-five years to build new housing to replace all abandoned units.

Again as figures clearly indicate, the number of abandoned buildings is increasing at such an alarming tempo, we could possibly face within the decade the total demise of 800,000 units. If present bureaucratic procedures continue to prevail, that would mean four hundred years to replace those units.

Why this continuing regression? Examine the Federal Housing and Urban Development Administration, the State Urban Develop-

ment Corporation, New York City's housing development super-
agency and each reveals itself as still one more example of how
government action from without dooms neighborhoods by its failure
to preserve existing housing, or to construct new housing consonant
with neighborhood characteristics.

In 1965, HUD authorized that New York City receive of the
1965 Housing Act's national allotment of 240,000 low-income
units, or 28,800 over a four-year period. This would come out to
7200 new units per annum—just barely maintaining the status quo,
given the demolition rate.

What has happened since that act came into force? Between
1965 and 1968 the NYCHDA bureaucracy requested only 12,600
units, only 58 per cent of the permissible 21,600. By September
1968, HUD had approved only 8990, bringing the percentage down
to only 42 per cent of the potential number of units.

Jason R. Nathan, administrator of the NYCHDA admits that
over 100,000 families are on waiting lists for public housing. A
hundred thousand families awaiting new housing while the city takes
four years to get under 9000 units through the bureaucratic labyrinth.

NYCHDA has not fared much better with the use of available
state moneys for both low- and middle-income housing. It used only
$12.6 million of the $25.6 million earmarked by the New York
Division of Housing and Community Renewal between December
1963 and early 1969. Consequently, a substantial amount of the
unused $13 million was irrevocably lost because the state diverted
such resources to other cities.

Bureaucracies operate solely from the point of view of determin-
ing where housing should be constructed or demolished, and what
kind of housing it will be. Occasionally, because of community or
individual pressure, some token neighborhood involvement is
granted. But the ability of neighborhoods to gain control of existing
housing, with the necessary financial resources to pay for the physical development of neighborhoods—streets, parks, gardens, plazas,
cultural centers is still virtually non-existent and will remain this
way under the present centralized arrangement.

We, therefore, suggest that New York City upon achieving statehood could move altogether away from any centralized approach to housing and toward the development in each neighborhood of a Neighborhood Housing Authority. Action on housing would then take its initiative from the street up, rather than down from the high government plateau of a NYCHDA.

Neighborhoods such as the West Village, Park Slope, Bedford-Stuyvesant, Fort Greene and others could provide examples of what has been done to delay the erosion of housing by indiscriminate destruction of abandoned buildings, bulldozing of historic community areas and their collective replacement by structures of concrete block and yellow brick. The success of these communities is directly attributable to citizens using their own time and resources in civic effort to improve existing buildings, prevent demolition, plant trees, beautify the area, sponsor block associations and activities, and, most of all, to elicit economic co-operation from local banks.

The virtue of every community having a Neighborhood Housing Authority would be its impact on present housing stock. Rather than a huge city housing administration trying to grapple with thousands of abandoned buildings, hundreds of thousands of substandard units, a neighborhood would have its energies and powers released for knowledgeable work on a block-by-block basis.

Immediately all housing owned already by the city-state (through tax default or receivership) could be turned over to the Neighborhood Housing Authorities. Owners of buildings recently abandoned would be obliged because of tax arrears to sell their property at land cost to Neighborhood Housing Authorities. In return they could receive a second mortgage. Under our present system, owners of these abandoned buildings rarely reclaim a cent from their properties due to the demolition lien which generally costs between $4000 to $6000.

The $20 million a year allocated for demolition would form the initial capital for establishment of Neighborhood Housing Banks. Each Neighborhood Housing Bank would create a revolving purchase-and-construction fund to provide low-cost interim financing for the restoration of abandoned structures; employing the present tool of FHA guaranteed bank mortgages, such moneys could be deployed over and over without any loss of original capital.

By reducing excessive administrative costs and channeling this gain with present sums allocated for housing construction into these neighborhood banks would assure an annual growth in capital. The estimated $400 million which comprises the amount welfare pays frequently for substandard housing could also begin to be placed into such banks. Federal grants, similar to the Federal Home Loan Bank, could be made on a per capita plus basis to increase the lending powers of such neighborhood-oriented institutions.

It can be foreseen that financial institutions which at present export the savings capital of Bedford-Stuyvesant, Harlem, and East New York out to the sands of Arizona or the shopping centers of suburbia could now be encouraged to invest in a Neighborhood Housing Bank. Large savings institutions which did not invest would then be obviously identified as refusing to replace even small amounts of their deposits into mortgages or improvement loans, and would be labeled as responsible for the decline of these neighborhoods.

Under this plan, the Neighborhood Housing Bank could become a regenerating and multiplying force on the local economy and its per capita income, its skill development, its job growth, and not inconceivably on the quality of its life.

What would be taking place, especially in the more troubled neighborhoods of our city, is the formation and retention of that most effective tool—capital; which would be used exclusively for the benefit of the neighborhood and its people.

The natural union of a Neighborhood Housing Authority, and a Neighborhood Housing Bank, would then be able to take action on absentee landlords of old- and new-law tenements which have become the typical abandoned building. If owners failed to comply with local housing standards, they could face violations and swift fines from the Neighborhood Housing Authority.

Since old buildings, in their present state, have a rapidly declining profitability, many are available in our city for a small amount of cash. In lieu of fines, landlords would be encouraged to sell such buildings at some coefficient of their assessed valuation, taking small cash and the rest in paper in the form of a second mortgage, subject to a new first mortgage based on rehabilitation and improvements.

Thus, say, in a typical eight-family old-law tenement, if the cash required for purchase is $1000, the expenditure per dwelling unit is little over $100—no more than two months' rent. People could then by the formation of either co-operatives or condominiums become owners with a stake in their home and neighborhood.

The restoration of neighborhood environments, rather than their destruction, would be the main objective of the city-state's housing policy. This would halt the senseless loss of substantial numbers of housing units which can be rescued and restored to livability.

Housing rehabilitation would become a local industry which would have a salutary effect on the neighborhood economy. It would readily provide jobs in well-paying fields like plumbing, carpentry, and electrical work. Educational manpower training would be related to programs and apprenticeships for youth, the unemployed, and the underemployed. Devoid of red tape, archaic codes, and time-consuming methods, rehabilitation under the direction of each neighborhood should begin to make significant break-throughs in improved ways of housing production.

Housing rehabilitation could open limitless vistas for the creative talents within neighborhoods. Tree planting, flower beds, small parks, colorful exterior wall murals, could summon men to be gardeners, horticulturists, landscapers, painters, sculptors, in an eternal exercise of beauty. Interiors could be adorned with ornamental plaster, carved woodwork, stained glass windows. A small percentage of the sums saved from bureaucratic administration could be devoted to such aesthetic and naturalistic pursuits.

We believe that people given the opportunity, the tools, and the incentives will do a better job when it comes to housing in their own neighborhoods.

It has been proven in certain neighborhoods with little or no governmental assistance that people are a more effective force for better-housing conditions than any centralized governmental agency.

We, therefore, offer those two logical and powerful proposals to resolve the existing housing crisis—the formation of Neighborhood

Housing Authorities and Neighborhood Housing Banks within the new city-state.

SUMMARY OF NEIGHBORHOOD EXPERIENCES

Harlem: A classic example of the tortuous route and the interminable gestation period between conception of a housing proposal and its completion via the baffling intergovernmental bureaucratic network is the Mary M. Bethune Houses in Harlem. From preliminary approval in 1962 by HUD through design, the project involved NYCHDA's selection of architects, approval by NYC Planning Commission, approval by NYC Board of Estimate, submission to HUD, approval by NYCHDA. Then NYCHDA approved the architect's preliminary plans, a contract was signed bteween HUD and NYCHDA, title thus being vested in NYCHDA, and finally construction bids were advertised. This design process consumed twenty-four months. From the award of construction contracts to completion of buildings took another twenty-six months.

Besides the array of bureaucratic hurdles, there is New York State's Wicks Law, which necessitates separate bids on major aspects of construction (plumbing, electrical, carpentry), thus making it difficult for a general contractor to negotiate with subcontractors. It does require NYCHDA to have another layer of administration which a private builder would be totally unconcerned with.

Thus we see how it took nearly six years to finish this housing project. And what was the total number of units? Two hundred and ten!

One can safely conclude that under the incalculable cost of the NYCHDA bureaucracy it will be decades before any sizable quantity of housing is constructed. Quality, design, and aesthetics are unfortunately not even an aspect of this incredible chronology.

East Harlem: Since World War II, East Harlem has received $300 million in public housing and related community facilities. Today after this massive infusion of capital, no less an urbanist than Jane Jacobs states in the *Economy of Cities* that the housing situation is poorer, unemployment is higher, and other related social maladies intensified. This capital was not used effectively nor creatively, because it failed to become part of the community's capital; which is to say it could not be deployed over and over again in a revolving developmental manner. Instead, this particular urban renewal destroyed and obliterated the fabric of neighborhood life. By razing the area, it eliminated over 1300 commercial enterprises of which many were owned by Puerto Rican residents.

West Village: The West Village was threatened during the Wagner regime with a Title I scheme which would have cost $30 million. Fortunately this community was eventually spared such a fate.

As a bulldozer plan, it called for leveling parts of the neighborhood, thereby expelling most of its residents and the removal of many established businesses. The final result would have been the obliteration of a historic community with a gain of only three hundred housing units.

Under the leadership of Jane Jacobs the people of the West Village thwarted this proposal. They drew up their own plan which demonstrated that for a cost of approximately $8.5 million (which provided for no personal dislocation nor displacement of business), the construction of 475 additional dwelling units was altogether feasible in a style harmonious with the character of the West Village.

Park Slope: Park Slope in Brooklyn is another illustration of how $400 can be more effective than a city expenditure of $250,000. In the late 1950s this brownstone community faced a dim future as predators and speculators raped once-elegant homes with illegal occupancies and blockbusting. The city gave hints of contemplating massive urban renewal. Community opposition stymied such an attempt.

Then the city came up with a Code Conservation District plan at a proposed cost of $250,000. It was suggested that instead of this, two housing inspectors at a total annual cost of about $20,000, be assigned to the community. This idea was never accepted and the original city proposal was eventually dropped.

The community proceeded to form a Park Slope Block Betterment Committee. Their plan of action was to publicize the virtues of urban living in Park Slope, to retain older residents and to attract new families to purchase homes on some of the more run-down blocks.

The committee advertised the community through inexpensive classified ads in the New York *Times,* sponsored walking tours, held conferences with bankers to encourage the placement of mortgages. Chase Manhattan through committee efforts made a commitment of $1 million in mortgage loans. Brooklyn Union Gas through the work of this committee invested $125,000 in a model brownstone house which received national publicity. The Brownstone Revival Committee is now using Park Slope as a model for the renaissance of some twenty other brownstone neighborhoods throughout New York City.

Block after block has been saved in Park Slope maintaining a mix of older and newer residents, white, black, and Spanish-speaking. The total cost of this whole effort was $400 and a lot of civic work. Probably some $5 million in mortgage money has now been attracted to Park Slope.

$400 for civic endeavor versus $250,000 for bureaucracy and then look at the results.

TABLE A-1
RESIDENTIAL STRUCTURES AND HOUSING UNITS
IN NEW YORK CITY
END OF YEAR, 1960 AND 1965

	No. of Structures		No. of Housing Units		Per cent Change	
	1960	1965	1960	1965	Struc-tures	Units
CLASS "A" TOTAL[a]	139,608	137,851	1,840,611	1,999,398	—1.3	8.6
Old-Law Tenements[a]	46,410	42,992	363,407	335,594	—7.4	—7.7
New-Law Tenements[a]	50,400	49,886	821,531	811,144	—1.0	—1.3
Multiple Dwelling after 1929	6,931	8,484	478,452	671,067	22.4	40.3
Misc. (including apt. hotels)	351	346	33,728	33,416	—1.4	—0.9
Converted Class "A"[a]	35,516	36,143	143,493	148,177	1.8	3.3
CLASS "B" TOTAL[a]	14,031	12,165			—13.3	
Converted Class "B"[a]	13,355	11,486			—14.0	
Lodging Houses	79	80			1.2	
Misc. (including hotels)	597	599			0.3	
ONE- AND TWO-FAMILY DWELLINGS TOTAL	567,055	591,720	762,864	802,163	4.3	5.2
One-Family	371,246	381,277	371,246	381,277	2.7	2.7
Two-Family	195,809	210,443	391,618	420,886	7.5	7.5
GRAND TOTAL	720,694	741,736	2,603,475	2,801,561	2.9	7.6

Class "A"—Buildings with three or more apartments used for permanent occupancy.
Class "B"—Buildings with rooms used primarily for transient occupancy.
Old-Law Tenements—Built prior to 1901.
New-Law Tenements—Built between 1901 and 1929.
Converted Class "A"—One- and Two-Family Dwellings converted to Class "A" Brownstones and brick-faced variations.
Converted Class "B"—Old- and New-Law Tenements and One- and Two-Family Dwellings converted to transient use. Primarily rooming houses.

Source: New York City Department of Buildings, *Annual Reports.*

Table A-2
MULTIFAMILY CLASS "A" STRUCTURES IN NEW YORK BY
BOROUGH
1960 AND 1965[a]

	No. of Structures as of December 31		Per cent Change
	1960	1965	1960–1965
Old-Law Tenements[b]	46,410	42,992	—7.4
Manhattan	18,247	16,309	—10.6
Bronx	3,409	3,117	—8.6
Brooklyn	23,330	22,204	—4.8
Queens	1,222	1,173	—4.0
Richmond	202	189	—6.4
New-Law Tenements[c]	50,400	49,886	—1.0
Manhattan	6,125	5,915	—3.4
Bronx	10,741	10,713	—0.3
Brooklyn	25,208	24,960	—1.0
Queens	8,276	8,248	—0.3
Richmond	50	50	—
Multiple Dwellings After 1929	6,931	8,484	22.4
Manhattan	1,098	1,522	38.6
Bronx	1,283	1,543	20.3
Brooklyn	2,001	2,353	17.6
Queens	2,455	2,932	19.4
Richmond	94	134	42.6
Converted Buildings	35,516	36,143	1.8
Manhattan	5,194	5,380	3.6
Bronx	4,765	4,827	1.3
Brooklyn	18,204	18,569	2.0
Queens	6,938	6,966	0.4
Richmond	415	401	—3.4
Total Multifamily Structures[c]	139,608	137,851	—1.3
Manhattan	31,006	29,461	—5.0
Bronx	20,198	20,200	—
Brooklyn	68,750	68,095	—1.0
Queens	18,891	19,319	2.3
Richmond	763	776	1.7

[a] See Table A-1 for definition of Class "A".
[b] Includes "single-room occupancy" structures.
[c] Includes "miscellaneous" category not shown.

Source: New York City Department of Buildings, *Annual Reports.*

Table A-3
QUALITY OF NEW YORK CITY HOUSING STOCK 1960

	All Units (Occupied & Vacant)		Owner-Occupied		Renter Occupied	
	Number	%	Number	%	Number	%
TOTAL HOUSING UNITS	2,758,000	100	578,000	100	2,077,000	100
Not Substandard	2,482,000	90	568,000	98	1,838,000	88
Sound,[a] with all plumbing facilities	2,205,000	80	537,000	93	1,600,000	77
Deteriorating,[b] with all plumbing facilities	277,000	10	31,000	5	237,000	11
Substandard*	276,000	10	10,000	2	239,000	12
Sound, lacking facilities	126,000	5	4,000	1	107,000	5
Deteriorating, lacking facilities	66,000	2	1,000	**	58,000	3
Dilapidated[c]	84,000	3	5,000	1	74,000	4

Definitions
[a] *Sound:* housing which is basically in good condition.
[b] *Deteriorating:* housing which requires repairs to items such as foundation, walls, roofs, floors, stairways, or ceilings, if it is to continue to provide safe and adequate shelter.
[c] *Dilapidated:* housing which endangers the health, safety, or well-being of its occupants.

Notes
* Substandard housing includes: (1) units in sound or deteriorating structures which lack private plumbing facilities (hot running water, a toilet, a bath, or shower) and (2) all units in dilapidated structures.
** Less than 0.5 per cent.

Source: Table IV-1, *Housing Statistics Handbook,* August, 1966.

IV. NEW YORK CITY STATEHOOD

LEON FRIEDMAN, ATTNY., AND PETER MANSO

1. The city of New York calls for an election of delegates to a constitutional convention to prepare a city-state constitution which, under federal law, must provide for a republican form of government.

2. This constitution is submitted for ratification by the people in a city-wide referendum.

3. Once approved by the people of New York City, the city-state constitution is submitted to the New York State Legislature for approval by a majority vote.

4. Adopted by the state legislature, both the legislature itself and the convention of delegates elected by the people of New York City petition Congress to admit the city as the fifty-first state.

5. By a majority vote Congress admits the city into the Union as the fifty-first state and provides for its immediate election of senators, representatives, and state-wide officials. This election completed, the city becomes the fifty-first state.

The establishment of New York City as the fifty-first state is not envisioned as a jest nor as an end in itself, but as a mechanism whereby the people of the city can begin to solve their most pressing economic and social ills. Statehood would carry with it the autonomy one needs to chart his daily life as well as the revenues to implement such a course. At the same time it offers advantages to our upstate neighbors, sparing them the fiscal and administrative responsibility of the five boroughs, a most demanding and unhappy burden to be sure.

But the point this morning—mark it!—is that the city's incorporation as a state is highly possible both legally and practically. The procedure for such partitioning is clearly defined in the U. S. Constitution and has been implemented several times in this country's history. And so we contend that this notion of city-state is as bold and real as the citizens of this city who would choose to forge it.

Article IV, Section 3 of the federal Constitution plainly provides that "no new State shall be formed or erected within the jurisdiction of any state . . . without the consent of the legislature of the States concerned as well as of Congress." Both the debates of the Constitutional Convention in 1787 and the Constitution itself anticipated that large states would break into more governable units for reasons of geography, economics, and political and social expediency. James Wilson, for example, one of the more important framers of the Constitution, foresaw the possibility and argued that "where the majority of a State wish to divide they can do so." The first two states admitted to the Union, after the original thirteen, were partitioned from larger states—Kentucky from Virginia, and Vermont from New York. In later years Maine broke off from Massachusetts to become a separate state as did West Virginia from Virginia.

The only requirement for separation established by the Constitution is that the state legislature of the larger entity give its majority consent. The Constitution also requires that the United Sates shall guarantee ". . . to every State in the Union a Republican Form of Government." Thus it has been traditional for new areas applying for statehood to present to Congress a proposed state constitution meeting Constitution standards.

The first step toward statehood by New York City would therefore be the preparation of a proposed city-state constitution. Delegates from each of the neighborhoods in New York City would be elected to a convention to draft a basic city-state constitution. The product of their labors would then be submitted to the people of the city for ratification. With the referendum successful, the city would subsequently petition Congress for admittance as the fifty-first state under the terms of the ratified city-state constitution. A simple majority consent of the state legislature in Albany would then be necessary. Granting this, Congress would then act upon the request and a majority congressional vote would admit New York City as the fifty-first state.

To the objection that the New York State Legislature would never approve this plan there are two answers. In the first place, upper New York State has much to gain by this procedure. The United States senators elected by New York have almost always been residents of the city. The fifty-first-state plan would therefore benefit the upstaters by giving them local representation in the Senate, which they have never had in the past. Then too a substantial majority of the present state legislature's time and energy is devoted to city problems. There is no reason why upstate legislators should be concerned about school decentralization and police organization in the city and even less reason why they should dictate the city's policies in these areas. Freeing Albany of these matters would allow the upstaters to take care of their own problems in their own way. Secondly, although the New York State Legislature has never been dominated by city representatives, they do constitute the largest single voting block, a near majority. Of the 57 state senators, 26 come from the city and 10 more from Long Island and Westchester. Of the 150 assemblymen, 68 come from the city and an additional 25 from the same surburban area. It can be assumed that most of these would support the city's application for statehood once their constituencies voted approval of the plan.

To the objection that Washington would balk at our statehood, there are a raft of answers. First, the election of Mailer and Breslin, two amateurs without funds and an organization of volunteers, would constitute an unignorable public mandate for statehood. The federal Constitution guarantees that "new states may be admitted by the Congress into the Union" with consent from the concerned state legislature. The demand for statehood from our country's largest, most important city could not go unheeded. One need only think of Prague!

Then, too, New York City's statehood, with its increased assets, its principle of neighborhood control, its ability to cope effectively with its financial and social problems, would spare Washington, and particularly the Department of Health, Education, and Welfare, one of its most persistent headaches. Federal funds now wasted through the bureaucracy of state administration would be saved, as would the countless man-hours regularly squandered by this creaky administrative machine. Washington could only gain by our becoming a state.

Statehood for New York City is therefore not an option but a necessity if we are to come to grips with our city's problems. The move is practical and possible and also entirely legal. On this the Constitution is clear, and the precedents have been set. Our statehood awaits only a mandate from the people. Then we've got it.

APPENDIX A: U. S. CONSTITUTION AS IT APPLIES TO THE ADMISSION OF STATES TO THE UNION

Article IV.

Section 3. New States may be admitted by the Congress into this Union; but no new State shall be formed or erected within the Jurisdiction of any other State; nor any State be formed by the Junction of two or more States, or Parts of States, without the Consent of the Legislatures of the States concerned as well as of the Congress.

APPENDIX B: HISTORICAL PRECEDENTS ADMITTING NEW STATES TO THE UNION

KENTUCKY
FIRST CONGRESS. SESS. III. CH. 3, 4. 1791

Chap. LV.—An Act declaring the consent of Congress, that a new State be formed within the jurisdiction of the Commonwealth of Virginia, and admitted into this Union, by the name of the State of Kentucky.

WHEREAS the legislature of the commonwealth of Virginia, by an act entitled "An act concerning the erection of the district of Kentucky into an independent state," passed the eighteenth day of December, one thousand seven hundred and eighty-nine, have consented, that the district of Kentucky, within the jurisdiction of the said commonwealth, and according to its actual boundaries at the time of passing the act aforesaid, should be formed into a new state: And whereas a convention of delegates, chosen by the people of the said district of Kentucky, have petitioned Congress to consent, that, on the first day of June, one thousand seven hundred and ninety-two, the said district should be formed into a new state, and received into the Union, by the name of "The State of Kentucky."

Section 1. Be it enacted by the Senate and House of Representatives of the United States of America in Congress assembled, and it is hereby enacted and declared, That the Congress doth consent, that the said district of Kentucky, within the jurisdiction of the commonwealth of Virginia, and according to its actual boundaries, on the eighteenth day of December, one thousand seven hundred and eighty-nine, shall, upon the first day of June, one thousand seven hundred and ninety-two, be formed into a new State, separate from and independent of, the said commonwealth of Virginia.

Sec. 2. And be it further enacted and declared, That upon the aforesaid first day of June, one thousand seven hundred and ninety-two, the said new State, by the name and style of the State of Kentucky, shall be received and admitted into this Unon, as a new and entire member of the United States of America.

Approved, February 4, 1791

Act of Febraury 4, 1791, Ch. IV,
III *Statutes at Large,* p. 189

VERMONT
FIRST CONGRESS. SESS. III. CH. 7, 8, 9, 10. 1791

Chap. VII.—An Act for the admission of the State of Vermont into this Union.

The state of Vermont having petitioned the Congress to be admitted a member of the United States, Be it enacted by the Senate and House of Representatives of the United States of America in Congress assembled, and it is hereby enacted and declared, That on the fourth day of March, one thousand seven hundred and ninety-one, the said state, by the name and style of "The State of Vermont," shall be received and admitted into this Union, as a new and entire member of the United States of America.

Approved, February 18, 1791.

Act of February 18, 1791, Ch. VII,
III *Statutes at Large,* p. 191

ALASKA
ADMISSION AS STATE
Alaska was admitted into the Union on January 3, 1959, upon issuance of Proc. No. 3269, Jan. 3, 1959, 24 F.R. 81, 73 Stat. c16, set out below, as required by sections 1 and 8(c) of the Alaska Statehood Law, Pub. L. 85-508, July 7, 1958, 72 Stat. 339, set out below.

ALASKA STATEHOOD
Public Law 85-508, July 7, 1958, 72 *Statutes at Large,* 339, as amended.

Sec. 1. Declaration; acceptance, ratification, and confirmation of Constitution.

That, subject to the provisions of this Act, and upon issuance of the proclamation required by section 8(C) of this Act, the State of Alaska is hereby declared to be a State of the United States of America, is declared admitted into the Union on an equal footing with the other States in all respects whatever, and the constitution formed pursuant to the provisions of the Act of the Territorial Legislature of Alaska entitled, "An Act to provide for the holding of a constitutional convention to prepare a constitution for the State of Alaska; to submit the constitution to the people for adoption or rejection: to prepare for the admission of Alaska as a State: to make an appropriation: and setting an effective date," approved March 19, 1955 (Chapter 46, Session Laws of Alaska, 1955), and adopted by a vote of the people of Alaska in the election held on April 24, 1956, is hereby found to be republican in form and in conformity with the Constitution of the United States and the principles of the Declaration of Independence, and is hereby accepted, ratified, and confirmed.

Sec. 2. Territory. The State of Alaska shall consist of all the territory, together with the territorial waters appurtenant thereto, now included in the Territory of Alaska.

V. EDUCATION

CLIFFORD ADELMAN AND PETER MANSO

New York schools have failed everyone—students, teachers, parents, and taxpayers alike. A few statistics make the point. Sixteen cents of every dollar spent on education in New York City go to administrative costs. Out of that same dollar only sixty-seven cents are eventually used in the schoolhouse. The present Board of Education disburses $3.2 million a year to hire proctors and application readers for teachers' examinations while allocating only $59,250 to develop curricula for disadvantaged children. Then, too, the board appropriates almost $500,000 yearly for its own budget, as compared, for example, to its total outlay of $941,000 for intensive teacher training.

What does it mean to be educated in the New York City schools? For the student it means entering an environment of overcrowded classrooms, meaningless study-hall periods, rigid and irrelevant curricula, frustrated teachers, and inevitably intimidating administrators. If the student is black or Puerto Rican, it also means being shuffled about from school to school because New York's Board of Education institutes different busing or pairing programs every year. It means, too, that 20 per cent of all Puerto Rican students who enter the first grade unable to speak English still cannot communicate in our tongue six years later because of the system's paucity of reading and speech teachers. And so one out of every four black and Puerto Rican kids entering the tenth grade is shunted off to a vocational high school where his chance of graduating is a mere 35 per cent. And in those academic high schools which, despite themselves, have managed to function in ghetto areas, a student's chance of going to college is one in 250.

No wonder it is, then, that the general dropout rate in New York's high schools is greater than 30 per cent, and that among black and Puerto Rican students, half again that figure, a full 45 per cent.

If the city has created a generation of students who are bored, browbeaten, frightened, and finally rebellious, it has, by the same token, victimized the teachers who have no control over what they teach and how they teach it. If the teacher is black or Puerto Rican —which is unlikely since less than 10 per cent of the city's teachers compared to 52 per cent of its students are in this category—he finds himself near bottom on the waiting lists for advancement, and his desire to educate children whose environment he comprehends thwarted by the city's curriculum and Board of Examiners. Faced with a plethora of duties which have nothing to do with teaching, a lack of facilities and materials, harassment from all quarters, and salaries hardly commensurate with training and responsibilities, the city's teachers pay dues to a union which many would claim merely aids the bureaucratic power structure. Like the students, the teachers, too, are victims of our schools.

When the Board of Education has responded to social change, it has done so only by creating additional bureaus, sub-bureaus and agencies, thus further removing the control of our schools from the people of New York. It has answered our problems piecemeal, and only in such ways as to safeguard its power. Its constantly shifting plans and programs have only served to increase racial tensions in the city. Thus, from 1964 to the present, despite pressure from all neighborhoods in New York City, we have been successively presented with busing and pairing plans, whereas what was really wanted by the people—by every group from PAT to CORE—was a return to neighborhood school management, to some form of meaningful decentralization.

The way of dealing with the problems of our schools lies, therefore, not in granting more money to the Board of Education or more cops to the corridors of the schools and to their surrounding streets. Neither is the solution to be had in token decentralization programs that do little to break the power of the bureaucracies and planners. These answers, offered by the politicians who created the present situation, do little to strike at the root cause of our school problems: the total irrelevancy of our academic curricula and environment, and the sense of alienation among parents, taxpayers, teachers, and students resulting from the all too-centralized control of the Board of Education.

Since our program envisions the political decentralization of New York City via Power to the Neighborhoods, decentralization of our school system would be a by-product of the city's over-all decentralization into smaller townships and neighborhoods. The centralized bureaucracy which now paralyzes our school system financially, educationally, and spiritually would no longer exist.

The new city-state would provide all moneys for education and distribute them to neighborhoods on a per capita school population basis. Under such an arrangement, individual school budgets would be markedly increased. At present, the federal government funds 6.1 per cent of our educational budget while Albany funds 38.8 per cent. We carry the rest, 55.1 per cent, or $801.8 million, $749.7 million of which comes from New York City tax levies. Were we to become a state, the federal government would match these tax levies for education on a fifty-fifty basis. Although we would lose $523.1 million in regular aid from Albany, our net gain after all adjustments in the regular budget ($1.34 billion for 1967–70) would be $211.5 million—a healthy increase, to be sure.

But as a city-state we would have a good deal more than this additional quarter billion dollars with which to provide quality education for our children. The three experimental decentralized districts recently in operation spent only 3 per cent of their budgets on Business and Administration, compared to 4.2 per cent for centralized districts. The difference, were all districts to be decentralized, would amount to $16 million city-wide. In addition, there would no longer be any excuse for spending nearly $500,000 on public relations for the central Board of Education, $9.5 million for a Bureau of Attendance which exists only because our students are so alienated from their schools that they won't attend them, and $260-000 for a Centralized Zoning Unit, which only hardens the worst flaw in our present school setup.

There would also be a marked reduction in waste stemming from capital projects. In a city in which school buildings are overcrowded and often in hideous condition, it is unconscionable that $16.9 million of $21.6 million appropriated in 1967–68 for non-mandatory repairs to buildings went unused. Under the new city-state, an incorporated neighborhood in Brooklyn, for example, could seal off and renovate five blocks of decaying brownstones and thereby create a local campus for nearly five thousand students for the very $16.9 million that was left rotting in the budget during 1967. On a per capita basis, this works out to a cost of $3400 per student, as opposed to the nearly $5000 per capita we spend at today's prevailing union rates for demolishing buildings and constructing faceless new high schools in their stead. Such construction could doubtless be done more cheaply under neighborhood control.

But we said that the answer was not more money alone. Our object is to bring the responsibility of the schools and their programs to the people of New York. Specifically, how would the decentralization of the public schools operate under the fifty-first state?

Any neighborhood that so elected would incorporate as a city or town and run its own school system. Neighborhoods that did not incorporate might choose to affiliate, for purposes of administering their schools, with incorporated neighborhoods. Small municipalities might agree to combine their school districts. Still other areas might choose to rely upon a central school administration.

Each school district would decide for itself on the composition and responsibilities of its local board. The total number of positions on the board, and the number of positions allocated to each group would be decided individually by municipality. These individual boards, like the school board of any suburb, would have full control of budgetary allocations, the hiring and firing of teaching, supervisory, and maintenance personnel within due process of law, and full control of curriculum. The city-state Board of Education—which will have little power—would act in an advisory capacity on curriculum if an individual neighborhood requested its services. For ordinary instructional services, plant maintenance, administration, books, and supplies, the local boards would submit their budgets to the city-state, whose only adjustments would be based on uniform per capita costs. For special programs, including capital projects and classroom services, in disadvantaged areas, individual neighborhoods would submit additional requests for funding, which would be granted after careful review of need and costs.

Each neighborhood would thus decide for itself on the education most relevant to its children. Poor neighborhoods, and black and Puerto Rican neighborhoods in particular, would have the funds with which to provide suitable programs. As parents and children in these neighborhoods realized that they had the power to influence their schools, dropout rates might diminish radically. No longer would children be shuffled unwillingly from school to school into neighborhoods deeply reluctant to receive them. City-wide racial tensions would doubtless be reduced.

Teaching certification requirements would be set by the city-state with some waivers for paraprofessional personnel now in existence. Minimum salary schedules would also be set by the city-state with a built-in cost-of-living clause. The UFT would bargain, on a city-state-wide basis, only on salaries and certification requirements. On all other matters, local chapters of the UFT would bargain with local boards. Sympathy strikes would be barred by city-state law, and, as in the case of all other municipal employees under the new city-state, *any* individual defying a court order enjoining a strike would be subject to prosecution.

It can be assumed that most neighborhoods would eliminate the tracking system, which determines whether a student receives academic or vocational training and which is partially responsible for such a high dropout rate in our high schools. In addition, state-wide educational examination similar to those of the present New York State Regents' Exams would be at the option of the local school boards. Students in a particular area might thus compete with other students in their neighborhood school system, and not against students from other systems with styles and vocabularies differing from their own. Such practices would most likely assure a far greater number of graduating high school students, and would naturally require a complete restructuring and expansion of our City University. It can be noted that such arrangements have been common in diocesan high schools in New York which take the best students from each parish.

It should be recognized that no matter how much we improve

primary and secondary education in New York, the value of a high school diploma continually decreases. Even the value of a college diploma is decreasing in our society due to the burgeoning number of graduates. Nonetheless, every graduate of the new city-state high schools should be able to attend what is now CUNY if he so desires. At present there are 53,000 graduates of our public high schools, and 24,000 places in the entering freshman class for all divisions of CUNY. We will need to double the number of these places by 1975 in order to accommodate all those students who wish to attend.

The ultimate disposition of CUNY would be up to the city-state's constitutional convention, but at this point it may not be remiss to suggest one possible plan. Each of the current *counties* of New York City would operate at least one senior university, one four-year state college, and a number of neighborhood "vest-pocket" colleges. All of these institutions would be administered by county boards composed of elected representatives from the neighborhoods to serve on the county board, the faculties of the colleges, and the students of the colleges. Such boards would have complete control over the allocation of funds. Curriculum and the hiring and firing of teaching and supervisory personnel would be in the hands of faculty and student bodies of the colleges themselves. The present Board of Higher Education, which recently began to decentralize some of its functions, would no longer exist.

The most promising solution to the shortage of college facilities, however, lies in the neighborhood "vest-pocket" campuses. These would consist of existing brownstone buildings, many now condemned and owned by the city, renovated by neighborhood manpower with on-the-job vocational training. They would be attractive, low in scale, and quite unlike the charmless buildings of our present campuses which, resembling factories and prisons in their architecture, seem only to promote dissatisfaction and rebellion among our students. Tailored to meet the specific curriculum and enrollment needs of individual neighborhoods, they could be built at a fraction of current college-construction costs. Exclusive of land purchase, the conventional eight-classroom building seating 240, for example, now costs $2 million whereas it is conservatively estimated that the purchase and rehabilitation of three red-brick buildings, accommodating the same number of students, could not exceed $200,000. An eight-building brownstone complex would accommodate 800 to 950 students for $500,000, and would include not only classrooms, two per floor, each seating no more than twenty students—but a library and an administration building, as well as a social and dining commons. On a per capita basis, the construction of these schools would work out to $550 per pupil as opposed to $8333 per head for a conventional campus building.

In addition to meeting the demand for increased college facilities, these vest-pocket schools would benefit the neighborhoods in other ways. They would provide college education locally, and for many ghetto youngsters would symbolize the immediate possibility of such an education. Then, too, their construction by local neighborhood manpower would considerably expand the Occupational Training Centers Program on which the city now spends a mere $1.6 million per year and eliminate the obvious discriminatory practices of the building-trades unions working on capital projects in black and Puerto Rican neighborhoods.

In the fall of 1969, there will be 4300 SEEK students at the various campuses of CUNY, and the Board of Higher Education plans an increase of 10,000 by 1975. Since it will take several years for the new neighborhood school system of the fifty-first state to produce students sufficiently educated to obviate the need for SEEK and similar programs, we suggest expanding these services, perhaps doubling their enrollment for the interim period. It presently costs the city $2700 annually to educate a SEEK student, as opposed to $1500 for a regular student, and thus we would need approximately an extra $30 million a year to finance such an expanded program. The expenditure is surely a wise one.

More immediately, the recently negotiated CUNY plan to admit an additional seven hundred students a year into supportive service programs would cost the city about $6.9 million per year by 1973. The substitute plan put forth by the CUNY Faculty Senate calling for a yearly increase of five hundred additional freshmen from disadvantaged areas will cost about $5.1 million by 1973. Unfortunately, neither plan stipulates the source of these funds, while both are conditional upon their being allocated, somehow, from somewhere. Nevertheless, whichever program is adopted by the CUNY faculty, we see its approval by the Board of Higher Education as essential. Out of a total CUNY budget of $215 million, its cost would be relatively small, its social implications huge. New York's school system has denied quality education to ghetto areas for decades. Of the eight hundred students, for example, who entered Benjamin Franklin High School in 1964, three hundred graduated in 1968, only fifty of these with academic diplomas and only three of these went on to college. The approval of either plan for CUNY is a necessary step toward correcting the long-standing injustices of our school system and, perhaps more significantly, a means of promoting a new sense of possibility in black and Puerto Rican high school students. Faced with the genuine prospect of attending college, more minority-group students could only take education more seriously.

It must be recognized too that neither plan is a "quota system." The entrance of a greater number of educationally disadvantaged students under either of the CUNY plans will not in any sense take place at the expense of white applicants. The projected enrollment figures for both the negotiated and Faculty Senate plans make this very clear, and we refer the reader to the appropriate chart on page 190 which outlines these plans.

As for the frequently voiced objection that these enrollment plans will promote a decline in college standards, we ask initially—whose standards? As a group, black and Puerto Rican students doubtless are academically deficient and have adjustments to make. But there is no reason these cannot be made under the proper programs. In the SEEK program, for example, the statistics suggest that the generally poor performance of first-year participants was very much improved during the program's second year. Then, too, black and Puerto Rican students usually have funds of experience lacking in their more insulated white counterparts. They can and, we expect, would offer an academic community an enriched campus life, as did the veterans returning to school following the Second World War.

The CUNY plan, like the decentralization of our present top-heavy school system and the creation of neighborhood-brownstone-college complexes, is therefore both necessary and just in time.

ESTIMATED DAY SCHOOL REGISTERS, 1969–70
(Average Daily Attendance)

	Total	Non-English Speaking 1966–67
Pre-Kindergarten	12,000	N.A.
Kindergarten	96,500	N.A.
Elementary—Regular	510,875	81,300
Elementary—Special Classes	8,800	N.A.
Elementary—Special Schools	8,000	N.A.
Junior High—Regular	228,525	16,300
Junior High—Special Classes	4,600	N.A.
Academic High	236,150	9,400
Vocational High—Full Time	42,750	2,600
TOTAL	1,148,200	109,600

SOURCES OF THE BUDGET, BOARD OF EDUCATION, 1969–70

	Amount (in millions)	Percentage
N. Y. State—Regular	$ 523.1	35.8
N. Y. State—Urban Education Aid*	45.0	3.0
Federal Government	13.5	0.9
Federal Government—Special*	76.5	5.2
N. Y. City Tax Levy	749.7	51.4
Capital Notes	17.8	1.2
Other	34.3	2.5
TOTAL	$1459.9	100.0

* Grants contingent on approval of special projects.

GENERAL ALLOCATIONS OF THE BUDGET, BOARD OF EDUCATION, 1969–70 (Exclusive of Special State and Federal Grants)

	Amount (in millions)	Percentage
Board of Education	$ 000.8	0.006
Superintendent of Schools	5.5	0.011
Personnel and Teacher Training	8.6	0.064
Curriculum Research and Evaluation	7.4	0.055
Instruction	908.0	67.7
Office of School Buildings	108.9	8.1
Business and Administration*	301.1	22.5
Total	$1340.3	98.436

* Includes $244.9 million for payments to Pension Fund, Health Plans, Social Security, Welfare Plans, and Pupil Transportation.

BUDGET INCREASES, 1969–70, DECENTRALIZED VS. CENTRALIZED ACTIVITY
(All figures in millions of dollars)

	Mandatory	Non-Mandatory	Total	Mandatory Business and Administration	
Decentralized Activity	$58.1	$31.0	$89.2	0.00	(0.00%)
Centralized Activity	$44.7	$20.1	$64.3	$33.3	(51.7%)

BUDGET REQUEST FOR DECENTRALIZED ACTIVITIES, 1969–70
(in millions of dollars)

Local School Boards	$ 0.84
District Headquarters	9.76
Elementary Education	366.08
Intermediate Education	176.31
Career Preparatory Education	139.18
Community Education	24.39
Plant Maintenance	14.53
Other	28.60
TOTAL	$759.69

Percentage of Total Budget, Exclusive of Special State and Federal Grants—
56.7 per cent

BUSINESS AND ADMINISTRATION BUDGETS, THREE
DECENTRALIZED DEMONSTRATION DISTRICTS

	Total Recommended Budget, 1969–70	Business and Administration	Percentage
Two Bridges	$4,442,914	$157,600	3.0
Ocean Hill-Brownsville	6,063,583	191,154	3.0
IS 201 Complex	3,444,627	110,668	3.0

PER CAPITA COST OF EDUCATION
(Based on Average Daily Attendance, 1967–68)

	Instruction	Books, etc.	Plant Admin., etc.	TOTAL
Kindergarten	$324.76	$ 8.81	$167.87	$ 501.44
Elementary School	574.10	19.66	273.73	967.85
Junior High & I.S.	742.64	47.35	347.88	1137.87
Academic High	743.47	41.81	423.24	1208.52
Vocational High	1097.31	62.52	524.33	1684.16
Overall (Estimated, 1969–70)				$1168.12

DROPOUT RATES, GRADES 10–12, ALL PUBLIC HIGH SCHOOLS*
(Board of Education Figures)

	Total	Simple Annual
Black	42%	12%
Puerto Rican	46%	13%
All Other	14%	4%
TOTAL	28%	8%

* Dropouts do *not* include those students discharged under the following categories: Graduation, Removal from City, to Parochial Schools, to Private Schools, to Institutions, Physical and Mental Disability, Death.

Running Against the Machine

CUNY ADMISSIONS PLANS, ENTERING FRESHMAN CLASS ONLY

	Present 9/69	9/70	Negotiated 9/69	9/70	Faculty-Senate Alternative 9/69	9/70
Competitive	1800	1800	1800	1500	1800	1800
Black & Puerto Rican*	8%	8%	8%	6%	8%	8%
100 Scholars Prog.	260	260	260	400	260	300
Black & Puerto Rican	60%	60%	60%	50%	60%	60%
SEEK	300	400	300	500	300	400
Black & Puerto Rican	90%	90%	90%	90%	90%	90%
Special High Schools	—	—	300	600	300	300
Black & Puerto Rican	—	—	90%	90%	90%	90%
TOTAL	2360	2460	2660	3000	2660	2800
Black & Puerto Rican	24%	29%	28%	42%	28%	37%

* These percentages are not dictated. They are simply projections based on current enrollments in each category.

COST OF SUPPORTIVE SERVICES FOR CUNY ADMISSIONS PLANS

	Tot. Entering Freshman Class 1969	1970	No. Freshmen Needing Supp. Services 1969	1970	Total No. Needing Supp. Serv. 1969	1970	Estimated Cost Supp. Serv.* (in millions) 1969	1970
Present	2360	2460	390	520	700	1090	2.1	3.0
Negotiated	2660	3000	630	990	1140	2280	3.4	6.9
Faculty-Senate Alternative	2660	2800	630	730	1030	1630	3.1	4.9

* Includes only supplementary reading programs, counseling (psychological and vocational), remedial teaching of English and mathematics, book money and transportation stipend.

ETHNIC DISTRIBUTION OF HIGH SCHOOL STUDENTS
NEW YORK CITY, 1968–69
(Figures based on total enrollment)

A. TOTAL	Black	Puerto Rican	Other	Total
Total High School	(19.5%) 79,699	(13.2%) 53,938	274,950	408,587
All Public	(24.0%) 74,856	(16.4%) 51,032	185,834	311,722
Academic	(23.2%) 62,499	(14.2%) 38,239	169,225	269,963
Vocational	(27.3%) 12,357	(30.6%) 12,793	16,609	41,759
Private	(5.0%) 4,843	(3.0%) 2,906	89,116	96,865
B. TWELFTH GRADE				
Total High School	(14.0%) 11,614	(9.1%) 7,577	63,663	82,854
All Public	(17.5%) 10,456	(11.5%) 6,882	42,364	59,702
Academic	(16.4%) 8,482	(8.6%) 4,472	38,878	51,832
Vocational	(25.1%) 1,974	(30.5%) 2,410	3,486	7,861
Private	(5.0%) 1,158	(3.0%) 695	21,299	23,152
C. GRADUATING SENIORS				
Total High School	(11.9%) 8,975	(7.7%) 5,767	60,419	75,161
All Public	(14.9%) 7,852	(9.7%) 5,093	39,751	52,696
Academic	(13.4%) 6,156	(6.6%) 3,032	36,750	45,938
Vocational	(25.1%) 1,696	(30.5%) 2,061	3,001	6,758
Private	(5.0%) 1,123	(3.0%) 674	20,668	22,465

VI. CRIME, NARCOTICS, AND THE POLICE

PETER MANSO

New York City has a parallel problem that meets at a most unhappy end. We speak of narcotics and crime. One would hope a solution could be offered for the first—but the answer cannot be found in the realm of a position paper. For the reasons of narcotics addiction are so profound only the superficial would offer an easy answer. Because those reasons are steeped in despair, surrender, and the denial of the pursuit of a good life. So for the moment we must deal from a stacked deck.

Our city's 50,000 to 100,000 addicts steal some two billion dollars worth of property each year and are responsible for at least half the city's crime. Fifty per cent of the cases coming before our courts —whether housebreaking, larceny, prostitution, or auto theft—involve addicts, and over 40 per cent of our prison inmates have narcotics records. A quarter of our police budget, half our court and jail costs, and a considerable percentage of our health and welfare expenses are attributable to addicts. The costs to New York, financial and spiritual, are incalculable.

And the situation only worsens. Despite the addition of 5000 new patrolmen over the past year and a doubling of the police budget by $300 million since 1963, addict crimes continue to increase. During 1967–68, for example, robberies were up by 52.7 per cent, burglaries by 24.9 per cent, and vehicle thefts by 29.5 per cent. As the police force has grown, so too has the crime. Additional personnel, funds, and publicity for New York's Police Department do not attack the problem itself. Only the recognition of the addict's extensive role in the city's crime can begin to reverse the trend. So extreme is the problem that extreme steps seem suggested for the solution.

Workable services for the care of addicts must be developed, regardless of the cost. Only this can reduce the city's crime to a tolerable level. An intensive program of methadone treatment, halfway houses and, unavoidably, the adoption of the English system of dispensing heroin at supervised neighborhood clinics is immediately necessary. No one of these programs is satisfactory. Combined, all three promise to reduce the crimes of drug addicts even if they will not end addiction. For the present, our only alternative to increasing addiction is to stop forcing the addict into the street where he must hustle for a fix.

Of the city's several programs aimed at breaking the addicts dependence on heroin, the most successful is the methadone-maintenance program started in 1964 by doctors Dole and Nyswander. The results of this program have been outstanding. The successful treatment of more than one thousand heroin addicts has demonstrated that the regular oral intake of methadone in prescribed dosages will block the need, desire, and effects of heroin. The synthetic drug is not taken in addicting doses, but it must be taken regularly. The patient becomes methadone-dependent but this does not interfere with his normal activities and is no more outrageous than other forms of habitual medication such as insulin, digitalis, and diphenylhydantoin for epilepsy. Of the twelve hundred addicts enrolled in the program between 1964 and March 1968, 87 per cent were stabilized on methadone during the four-year experiment. The remaining 13 per cent were discharged as ineligible for treatment (dependence on amphetamines, barbiturates, or alcohol), died, or dropped out for unknown reasons. Sixty-five per cent in the program longer than four months are in school, working, or both.

Prior to treatment the average patient in the program had a history of addiction for twelve and a half years, and 92 per cent had one or more criminal convictions, with an average of 4.84 convictions per patient. At present only 3.4 per cent of these patients have been convicted for offenses committed while in the program. It is estimated that the city has saved $18 million annually on thefts alone, plus the savings in jail, court, and welfare costs. The city's initial investment totaled a mere $250,000. Because of its success the program now receives $2 million yearly from the State Narcotic

Addiction Control Commission. These funds, however, are severely inadequate as there is now a one- to two-year waiting list for methadone treatment.

Methadone maintenance, however, has several significant limitations. It assumes an addict willing to abandon heroin. Many addicts, particularly those under the age of twenty, are not in this category. Methadone is also of no effect against drugs other than heroin. For addicts taking barbiturates, amphetamines, or alcohol in addition to heroin, the treatment is worthless.

Appropriate programs must be developed for those unwilling or unable to undergo methadone maintenance. The city must recognize the need to supply legal heroin at neighborhood hospitals. For certain types of addicts there is no alternative. As in England, these addicts would be registered and for each patient complete records would be kept. Heroin would be dispensed under the most rigid conditions, and administered either intravenously or in solution at the clinic to prevent overdoses and the resale of the drug.

Such a program could be expected to stabilize otherwise alienated and criminal lives. It would reduce if not eliminate the vigorous subculture of crime and drugs, and reduce the more than eight hundred annual deaths of addicts resulting from impure heroin and overdoses. Most importantly, it would grant the addict his drug without forcing him to crime. To the objection that the "legalization of heroin" would turn New York into a mecca for addicts, it can be noted that our city has already the largest junkie population of any metropolitan area in the western world, and an estimated two thirds of all the addicts in this country. To reach the ceiling and reduce the crime might be less odious than the present ill.

Group residential centers such as Phoenix House have been in operation for two years and offer a third approach to the addict problem. Here ex-addicts pool their resources (mostly welfare checks), purchase and renovate brownstone buildings, and live together in a therapeutic community. The stress is on group therapy and the addict is kept off drugs by his fellows as well as through his own efforts. No drug substitutes are used. The advantage of such a program is that it offers the addict a potential measure of control over his existence, a sense of identity and insight not possible under other programs. Even more than the methadone plan, however, it presupposes the addict's desire to abandon drugs, and so does not work for many younger addicts. Nevertheless, the success of Phoenix House recommends its expansion. In conjunction with methadone treatment such halfway houses promise an even more positive approach to treating our city's addicts.

The point is that the city must alter its attitude toward addicts. Addiction is the most profound form of alienation in our city, the junkie the severest victim of the general powerlessness felt by anyone living in New York. Giving individuals control over their schools, police departments, housing projects and training programs can only lessen the initial cause for addiction. Similarly, any drug-treatment program must itself be administered by the neighborhoods. The city would give priority to these programs and fund any reasonable plan proposed by individual communities. One area, for example, might choose to rid itself of illicit drug traffic and its related ills by opting for heroin centers, while another might wish to set up a series of corner methadone clinics. Still another might opt for a combined program of halfway houses, vocational-training centers, and extensive methadone treatment. Thus neighborhoods would have both the power and responsibility for their addiction services. The city would finance these one and all as long as they promised to stabilize addicts and cut addict crime. No doubt most would.

In short, the city must cope with crime as the symptom of a deeper ill. This is implicit to the concept of neighborhood control. The premise is that only by relieving the ill—the purposelessness of many of our citizens—can we relieve its symptoms, whether drug addiction, larceny, assault, or homicide.

Under the fifty-first state, neighborhoods would be given the power to control their own police forces. Hopefully these would be local to their communities. Policemen might be remunerated for living in the area in which they worked, or perhaps certain neighborhoods would choose to make local residency a requirement for its police officers. Neighborhoods not wanting a local force could, of course, rely on municipal policemen assigned to their area. The advantages of the local police force, however, would be many. With such an arrangement, community relations would improve immeasurably. Both cops and citizens would know each other not just as potential antagonists but as neighbors. In ghetto areas, particularly, policemen would no longer be regarded as intruders, and in black and Puerto Rican neighborhoods there would surely be a dominant percentage of black and Puerto Rican cops. Racial tensions might thus diminish considerably. For the policeman himself, local residency could assure more respect from the community as well as a conceivably more satisfying job. Both the local cop and his family would live with a set of neighborhood conditions improved or impaired by his performance; not only would his sense of responsibility increase but so too might his sense of accomplishment. The policeman would no longer be oblivious to the results of his labor.

A city is only as good as its cops, but a cop can be better than his city. This is his responsibility—and the paradox of his job. As a buffer for society he must live with criminals and suffer a double standard. The adjustment is difficult. Maybe it's the stuff of heroism, maybe more often than not the basis for corruption. The cops have a saying: "We're damned if we do and we're damned if we don't." By this they mean their performance pleases no one. One side plasticizes them as saints, the other dehumanizes them as pigs. With their tough street intelligence they realize that politicians have been working them, like everyone else in this city, on both sides of the street.

A good administration would encourage the best cops. Local neighborhood recruitment offers another possibility. Still others, suggested by Mr. Breslin though skeptically received by Mr. Mailer, are that the city grant draft exemptions for short-term police service, encourage law students to work as part-time cops during high-crime hours, and aid neighborhood high schools offering police training for interested students. Then, too, getting closer to the problem, the citizen should be the recipient of the action that goes on in this city. We would do this by legalizing all gambling. Coney Island could become the Las Vegas of the East, for gambling is natural to man. As well, the city must investigate the malpractices of loan agencies and city marshals. A police force can be expected to move only on its lack of corruption and the honesty of the institutions it serves. While we ask the police force to improve, we must ask the same of ourselves.

VII. CITY-STATE FINANCES

WHIT SMITH AND PETER MANSO

New York City is the legal creation of the state. In no area is this fact more evident than in the city's limited fiscal and monetary powers. The taxes which the city levies and the rates of taxation are determined by state law and the Constitution. The city cannot default on its obligations to meet interest and amortization payments on its debt. State law requires full payments to employee pension funds and obligations under outstanding collective-bargaining agreements.

The inability of the city to govern itself financially is best dramatized by annual budgetary rituals. The mayor implores Albany to increase local assistance or legalize off-track betting or restore cuts in education. With rhetorical passion, he warns of the immediate collapse of essential services and the halt of priority programs. The response of upstate legislators and the governor is usually minimal: slight increases are provided and the city struggles along in its habitual impotency.

The city's fiscal dependency and weakness is ironic considering its financial resources and potential. It is the wealthiest city in the world. With annual retail sales in excess of $12 billion, New York accounts for more than 5 per cent of the United States market and possesses a buying power greater than that of all but eight foreign nations. The city has a budget second in size only to the federal government's and provides Washington with approximately $20 billion in personal and corporate-income taxes, almost one fifth of all the income revenue collected by the federal government.

While the litany of the city's fiscal problems has been well enunciated by numerous mayors, commissions, and other public officials, concrete proposals have been few and progress limited. Confronted by the dilemma of a constituency already financially overburdened yet underserviced and the need for additional funding sources, the city has nearly exhausted the possibility of new or increased taxes. In vain it has turned to Albany and Washington.

The creation of the city-state represents New York City's only viable alternative, the only method of achieving financial independence and security. As every annual budgetary crisis demonstrates, all other means have been expended.

THE CITY BUDGET: EXPENSES

In the past ten years New York City's expense budget has tripled, from $2.2 billion for 1959–60 to $6.6 billion in the 1969–70 proposed budget. During this decade, the Sanitation and Police departments have more than doubled their budgets, welfare expenses have more than quadrupled, and public-education expenditures alone have tripled since 1960.

Yet these massive increases for city services do not provide an adequate index of the distribution of costs in the budget. In 1959–60, education, police, and sanitation all claimed larger portions of total expenditures than they will in 1969–70. The changing pattern in distribution allotments is based on three primary changes: (1) technological advances in areas such as sanitation have made it possible to concentrate a smaller share of the city's money in those fields; (2) the emergence of new programs has required city funding; (3) a few services have increasingly necessitated a larger share of city expenses. This last phenomenon is best exemplified by the increase of welfare expenditures from 11.9 per cent of the 1959–60 budget to 16.5 per cent for 1969–70.

Massive budgetary increases also do not indicate the actual changes in levels of service provided by the city. Even when new programs are not instituted nor services expanded, the city's budget continues its inexorable rise. Three major causes produce these mandatory increases:

1. Wage and salary levels must increase; the rising cost of living and collective-bargaining agreements are primarily responsible for these increased costs which must be met by the city. Similarly, expenditures for pensions and other fringe benefits result in annual increases. The result of the growing union militancy of the city's 354,600 employees has been an increase of labor costs to roughly 60 per cent of the budget.
2. The growing number of participants in such open-ended programs as public assistance, Medicaid, and public education produces automatic increases in city expenditures.
3. As part of the general national inflationary trend, the city must pay higher interest rates on its debt and reach higher contractual agreements on goods and services provided.

These mandatory budget increases often produce a paradoxical situation characterized by cuts in city programs even though the total budget figure increases over the previous year.

THE CITY BUDGET: REVENUES

The city's present revenue sources are unable to maintain adequate service levels. This situation will only deteriorate over the next decade unless major fiscal revisions are made. Without increases in the coverage or rates of present taxes, city revenues should exhibit a natural annual growth of 5 per cent. Yet at the same time, city expenses are now increasing at a rate of approximately 15 per cent per year.

The principal sources of revenue generated by the city itself are real estate taxes, sales and other taxes on doing business, user charges, and the city income tax.

Until the mid-1950s, real estate taxes accounted for more than half of the city's revenue. But rates have not increased in comparison with the economy's growth or the city's expenditures, and real estate taxes now comprise less than 30 per cent of the city's revenue. This decline also represents the impact of new taxes, primarily levies on doing business such as the stock-transfer tax. The regressive nature of the real estate tax has been only partially mitigated by the city's sales tax. Because it excludes food, housing, and transit fares —major expenditures for low-income individuals—the sales tax can be characterized as slightly progressive. However, it does not seem likely that sales and other city excise taxes will account for a larger share of the city's future revenues. Between 1959–60 and 1969–70, the portion of city revenues resulting from excise taxes decreased from 24.9 per cent to 14.7 per cent. These taxes are usually sluggish in responding to the city's over-all economic growth; they increase by less than one per cent for each single percentage rise in total income generated by the city's economy.

In 1966, the city income tax was instituted. This tax will account for approximately 3.3 per cent of the city's 1969–70 revenues. The introduction of the city income tax and reduced dependence on the real estate tax represent a limited but notable trend toward the use of more progressive taxation methods. A New York University study of the distribution of the burden of city taxes in 1960–61 disclosed that the real estate tax, usually passed on to tenants by landlords, absorbed about three times as much of the income of a family with $4000 or less per year as for the family with from $10,000 to $15,000 per year.

On the other hand, an income tax is more responsive to economic growth than virtually any other kind of tax. As total income rises, an increasing proportion of it is subject to taxation since personal exemptions are flat dollar amounts and do not rise with income. As a result, taxable income over-all increases more rapidly than total income. Under a progressive-rate structure, income tax collections would also be highly elastic, with each increment of added income producing a proportionally larger increment of tax. The federal income tax, because of its progressive-rate structure, yields a 15 per cent increase in revenue for every 10 per cent in the total output of the nation's goods and services. Unfortunately, under the present local tax system, the income tax will probably not be utilized to reduce or replace the property tax, but merely to supplement it.

The city's present fiscal crisis is primarily attributed to the inability of the local administration to receive adequate funds from locally generated revenue, and future projections portend no immediate relief. One New York University study has estimated that between 1964–65 and 1974–75 the total money income of New York City residents would increase by 57 per cent, yet excise-tax collections, for example, would grow by only 24 per cent. If recent expense trends continue or intensify, expenditure increases would far outdistance revenue growth.

While some remedial actions—such as increased reliance on income taxes—are available to the city, with the consent of the state, of course, major revisions in local-generated sources of revenue seem remote. Faced with the unacceptable possibility that increased taxation rates would produce detrimental economic effects, the city's present fiscal dependency on the "good will" of Albany legislators and Washington bureaucrats seems likely to grow.

STATE ASSISTANCE AND REVENUE

For the privilege of electing one governor, two senators, ninety-four legislators, and an assortment of other state officials, New York City residents contribute approximately $2.5 billion to the state of New York.

In return, for the year 1969–70 New York City will receive approximately $1,385,000,000 in state aid for numerous programs, including health, education, and welfare. The state also contributes $197,000,000 of per capita aid to be distributed at the city's discretion. These amounts represent roughly 60 per cent of the total funds it is estimated that the city provides to the state in taxes and fees. The city, of course, receives additional benefits in the form of state-conceived and -administered services provided in and for the city. However, the city's $.60 return on every dollar paid to Albany, including roughly $.07 in the form of per capita assistance, compares unfavorably with the $.69 return to the rest of the state.

This year's state-budget cuts clearly illustrate the city's need for a dependable source of revenue which is not subject to the annual legislative whims of Albany. The present system of per capita aid does not meet this need. This formula is based upon a set amount which increases only if the population increases and bears no relation to increased service costs or economic expansion. For example, in

1948, per capita aid comprised 7 per cent of local revenue sources in the state, but by 1965 this figure had decreased to 2.3 per cent.

The creation of the city-state would have two immediate effects in terms of the city's fiscal relations with Albany. First, approximately $2.5 billion which the city now contributes to Albany would be retained by the city-state, assuming that all existing taxes and rates of taxation were maintained under the new legal entity. The continuation of present state income tax rates by the city-state would produce over $600 million in annual revenue; the estate tax, $59 million; alcoholic licenses, $17 million; cigarette tax, $107 million; sales tax, $254 million; motor-fuel tax, $81 million; motor-vehicle fees and licenses, $54 million; and pari-mutuel taxes at Aqueduct, over $80 million in additional revenue. After subtracting the amount of state aid which is directly contributed to the city, the net saving to the city-state would be roughly $1 billion.

Second, the city-state would achieve full fiscal independence, with the power to control tax levies and their distribution. The city could then, without the present necessary approval of Albany, possibly enact an off-track betting bill which would yield $25–$50 million in the first year and $150–$200 million annually in subsequent years.[1] Or the city-state could increase the income tax while offering lower real estate taxes to landlords who make property improvements or provide other benefits for tenants.

A number of initial costs would result from the creation of the city-state involving the gearing up of administrative machinery to handle, for example, the collection and distribution of additional revenue; the purchase of certain property and facilities now owned by New York State; the hiring and training of city-state employees to administer programs; and the assumption by the city of certain services now provided by the state such as penal institutions and higher judicial levels.

The costs of this transfer of power, however, would hardly be prohibitive, particularly in view of the additional funds available to the city-state. New York State, for example, now spends $22.37 per capita for General Control and Financial Administration, ranking as the sixth highest figure among all the states, and compared to a national average of $16.68 per capita.[2] If the city-state met these administrative costs at the national average per capita level, then a total expenditure of $132 million would be required, a high estimate in consideration of the reduced administrative costs resulting from the decentralization of city services.

Other problems could similarly be resolved. The state's substantial property holdings in the city and its desire to divest itself of them would be an adequate incentive for the state to reach a reasonable settlement on the provision, for example, of water resources to the city-state. With proper budgeting and planning procedures, the costs involved with the implementation of the city-state's powers should not consume more than $700 million a year, leaving an immediate budgetary surplus of $300 million for the city's discretionary use.[3]

THE FEDERAL GOVERNMENT: EXPENSES AND REVENUE

In fiscal 1968, New York State contributed over $30 billion in taxes to Washington while the city provided approximately $20 billion, two thirds of the over-all state contribution. From an economic viewpoint, during this same period the federal government expended $19.4 billion in New York State and $7.1 billion of that total in the city. These figures represent total federal disbursements and include such items as veterans' payments, government contracts, expenditures for operating federal offices, etc.; they are primarily characterized by programs or appropriations over which state and local governments have no control.

On a per capita basis, the average New York State taxpayer receives $1156 in federal funds. The per capita average for New York City residents is $917, while the level for state taxpayers living outside the city is 48.6 per cent higher, a total figure of $1363.

A number of related causes have produced this gross inequity in the distribution of federal funds. First, state officials and upstate bureaucrats lack a direct incentive for getting federal funds for the city. Second, New York City's congressional delegation has exhibited a tendency toward involvement in intellectual pursuits concerning national and international policies, while other regional coalitions have devoted themselves to committee work related to gaining additional funds for their areas. Third, most urban-aid legislation stipulates that only 12.5 per cent of the total appropriation may go to a single state, producing a situation in which New York cities may share the same amount of money as urban areas in North Dakota. With the power of statehood, the city of New York would be in a position to substantially eliminate this imbalance. Represented by two senators and twenty congressmen, the city-state could bring its full economic leverage directly to bear on Washington to receive its fair share of federal aid. Its representatives would be unified by the city-state's common interest in more urban-oriented federal programs and would directly negotiate with Washington bureaucrats on the basis of need and self-interest. Moreover, the 12.5 per cent limitation on urban-assistance programs would no longer inhibit the funds allocated to New York City due to the elimination of competition with upstate urban areas.

It is possible on this basis to provide gross estimations of the increased assistance available to New York City once statehood was achieved. If the city-state received the same rate of per capita assistance as is now provided for New York State, the total amount of federal disbursements would increase by $1.9 billion. If the rate of aid to the city was the same as that now received by state residents living outside New York City, then federal appropriations would increase by $3.5 billion.

With the addition of $300 million which now goes to Albany, the total increase in city-state revenue would range between $2.2 billion and $3.8 billion.

Participation in federal programs will, of course, require substantial revisions in budgetary allotments, which can be determined only on a program-by-program basis. The city-state would, for example, be eligible for participation in the Interstate Highway Program with the federal government contributing 90 per cent of costs. Some programs, such as the School Lunch Program, would not require substantial increased costs to the city-state since the primary source of the state share of expenses is the contribution of participants. Other open-ended programs such as public assistance and Medicaid would necessitate increased city-state contributions under federal formulas.

Beyond the specific and calculable financial advantages of statehood, a number of hidden economic effects would result from the creation of the city-state. Administrative efficiency would represent one major improvement. The present duplication of functions as the result of bureaucratic levels in Albany and New York City could be eliminated and replaced by a single administrative structure. For those neighborhoods which did not seek to incorporate, the city-state would provide and administer services, aided by local representatives who checked the equity and efficiency of financial allotments. For incorporated communities, the city-state would simply pass along funds and allow neighborhoods to administer their own programs. The end result would be substantial savings through efficient and responsive administrative practices.

Statehood offers other intangible economic rewards. The people of New York City would no doubt experience a new confidence and pride in themselves and their institutions with the city claiming its proper fiscal prerogatives. No longer would there be the feeling that one's tax dollars were supporting spurious projects mainly benefiting the upstaters.[4] The progress of neighborhood projects funded by the city-state would be tangible evidence to New Yorkers that their taxes were being used for their own benefit, without the depressing waste that now characterizes so many municipal undertakings. Having the power to spend what it had earned, the city might just sense the full possibilities of its imagination; it might, indeed, come to see its own potential and progress.

FOOTNOTES

[1] This estimate was provided by Mayor John V. Lindsay, "Message of the Mayor," *City of New York: Executive Budget for 1969–1970.* p. 3.

[2] Tax Foundation, Inc., *Facts and Figures on Government Finance: 1969* (New York, New York: 1969). p. 226.

[3] A wide range of expenditures must be considered as a result of the creation of the city-state: the cost of purchasing state-owned properties and facilities; the loss of parking-meter revenue once private cars are banned from Manhattan; the cost of negotiating water rights with the state of New York; expenditures for the construction of facilities which would house neighborhood service and administrative functions; the creation of administrative machinery to handle the distribution and allocation of additional revenue; the cost of training programs for neighborhood administrators; expenditures for the construction of a city-state penal system; the creation and operation of city-state judicial offices; increased administrative costs if the Constitutional Convention creates a bicameral legislative structure; etc. These costs would require an annual expenditure of roughly $700 million.

[4] Such projects include the South Mall Complex which will cost New York State taxpayers $610 million as well as the numerous expressways which connect upstate rural villages.

NEW YORK CITY EXPENSE BUDGET: FISCAL YEARS 1960-1970
(IN BILLIONS OF DOLLARS)

Fiscal Year	Amount
1959-1960	2.179
1960-1961	2.353
1961-1962	2.547
1962-1963	2.794
1963-1964	3.091
1964-1965	3.383
1965-1966	3.965
1966-1967	4.599
1967-1968	5.178
1968-1969	6.007
1969-1970	6.604

NYC EXPENDITURES FOR SELECTED SERVICES, 1960–1970

($millions)

	Education (incl. Higher Ed.)	Welfare	Police	Sanitation
1959–1960	579	254	215	92
1960–1961	635	248	235	97
1961–1962	509	300	249	102
1962–1963	808	299	265	111
1963–1964	898	346	302	118
1964–1965	990	419	330	123
1965–1966	1048	535	364	126
1966–1967	1151	607	351	129
1967–1968	1440	696	456	152
1968–1969	1557	1016	467	182
1969–1970	1606	1092	568	212

STATE AID: 1969–70 EXECUTIVE BUDGET

Department	Amount	*Increase or (—) Decrease
Housing and Development Administration	$13,568,029	(—)$471,697
Comptroller	15,856	*315
Law	. . . . . .	(—)55,000
New York Public Library	1,643,500	(—)645,112
Brooklyn Public Library	1,524,832	(—)299,286
Queens Borough Public Library	1,218,479	(—)106,988
Education	576,971,861	(—)21,839,547
Higher Education	89,280,388	*7,501,397
Police	500,000	. . . . . .
N. Y. C. Division of Veterans Affairs	108,801	(—)12,929
Health Services Administration	128,857,106	*11,038,718
Environmental Protection Administration	5,689,031	*187,455
Addiction Services Agency	4,848,763	(—)3,545,339
Social Services	440,104,900	*8,869,650
Youth Services Agency	3,752,790	(—)195,000
Charitable Institutions	84,270,718	*15,257,739
Correction	4,000,000	1,000,000
Criminal Court	980,000	*100,000
Family Court	390,000	*30,000
Civil Court	1,200,000	*125,000
Probation	6,542,419	(—)550,542
Supreme and Surrogate Courts	1,661,189	(—)218,786
Debt Service	3,911,918	*95,721
Miscellaneous	6,794,814	*1,049,288
Mayoralty	143,145	(—)23,105
New York City Retirement System	68,525	*39,775
Total	$1,378,047,064	*$17,331,725

* State aid does not include $196,700,000 New York State Per Capita Allocation, $48,800,000 State Motor Vehicle and Motor Fuel Revenues, $1,100,000 Highway Maintenance and $48,800,000 State Motor Vehicle and Motor Fuel Revenues, and $6,000,000 reimbursement from the state for one-half of the railroad relief from assessments, which are shown as General Fund Revenues in this table, it also does not include $7 million contained in pending legislation. These items reflect a reduction of $13.4 million in New York State Local Assistance.

FEDERAL AID: 1969–70 EXECUTIVE BUDGET

Department	Amount	*Increase or (—) Decrease
Mayoralty	$564,102	*$188,673
Comptroller	64,197	*2,050
Housing Development Administration	5,543,025	*725,167
Law Department	400,000	*160,000
Municipal Service Agency	510,979	*86,249
Education	89,785,138	(—)633,067
Police	25,540	
Environmental Protection Administration	914,000	*114,000
Health Services Administration	145,380,859	*19,222,257
Social Services	639,741,668	*122,729,734
Charitable Institutions	54,612,343	*23,014,646
Correction	171,711	*9,000
Human Resources Administration	67,601,938	(—)18,975,887
Miscellaneous	41,376,000	*1,414,000
Addiction Services Agency	5,207,864	*1,742,493
New York City Retirement System	68,525	*39,775
Economic Development Administration	. . . . .	(—)109,100
Total	$1,051,967,889	*$149,730,090

VIII. A MISCELLANY OF IDEAS FOR THE 51ST STATE

Monorail around Manhattan and free jitney service in midtown Manhattan.

Vest-pocket neighborhood colleges.

"Sweet Sunday."

Neighborhood Housing Banks.

Legalized gambling.

Vegas East at Coney Island.

Free bicycles in all city parks.

Roof forest and ivy program for housing projects.

A referendum calling for the fifty-first state and subsequent constitutional convention.

Recognition of the necessity for a free and open system of higher education for the city's neediest as continuation of free and open elementary and high schools.

U. S. Grand Prix in Central Park—once yearly.

Weekend jousting matches for adolescents in the city's parks.

Call for a passage by the City Council of a resolution recognizing Muhammad Ali as still Heavyweight Champion of the world.

Support of Mr. John Seder's program for the federal government's contributing 90 per cent of city welfare dollars.

Cable TV to be controlled by neighborhoods.

Day-care centers and nurseries.

The city-state to investigate the possibilities of taking over Port Authority.

Strict pollution control of vehicles, apartment house, and Con Edison smokestacks.

A central-city farmer's market offering ethnic foods of all varieties.

Mayor Mailer promises to plead with Mario Procaccino to serve as Official City Greeter.

A zoo in every neighborhood.

Rebuilding of our dilapidated neighborhood water fronts as waterfront housing.

Concerted ecological improvement of the city's water, vegetation, and air resources.

The city to investigate and, where actionable, eliminate loan agencies and city marshals.

Abolishment of Surrogate's Court and Traffic Court. Traffic fines to be paid by mail or at conveniently located banking windows.

Nighttime truck deliveries permitted in midtown Manhattan with trucks using what are now off-limit thoroughfares such as the West Side Drive.

The park in Fort Greene as New York's equivalent to Arlington's National Shrine in memory of the men who died aboard British prison ships during the Revolution.

Neighborhood school curriculum could include courses in local history, architecture, and neighborhood life.

Craftsman training in gardening, and stained glass windows to enhance the appearance of parks, streets, gardens, fountains, and public buildings.

Police-cadet training in ghetto high schools instead of physical education courses.

A neighborhood world series of stickball to be held on Broad Street every weekend.

An effort will be made to return national baseball teams to Brooklyn and Manhattan.

Policemen will be encouraged to live in the precinct in which they work.

PART FOUR

The Daily Round, a Miscellany of Ads, Handouts, and Schedules

SHOPPING LIST FOR THE CITY-STATE

An additional $3,000,000,000 in revenue to the city-state means:
1. 136,356 units of new low-income housing ($22,000 per unit).
2. 200,000 units of rehabilitated housing ($15,000 per unit).
3. 250,000 sanitation trucks ($12,000 per truck).
4. 150,000 bulldozers for snow removal ($20,000 per bulldozer).
5. 75,000 vest-pocket parks ($40,000 per park).
6. 60,000 day-care centers ($50,000 per center).
7. 75,000 hospital beds ($40,000 per bed); 300 hospitals (250 beds per hospital).
8. 100 libraries ($30 million per library).
9. 15,000 superpumpers ($200,000 per superpumper).
10. 40,000 hook and ladders ($75,000 per hook and ladder).
11. 1500 new college classrooms for 360,000 students (conventional college classrooms for 240 students cost $2 million).
12. 15,000 classrooms for college students in rehabed brownstones, accommodating 3,600,000 students (rehabed classrooms for 240 students cost $200,000). This equals 30 CUNYs (present CUNY enrollment: 125,000).
13. 150 new high schools (average cost: $20 million per h.s.).
14. 500 new intermediate schools (average cost: $6 million per school).
15. 1000 new public schools ($3 million per school).
16. 428,571 new teachers (starting salary approx. $7000 per year).
17. 250,000 cops on the beat ($9000 approx. starting salary plus $1000 retirement per year, plus $1000 training, plus $1000 equipment and miscellaneous: $12,000 per cop).
18. 375,000 new sanitation workers (approx. salary $8000 per year).

19. Fiscal 1969–70 Expense Budget: $568.4 million for police; $269.9 million for fire; $212.0 for sanitation; $1.481 billion for education; $221.6 million for CUNY.
20. 5.2 times present police budget.
21. 11.1 times present fire budget.
22. 14.1 times present sanitation budget.
23. 2.025 times present education budget.
24. 13.5 times present CUNY budget.

AQUEDUCT

RAILBIRD'S PICKS

THE MAYORAL HANDICAP

June 17, 1969

P.	Horse	Comment	Pr. Odds
	WAGNER 12-yr.-old gelding by Meade Esposito—Out of Machine	Knows the Track	8–5
2	**PROCACCINO** Bronx Ridgling by Fear—Out of Law and Order	Moves Up on Sloppy Track	2–1
3 3A	**SCHEUER** by Liberal—Out of Loser **BADILLO** by Liberal—Out of Loser	Can't Tell Them Apart	11–1
4	MAILER ***BEST BET*** by Amateur—Out of Statehood	First-time Starter Good Barn	20–1

TAKE A SHOT

MAILER—BRESLIN AND THE 51ST STATE

Democratic Primary—June 17

(Distributed at the Betting Windows at Aqueduct. —Ed.)

IF THESE GUYS WIN—

They'll never pass the

Urinalysis.

VOTE MAILER-BRESLIN!

DEMOCRATIC PRIMARY, JUNE 17th.

(Also distributed at Aquaduct... Ed.)

Power to the Neighborhoods!

Local control of Education, Housing, Sanitation, Parks and Police!

Kiss off the boredom of the Democratic Machine!

Photos courtesy Shirley Ransdell (N.Y. Press Service) and Jill Krementz

Give a vote to—

MAILER-BRESLIN!

NOTES TO CANVASSERS

Two men . . . Norman Mailer and Jimmy Breslin . . . propose to return political power to the people of this city.

The idea was once defined as ". . . government of the people, by the people, and for the people . . ."

Your job as canvassers is to go to the people (registered Democrats), explain our program, listen, and feed back what they are saying.

To do this, you must know what we are trying to do and how it can be done.

Simply stated, Mailer and Breslin want to make New York City the 51st state. Then they propose to divide the city into municipalities of about the size of local neighborhoods. The municipalities would be administered by the people who live there.

To do this we must win the mayoralty and City Council presidency in November with a majority vote. That gives us a mandate from the people of New York City to pressure Albany and Washington so that they will, according to the provisions of the U. S. Constitution and the precedent of the case of West Virginia, grant our request to become the 51st state of this Union.

If we do not win that election by a clear majority we pass the election back to the people of New York City until they give us that mandate.

After we become the 51st state any neighborhood in the city which so wishes can declare itself to be a municipality, and can begin the task of setting up its own local government, services, and life-styles.

Any area of the city that does not choose to declare itself a municipality retains a status like that of unincorporated rural areas until such time as it does incorporate.

Local services for such unincorporated areas will be provided by what is now the New York City pool.

The candidates and their position papers will, of course, spell out the details. But you are going to be asked a lot of questions now. "Notes to Canvassers" gives you the answers to as many of those questions as possible. You will also be given a short summary of our program to leave with each voter.

Bring back the questions you can't answer to your A.D. captain.

It is essential, however, that every registered Democrat you visit understand the two basic steps by which we intend to return the power of government to the people; to the wisdom of our neighborhoods.

1. Make New York City the 51 state.
2. Break up that state into incorporated municipalities.

Under the present status of this city, the same style of life is being forced on both the lion and the ox, and that, as the poet Blake said, is oppression.

FINANCES

The city of New York presently pays the state of New York and the federal government $14 billion in taxes and receives only $3 billion in revenue.

That means the state of New York, on a per capita basis, gives New York City only 30 per cent of its total revenue. On the same basis, the state provides 40 per cent of Rochester's total revenue.

The creation of the city-state would significantly reduce these inequities and automatically provide an extra $2 billion for the 51st state. As an independent legal entity, the city would no longer be subject to the financial whims of Albany.

The city-state would be eligible automatically for direct participation in federal funding programs. It would be free from the fiscal and budgetary impositions of the state of New York. The city-state would then receive direct assistance under all federal programs, participate in revenue sharing, and use direct economic leverage on the federal government.

HOUSING

All dwellings of two or more families in New York City-State would be subject to mandatory rent controls.

To encourage renovation of substandard housing, real estate taxes should be lowered, not raised, after improvements are made.

Neighborhoods which incorporate into municipalities will set up their own real estate tax structures, and their own systems of rent control.

On a city-state-wide level we would favor encouraging the rehabilitation of existing buildings over construction of new ones. To achieve this goal, the new city-state would provide direct loans to individuals and municipal (neighborhood) groups.

We would also propose programs to stimulate ownership of apartments by tenants, believing that occupant ownership is the basis for pride in one's home and neighborhood, the preservation of the existing housing stock, and the economic survival of our cities.

Specifically, we propose the following elementary steps for the new city-state program:

1. City-state funds will be made available to tenants living in substandard housing units. These funds will be used for the restoration and maintenance of the tenants' homes by their own labor and/or with labor forces assembled for this task in each neighborhood.

    To the extent that the tenants invest work and money in their homes it would serve as a down payment toward complete purchase. Thus, they would acquire an equity in their homes by restoring and maintaining them.

2. Loans at a fraction of the prime interest rate will be made available by the city-state for the direct purchase and renovation of apartment buildings by tenants and neighborhood administrations.

3. Landlords will be compelled to maintain their buildings under penalty of losing the property. If they do not wish to maintain their buildings, the law would force them to sell the apartments to the tenants or neighborhood administrations who, in turn, would exercise their privileges under #2.

4. All recoverable property currently in New York City receivership units wil be turned over to the neighborhoods and tenants for action under #1.

WELFARE

Under the city-state neighborhoods would administer all welfare programs, tailoring them to the specific needs of the community and recruiting local recipients into the administrative process. For instance, a recent survey showed that 70 per cent of ADC mothers expressed a desire to work. City-state funds should be provided to neighborhoods as an incentive to employ these individuals in day-care facilities, permitting other neighborhood mothers to seek work in the community. But in no way will people be forced to work.

The present centralized welfare bureaucracy degrades and de-humanizes recipients. Fifteen per cent of welfare costs is spent on investigations into the private affairs of participants. The neighborhood administration of public assistance programs would substantially reduce the need for investigatory expenditures and also provide for a more simplified, responsive, and humane welfare program.

It is unfortunate that over 90 per cent of the public assistance recipients in New York City are unemployable: the aged, handicapped, children and their mothers. Increased federal reimbursements are necessary to provide a livable income for these individuals.

Our view is that welfare is a national responsibility. It requires a more equitable national revenue source, national standards, and eligibility criteria.

CONSTRUCTION OF CAPITAL PROJECTS

There should be no approval of any city-state capital projects until all plans and final estimates have been submitted. Only at that point will funding take place.

The administration of local capital projects will rest solely with the governments of the individual neighborhood-municipalities.

State contracts would tend to encourage firms giving preferred employment to residents of the city-state.

CRIME

Our program for the political decentralization of New York City will serve as an antidote to crime.

We will encourage police to live in the neighborhood in which they work to provide them with a better understanding of the problems of the neighborhood, and to increase the respect accorded to them individually. The city-state will provide grants to incorporated neighborhoods for police training and for supplementary salary bonuses to those policemen who continue their formal education beyond high school.

The dropout rate among juveniles, who today are responsible for a large number of crimes, will be vastly reduced because the education systems will improve under local neighborhood control.

Neighborhood vocational and building programs will also serve to involve youths in projects that could be meaningful to the community.

We will also institute a system of trials by lay arbitrators and judges from the neighborhoods themselves. Since court congestions and case backlogs have been one of the chief causes of individual dissatisfaction with the legal system, skilled legally trained lay arbitrators acting swiftly can solve many disputes and grievances that ordinarily take years to be heard. Such a plan is already in effect in small claims cases and should be greatly expanded.

All judges will be appointed for fixed tenure periods of a maximum of ten years. Judges must be practicing lawyers with legal backgrounds commensurate with the nature of the court to which they are appointed.

We also advocate a program that would transform our jails from mere inhuman detention centers to environments conducive to genuine social rehabilitation. Inmates should be provided with opportunities for academic, artistic, and vocational education. In addition, apartments or halfway houses shall be set up in family situations on social visits.

TRANSPORTATION

We will increase the variety and amount of *surface* transportation services.

All private automobile traffice will be barred from Manhattan.

All forms of mass transportation would be for the free use of the public.

The city-state would also provide 100,000 free public bicycles.

A monorail will be constructed around the city.

A superhack bureau will be created:

The increased demand for taxi service would result in heavier business for medallion and non-medallion operators. Gypsy cabs would be incorporated into the present force through more flexible licensing policies.

Cab drivers *alone* will be able to purchase gasoline at wholesalers' prices, without state taxes.

Until more effective smog-control devices are developed, the new city-state will replace such devices on all cabs once a month. Cabs will be inspected at the same time.

MUNICIPAL UNIONS

Under the new city-state system, strikes by local municipal eployees against individual municipalities would be legal, subject to due process. Sympathy strikes or strikes against all municipalities in the city-state, however, will be forbidden by law.

The new city-state will require all incorporated neighborhoods to insert automatic cost-of-living-increase clauses in all their contracts with municipal unions.

RECREATION PROGRAMS

Most recreation programs would be under the control of the local neighborhoods. The city-state would also have a department of recreation, which would, for example, arrange for athletic and other competitions among the various neighborhood groups.

We would also encourage the complete decentralization of the theater establishment, and non-professional involvement in the performing arts. The new city-state would make significant sums available to the neighborhoods for local theater and art programs. A range of new games and recreational concepts would be encouraged for competition between neighborhoods. We could, for instance, have horse races through specified city streets on particular Sundays, comparable to the annual race of the guilds in Siena, jousting contests in Central Park, perhaps even a World Series of stick-ball teams from neighborhood leagues to be played on Broad Street on Sunday. We could help, but the neighborhoods will discover their own athletic preoccupations.

RACIAL AND RELIGIOUS ANTAGONISMS

We do believe that much of the real fear of the white middle class, as well as the justifiable anger of the blacks, Puerto Ricans, and poor will be considerably abated if all these groups are allowed to run their own affairs.

Our existing antagonisms have resulted, in part, because professional politicians, totally out of contact with the people, have tried to *force* groups with differing styles of life to live together. This policy is manifestly bankrupt. If it continues, we will have a domestic Vietnam in New York City.

There may be groups, indeed, large numbers of people, who wish to found and incorporate neighborhoods which are racially, economically, and socially integrated. By all means let them do so! As for the rest, whether they live in Bay Ridge or Bed-Stuy—let them assert their independence and identity, allay their fears and tensions, and establish some form of psychological security before they become interdependent. We can only hope that after such a period of regroupment and consolidation, patterns of neighborhood integration will begin to emerge. But it had better come naturally or not at all. For to force integration, of whatever sort and by whatever not-so-subtle means, is only to increase the tensions which, given the essential speed and violence and obscenity (any assault on human sensibilities) of urban life today, will only lead to mass bloodshed and the complete destruction of our cities.

ANOTHER NOTE ON TECHNIQUE

If a voter is for Mailer and Breslin, but does not seem likely material for volunteer work through the organization, put them on their own. Give them twenty to thirty pieces of literature. Encourage them to talk to, visit, write, and call all their friends to convince them to vote for Mailer-Breslin.

Emphasize the value of spontaneous chain reactions like this from people for Mailer and Breslin.

NEW YORK GETS AN IMAGINATION–OR IT DIES!

CRIME, WELFARE, POLLUTION, HOUSING, TRANSPORTATION, TAXES, EDUCATION: NEW YORK CITY IS STRANGLING. MAILER AND BRESLIN ARE THE ONLY CANDIDATES OFFERING A PROGRAM THAT LEADS TO SOLUTIONS FOR THESE PROBLEMS.

MAILER AND BRESLIN WANT TO MAKE NEW YORK CITY THE 51ST STATE—TO FREE THE CITY FROM THE CONTROL OF UPSTATE LEGISLATORS WHO DON'T CARE ABOUT THE CITY BUT CONTROL OUR SCHOOLS, POLICE, HOUSING AND MONEY.

MAILER AND BRESLIN WANT NEIGHBORHOODS TO GOVERN THEMSELVES. POLITICIANS HAVE RIDDEN THIS CITY RIGHT INTO THE GROUND. MAILER AND BRESLIN WANT TO RETURN POWER TO THE PEOPLE—POWER OVER THEIR SCHOOLS, POLICE, SANITATION, HOUSING, PARKS AND LIFE STYLES.

TAXES

Each year the New York City taxpayer pays $14 billion to the state and federal governments, and gets only $3 billion back. The creation of a City-State would help to correct this imbalance and bring at least $2 billion in additional revenue to the city.

TRANSPORTATION

All private cars will be banned in Manhattan. The number of cabs will be increased. All city bus and subway transportation will be free. A monorail will be built around the City-State. Publicly owned bicycles will be available to all without cost.

POLLUTION

The elimination of private cars in Manhattan will reduce pollution there by three-fifths. All vehicles and incinerators in the city will be required to have pollution control devices. Sweet Sunday will give the city breathing room once a month.

EDUCATION

The neighborhoods will have complete control over their school systems. The education of our children is not a political football–it must be left to the parents and students themselves.

HOUSING

Immediate rent control will be extended to all dwellings with two or more families. Neighborhoods will manage all rent control housing programs. The City-State will fund programs for rehabilitation, not demolition, and home-ownership for tenants.

CRIME

Local neighborhoods best understand how to control crime in their communities with policemen who have the respect of the community because they live there. The City-State will fund neighborhoods to administer their own crime control programs.

WELFARE

All welfare programs will be administered by the neighborhoods, eliminating most of the 15% of money spent for welfare case investigations. The City-State will fund neighborhoods to employ residents in local day-care centers, housing rehabilitation, on-the-job training, and recreational programs.

Vote Mailer-Breslin!
in the Democratic Primary, June 17th

Headquarters open at 989 8th Ave. (Columbus Circle & 58th St.)

Telephone 765-9257-8-9

New Yorkers for Mailer-Breslin, 989 8th Ave., N.Y. N.Y. 10019

PAYING OUR DUES

JIMMY BRESLIN

DAILY NEWS AD, JUNE 16, 1969

They were smoking cigarettes on the steps of the school, Theodore Roosevelt High School in the Bronx, and when Norman Mailer and I came walking toward them they stopped talking. Their faces said nothing, but you could feel the alertness of the streets coming out of them.

"Say there," one of them finally called out. He was with a group over at one end of the steps and he summoned me with a regal wave. By this time I had accepted the obvious, that I not only would most certainly win tomorrow's Democratic primary for City Council president, but that I also would win in November and thus become a servant of the people. So I picked my way through the crowd on the steps and presented myself to the young man who called.

"You in some election?" he asked.

"Yes, I am, and I wish you'd tell the people home about me."

Somebody had handed him a campaign leaflet and he looked at it. "So you runnin' for office," he said, studying the leaflet.

"I'm out every morning and I don't stop running until late at night."

"Uh huh," he said. Then slowly, his eyes came up from the leaflet and ran over me. "Well now, if you runnin' so hard, then how come you got such a fat *be*hind?"

Everybody around him shrieked and began slapping his hand. Another stranger had just stumbled over this sense of timing which kids learn so naturally in crowded neighborhoods.

Mailer and I left and the kids went back inside to the classes in a school from which, my friend John Doar points out, only 12 per cent graduate with an academic diploma. And Theodore Roosevelt High is really Harvard when you compare it with places like Haaren High or Benjamin Franklin.

In walking around this city for so many days and nights now, Mailer and I have noticed that young kids from run-down, crowded neighborhoods have the good ears and great word choices that this city needs so badly as we go into a time when sight and sound, film and tape, take over much of the work of the printed word. They are, these kids from the Harlems and Brownsvilles of the city, far ahead of the pasteurized, homogenized level of speech directed at us from the Scarsdales. For the oral years ahead, the kids of the ghettos are our treasure. And we are spilling our treasures across the floors of the criminal courts buildings.

The Corrections Department bus taking the prisoners from police headquarters in Manhattan to the court of Queens sat in the exhaust fumes of stalled traffic on the expressway. The very young face stared through the screened windows of the bus at the car in which I was riding.

"Well," I said. I moved one of my hands to show helplessness.

"Room and board," the young face said. The ones around him in the bus broke into laughter and the bus lurched forward and they laughed while they rode to court in handcuffs in a prison bus.

Like everybody else in the city of New York, I'm afraid of crime, and I hate what it has done to the life of the city. I still remember the night a junk pusher with a shotgun caught a detective named Pollins in a dark hallway and fired a couple of feet away. They took Pollins to the Hospital for Joint Diseases and this one little nurse tried so hard to help save him, but it was useless. At the end, exhausted, she stood in the doorway leading to the street and she refused to go home unless somebody drove her. She said a nurse could not go through the small park across the street from the hospital and come out alive.

This kind of feeling is everywhere in New York. The woman

around the corner from me came home from shopping the other afternoon and a prowler was at her the moment she closed the front door and tried to kill her with a tire iron. A day later, my friend Mabel came home from scrubbing somebody else's floors all day and three of them pulled her into a doorway on Franklin Avenue in Brooklyn, took her purse, and then started punching. One of the punches left Mabel's ear damaged. Mabel is black. About 70 per cent of the crimes in this city are committed by minority people against other minority people. So I think you'll find Mabel is just as enthusiastic about adding 5500 more policemen to the force as are the people in Staten Island or Queens Village.

But it is either enormous ignorance or an enormous lie to tell people that 5500 more policemen, strategically placed, will stop the crime in New York. For we in this city grow, in the soot and chipped plaster and spilled garbage of the ghetto, a breed of kids who have so much to give us, but are given so little of life to lead that some of them give up. They have nothing at home, and they sit in schools where white teachers don't know how to teach them, and when they think ahead, they see nothing. The trade unions give an automatic apprenticeship to any black kid who takes the Sunday *Times* to Central Park and reads it inside the lion's cage. The union leaders spend Sunday in church, praying against people.

The trouble for the city of New York starts when these kids give up. Mindless, desperate, often deranged for want of heroin, they are the ones who are out stealing all over this city. And if we keep making these kids give up, as a walk through any junior high school shows you, we will be hiring 5500 more policemen from now to forever. Perhaps, right away, we can open clinics and give heroin to addicts so perhaps they won't hide in alleys or behind staircases and wait for women with purses. Perhaps properly funded rehabilitation centers will work—the upstate farmers always vote against giving the city any money—and perhaps we can hospitalize and cure addicts who are criminals. Narcotics is at the bottom of 60 per cent of the crime in this city. Perhaps these immediate moves will help. But always use the word "perhaps." Any man who claims he has an immediate, outright solution to the crime problem is a liar. Mention jail to these young people we worry about; particularly mention jail to the youngest of them; and they look at you and they laugh. Jail is a place they want to be able to say they come from.

And so they steal, these young guys do. Steal cars and purses and they steal in the daytime and they steal at night and they steal on the street or they come into your apartment and they use a knife or a lead pipe or even a gun. They steal with the same absence of feeling that a union leader has when he makes sure blacks do not get work; that white merchants have when they sell defective goods at immense prices to bewildered black people; that a plainclothesman has when he takes money from a narcotics seller or a policy numbers man. And then these kids step out, which is street talk for going on a holdup, and they come into drugstores and liquor stores with pistols shaking in their wet hands and the clerks behind the counters have heart attacks and enough of them get slugged and shot to keep a city of eight million living in degrees of fear.

Norman Mailer and I cannot understand why we all have to continue living this way. We think human beings can do a lot better than to live with a Fox lock on every door. Norman Mailer and I were born in this city, we have lived in this city all our lives, and we owe all of our success to this city. We now stand ready to pay our dues to this city. We would give up an awful lot of our lives for the chance to try to get New York to the start of the beginning of the process which, someday, will make all these empty law-and-order phrases become real.

MAILER-BRESLIN HEADQUARTERS   PLEASE CONFIRM:
989 Eighth Avenue   Alice Krakauer
New York, New York   Niles Peebles
Telephone: 765-9257

Schedule for Norman Mailer, Friday, April 25

11:00   Press Conference for neighborhood newspapers (Mailer home)

12:00   Brooklyn College

1:00   Long Island University (Flatbush & DeKalb, Conference Hall, Humanities Building)

2:30　Hunter College (65th Street & Park)

4:30　WNEW Radio (565 5th Avenue, 2nd fl.)

6:15　Staff meeting at Steinem's

8:30　Fund-raising party for Harlem Six (Hotel Diplomat, 108 West 43rd Street)

9:45　WNEW, Channel 5—Newsline (205 East 67th Street)

10:30　Park Slope Independent Democrats—"Easter Uprising" party (Prospect Hall)

MAILER-BRESLIN HEADQUARTERS	PLEASE CONFIRM:
989 Eighth Avenue	Niles Peebles
New York, New York	Alice Krakauer
Telephone: 765-9257	

Schedule of appearances by Norman Mailer, Friday, May 2, 1969

7:00　CBS-TV　Joe Benti
　　　524 W. 57th St.

11:30　United Bronx Parents
　　　791 Prospect Ave.　(Evelina Antonetti, Pres.
　　　　　　　　　　　Mrs. Tilly 842-1484
　　　　　　　　　　　Arnoldo Segurra arranged this)

12:30　Luncheon with group—discuss school lunch decentralization—serve ethnic dishes to students—soul food

3:00　I.S. 201 Meet with governing board
　　　185 E. 116th St.

4:30　Students for Political Action (college)
　　　173 E. 83rd St. (Lex. Democ. Club)
　　　Charles Bell 799-7484; TE 1-9200

5:00　Youth group drop-ins in East Harlem (time permitting)

7:30　Liberty Bell Civic Assoc. (Candidates Forum)
　　　IHM School
　　　Fort Hamilton Ave. & E. 5th St.

9:00　East Harlem Democ. Club
　　　2057 Second Ave.

10:00　Black Panthers benefit
　　　293 Riverside Drive

MAILER-BRESLIN HEADQUARTERS   PLEASE CONFIRM:
989 Eighth Avenue   Alice Krakauer
New York, New York   Niles Peebles
Telephone: 765-9257

Schedule of appearances by Norman Mailer and Jimmy Breslin

MONDAY
MAY 26   4:25–   Victor Riesel   nm

            5:30 P.M.   WEVD Radio
                           117 W. 46th St., 5th fl.

            8:15 P.M.   East Midtown Reform Dem.   nm/jb
                           300 E. 28 St.

            8:50 P.M.   League of Women Voters   nm
                           Manhattan, Donnell Library
                           20 W. 53rd St.

            9:45 P.M.   East Side Democrats   nm/jb
                           350 E. 85th St.

            10:00 P.M.   West Side Democrats   nm/jb
                           2390 Broadway

TUESDAY
MAY 27   10:00 A.M.   Press Conference   nm/jb
                           Overseas Press Club
                           54 W. 40th St.

            12:30 P.M.   Dutch Treat Club   nm
                           Regency Hotel
                           Park Avenue & 61st St.

            2:00 P.M.   Electric Circus Storefront   nm/jb
                           Campaign Headquarters Opening
                           St. Marks Place
                           between 2nd and 3rd

            5:00–   Rockefeller University   nm

            7:00 P.M.   "Environmental Pollution
                           Solution"
                           Caspary Aud., York & 66th St.

            7:30 P.M.   Albert Einstein College   nm
                           of Medicine
                           Robbins Auditorium

            9:30 P.M.   Riverdale Jewish Center Men's   nm
                           Club
                           3700 Independence Ave.

MAILER-BRESLIN HEADQUARTERS   PLEASE CONFIRM:
989 Eighth Avenue   Niles Peebles
New York, New York   Alice Krakauer
Telephone: 765-9257

Tentative schedule of public appearances by Norman Mailer on Monday,
June 9, 1969

MANHATTAN DAY

7:45–8:30 A.M.	Subway station—IRT 72nd and Broadway
8:45–9:30	Subway station—IRT 34th and 7th Ave.
9:30–10:00	Breakfast
10:00–11:30	Area walk—Union Square Start at Klein's front entrance Union Square East (main entrance)
12:00–1:30 P.M.	Area walk William St. and John St.
2:00–2:30	WNYC Radio Municipal Building, Chamber St. 25th floor, Studio C
3:00–4:00	Area walk 34th and 7th Ave.
4:15–5:15	Area walk 116th and 3rd Ave.
5:00–6:00	Area walk 125th and 7th Ave.
7:30	Private Dinner
9:30–midnight	Block Party 104th bet. West End Ave. and Riverside

MAILER-BRESLIN HEADQUARTERS   PLEASE CONFIRM:
989 Eighth Avenue   Alice Krakauer
New York, New York   Niles Peebles
Telephone: 765-9257

Schedule of public appearances by Norman Mailer Friday, June 13, 1969

BROOKLYN

7:30–8:30 A.M.	Nostrand Avenue and Flatbush Avenue IRT Subway
8:45–9:30	Fulton and Jay IND subway station
9:30–10:00	Breakfast
10:30–11:30	Walking tour from Court and Montague to Court and Atlantic
11:30–12:30 P.M.	Walking tour from Fulton and Jay to Albee Square
1:00–2:00	Walking tour of Flushing and Broadway
2:30–3:30	Walking tour of Fulton Street and Nostrand (to Nostrand and Atlantic Aves.)

MANHATTAN

| 5:00–7:00 | Harlem Rally West 125th and 7th Ave. |

BROOKLYN

| 7:30–9:00 | Open house at Bedford-Stuyvesant headquarters 1190 Fulton Street |
| 9:30 | Brooklyn Heights synagogue 65 Remsen Street |

PART FIVE

Some Arguments and Impressions

AFTER THE BALL IS OVER
OR REFLECTIONS BY THE PERLE MESTA
OF THE MAILER-BRESLIN CAMPAIGN

LINDA FRANCKE (JANE EDMUNDS)

Trying to raise money for the Mailer-Breslin campaign was as close to masochism as I ever care to get. For two reasons. First, the people attracted to the various fund-raising parties, rallies, happenings, et al. were types that didn't have any money, but simply wanted to say that they had shared a living room with Mailer, and that had the money plus enough smarts not to throw it away on a futile candidate. They were mostly ex-McCarthy or ex-Kennedy people in search of a new intellectual hero, or people on the fringes of the artistic world who would otherwise not be privy to Pulitzer prize-winning authors. For the latter, it was purely a social and "in" coup, and their wallets remained irrevocably sealed to their jeans. The second reason for the futility of the money end was Norman Mailer. Proud as he and the rest of the campaign workers were about his "non-politician" standing, it made the practical side of the campaign impossible. The majority of voters considered him a "joke" candidate, and delighted as everyone is to have a good laugh, not too many people are willing to pay for one. The credibility gap which obsessed the campaign committee meetings became the credit gap in our bank account.

But Norman tried to close the gap. God, how he tried. He stopped his longshoreman's mouth. He stopped campaign drinking. He got his hair cut. He even made his sidekick, Jack Banning, cut off his beard. And he became so serious in speeches and debates that in the end, he turned into a crashing bore. But as a magnet for money he remained eternally a flop. The hard fact of cash, and doing a soft shoe to bring it in, was beneath the behavioral pattern of a Pulitzer prize winner. He was a purist, delighted to expound at length about the "fifty-first state" and "power to the neighborhoods" and "alienation in our society" to an audience of peers, but to mouth the platitudes that soften up wallets would have been too crass. And even to go along with various schemes that we dreary, practical people thought up to raise money was too humiliating for his ego. I was Sisyphus shouldering the boulder up the hill only to lose it. Norman was the boulder.

In the six weeks I was the Perle Mesta of the Mailer-Breslin campaign, I raised a grand total of $473.51. And we missed out on about $25,000. It's a long, sad story.

SUNDAY, MAY 4:

Ah, how well I remember that day. The sun was shining, the dogwood was blooming in Central Park, and I was bursting into my sixth month of pregnancy. Then Gloria Steinem called. She talks very gently on the phone and that day she said things like: "it won't be much work" and "you'll have lots of people to help you" and "if you could just help organize a few fund-raising parties for Norman" and "I'm going to be away for a few weeks." So I said merrily to my husband things like: "what a gas" and "just a few fund-raising parties" and "it's just till Gloria gets back." But he was not merry. He was bleak and sour. That's because he ran part of the first Lindsay campaign and he knew there was no such thing as "just helping out for a few weeks" in a political campaign. But he is a good and kind husband, and he didn't say anything till I was one step short of weaving footstools in the Hartford Institute for Living.

So off I went to headquarters over Childs Restaurant on Columbus Circle that night. There were empty coffee cartons, newspapers, paper bags, and the accumulated filth the McCarthy people had left behind all over the floor; two dogs were nosing their way through the debris, hopefully on the trail of a doughnut and not a rat, a little kid was watching "Bonanza" on the tube, and the one john gurgled ominously under it's "out of order" sign. The campaign committee members straggled in, all bristling beards of varying shapes and colors, and as we sat down around two overflowing ash trays, it looked like a Smith Brothers convention. I struggled to match name to beard, but to no avail. (In the course of the campaign so many of them quit, shaved, or just wandered off into the night that it didn't matter anyway.) Just as I decided the campaign was going to be the gas I had hoped, we got down to business. Already on the schedule was a rally at the Village Gate for Wednesday, May 7, three days hence. There had been no time or money for publicity. Yet still it was decreed that there be two thousand people there. My job was to get them. Sure. Then there were two fund-raising parties scheduled for May 9 and the following Tuesday, May 13, which I was now in charge of. And I was handed a list of twenty women which read like the patroness list of the Paris Review Ball. They had come to a lunch for Norman, and had supposedly said they'd also like to give parties. And while I was at it, how about rallies in Brooklyn, Queens, and the Bronx, and what about Yankee Stadium? The list of campaign titles was handed out. There I was—Finance Co-ordinator. And I'd been had.

WEDNESDAY, MAY 7:

The rally at the Gate started at midnight and ended in disaster. In spite of the lack of publicity, the word had gotten around to all the kids, and they arrived in vote-less droves. With them came hecklers, drunks, and several serious Democratic biggies who wanted to see if Norman was going to be for real. He was real, all right. Sensing the crowd had come to see him perform, he went into it like a herring-happy seal. The crowd yelled obscenities at him, and he joyfully roared them back at the crowd. The kids loved it, the press loved it and never forgot it, and neither did the serious Democrats. Right then and there, while the campaign countdown was just beginning, Norman turned off the pocketbooks and the supporters that might have bridged the credibility gap later on. He also turned off his own running mate, Jimmy Breslin. Breslin reportedly stomped out with his wife because he thought the language offended her.

Breslin stomped out? Man. (I turned into a pumpkin by 10 P.M. those days, and therefore missed it, thank God.)

So there we were. First rally. First disaster. I should have learned something.

FRIDAY, MAY 9:

My dialing finger has a blister on it. Of the twenty women on the potential party-giver list, not *one* says she ever was interested. Zero. But there are other leads. Ursula Pinkwater, whom the list says is a "high school friend of "Jimmy's" turns out not even to know Jimmy. But she has some action in Church, a brand-new discotheque in Hell's Kitchen. But it turns out Church has already lost its liquor license, and when it reopens (under the name Sanctuary) they're going to be more buck-minded than Mailer-minded. Scratch that one. The Plaza Pub around the corner from headquarters wants to throw a cocktail party. And a young Englishman with a stutter wants to give a party for his "g-g-g-groovy friends."

But it is with high spirit that we swing into the evening's fund-raising party, being given by two girls, Laura Stevenson and Daphne Davis. They've sent out fifty invitations and expect a $50 contribution from each person. That's a cool $2500 in the till and a nice feeling for this pregnant Perle Mesta. I've provided them with buttons, bartenders, and literature, and they, in turn, expect Jimmy and Norman to come. Norman comes. Jimmy doesn't. Jimmy never will unless there are at least three television cameras there. He's obviously been reading McLuhan.

And so the party goes. Out of the fifty invited, around twenty show up. Everyone else there is free-loading from headquarters. Norman, still wincing from the Gate, talks very nice to them. But the total take is just over $100. One hundred dollars. I'm beginning to learn something.

TUESDAY, MAY 13:

Barbara Held, Charlotte Sheedy, and Sonia Weil, all ex-McCarthy people, are throwing this party on Central Park West. I suggest, very sternly, that they charge a $5 head tax at the door to separate the culture climbers from the Mailer supporters. Horrified purists as they are, they reject that as beneath them, claiming that their friends, again all ex-McCarthy people, would be insulted and not give a penny as a result. So once more into the breach, this time armed with blank checks, self-addressed envelopes, and the normal party package of "No More Bullshit" buttons, girls, and bartenders.

And they came—oh, how they came—over one hundred bearded, beaded, jeaned, fun-loving types. And they laughed and drank and waited two hours for Norman to finally show up. When he did, Norman asked for a drink in a "real" glass instead of the throw-away types, and striding to the front of the crowd, announced, "I stand before you, drink in hand . . . the only candidate who dares drink in public." Now there's a great slogan. But the crowd loved it. And they giggled and chortled the whole way through the "fifty-first state" and "Sweet Sunday." When Norman left an hour later, we moved in with the breadbaskets, casseroles, and empty vases to capture in green the blithe spirit of the party. Sure. The cry had been to write out checks for $51 for the fifty-first state. We got one check for $51, three checks for $5.10, and a plethora of $.51'ers. The biggest contributors were a couple of out-of-towners, from Cleveland and Bedford, who were willing to pay for the groovy time they'd had. But the New Yorkers? Oh no. "Stop spoiling the party," one producer from a film house said, as I was trying to pry his wallet from under his beaded vest.

The hostesses stood either side of the front door with their breadbaskets. Gone was their air of "purity shall prevail." "You cheap bastard," one of them yelled, as the happy, untouched crowd surged toward the elevators. "What did ya come for anyway, ya cheap son of a bitch?" echoed in the hall as we counted the take— $373.51. A big, two-hour chunk out of a heavy campaign schedule for Norman for $373.51.

Now I have learned something.

THURSDAY, MAY 15:

Bravely I face the beards at headquarters with my miserable pittance. The scene there looks like a hippie commune. The Sanitation Department has refused to pick up the garbage, which has now reached typhoid proportions. The john is still gurgling. Blank-eyed kids lounge in corners while the phones jangle with the cacophony of the "Hallelujah Chorus." An incoherent young black is stumbling around pointing his finger at the white volunteers saying, "When the revolution comes, you're going to be the first to go." Beautiful. It's a zoo.

At the meeting we decide that there shall be no more parties without at least a $10 head tax. We discuss the remarkable disappearing acts Breslin has been pulling whenever he's scheduled to show up at something he doesn't want to. We decide the most reasonable way to keep tabs on him is to send a beautiful meter maid with him who will charm him into accepting her, then give him a karate chop when he wanders off the schedule. I'm given three blocks of time to fill—May 28, June 3, and June 9—and the meeting's over.

MAY 16–MAY 27:

No more screwing around with little parties. Now the negotiations become intense for the real extravaganzas. We are in desperate need for bread with a half-page ad scheduled for the Sunday *Times,* a fifteen-minute television spot, and twelve hours worth of radio spots. And all the cheery bell-bottom jeans in New York aren't going to come up with that amount.

So think big. One of the volunteers at headquarters who is also a waiter at Arthur proposes that we run a club like the "Club Eugene" in a private room at Arthur. Beautiful. He works it out with the agent and we end up with a promise of all the profit off the bar and whatever admission charge we slap on, out of which we pay Arthur to staff the room, provide a bouncer, and pipe in the music. We name our new discotheque "The 51st State." Now we're beginning to get somewhere.

Dave Maysles calls and offers us *Salesman* for a night as a benefit for Norman. There are 360 seats in the 68th Street Playhouse, which, at $5 a head, brings in $1800. The theater wants $500 for itself, which still nets us $1300. We put the movie and The 51st State opening together as a package, and schedule it for May 28.

The Fillmore East calls and offers themselves to us for a night. It seems Lindsay had approached them, but they had turned him down because they were for Mailer. So for $900, which was their cost for personnel, tickets, the light show, et al., we got the Fillmore East and any profit thereafter. All we had to provide was the talent. That would be simple. So the Fillmore East slides into the June 3 slot.

The phone rings. Says the voice, "This is Mrs. Norman Mailer." Now, just the day before, my Row A all the way father-in-law had called my equally Row A mother, and knowing her paranoia for my role in the Mailer campaign, had announced that he was Norman Mailer. He invited her out to dinner and was so cool about it she had bought it and said she was very busy that week but maybe some other time. This coup had of course caused great brouhahas around the dinner table, so when my call came through from "Mrs. Mailer," I naturally assumed it was my mother-in-law. "Can't catch me, dearie," I said back on the phone. There was silence. Then she said, "but this is Norman Mailer's *mother,* and my neighbor wants to give a tea for Norman." Clunk. I scheduled the tea for late afternoon, June 3.

Then came the call from the Electric Circus. Would we be interested in the Circus for a night? Would we indeed! I hoist my ballooning body into a taxi and speed down to the East Village. By sitting down on the landings, I make it up to the fourth floor, where they meet me with a desk chair and wheel me into the office. Feeling more like Agnes Gooch than a zappy party arranger for Mailer, we get down to some very profitable business. We decide to run a private dinner for five hundred from eight to ten and then open the doors for a rally. The dinner will weigh in at $25 a head, the rally afterward at $5 each. Nathan's will cater it, they'll arrange for the liquor, the publicity, the personnel, etc. and will take 25 per cent of the profit after expenses. Not too hot a deal, but they also throw in a free storefront right in the Circus for a Village headquarters. This party's going to be the big moneymaker. Nothing delights the squares north of Fifty-seventh Street more than doing something kinky. And the money is north of Fifty-seventh Street. Even with Nathan's costing us $1000 worth of hot dogs and potato salad, and the liquor costing another $1000, we stand to make $10,500 from the dinner party alone. We schedule it for June 9, and they wheel me back out to the top of the stairs. "You get the talent," they yell as I lumber down. "Sure. Sure," I call back.

WEDNESDAY, MAY 28

The night of the Maysles/51st State opening.

The night of the no Maysles/51st State opening.

Sybil and Christopher are supposedly selling Arthur the very day of the benefit. Thud. And *Salesman* without a follow-up is like dead. So I call all the neighborhood pubs. The Sign of the Dove wants $1000 before I even hang up the phone. So does Yellow-fingers. Harlow's won't do it. Nothing.

I cancel *Salesman.*

MAY 29–JUNE 1:

The talent hunt is on. I call Jimmy to ask him to get Namath for either the Circus or the Fillmore East. Rosemary (his wife) says she'll tell him. Either she doesn't or he didn't. I call Norman and ask him for help. Instead I get in the mail his guest list. I call back and beg his secretary to get him moving on talent. She calls back and says the only person he wants at the Circus is Francine Gottfried, the Wall Street bosom. Ah, Norman the purist. Who's going to pay $25 a head for one Nathan's hot dog? We need names, names, NAMES! Nothing. I'm getting closer to weaving footstools in Hartford every minute.

Points! Viveca Lindfors says she'll come to the Circus. And Zero Mostel says he'll endorse him. Wow. Nothing.

One of the volunteers says she studied math with Bob Dylan in high school. Would he come out of hiding for his math seatmate? She calls his neighbor in Woodstock (Dylan obviously wouldn't keep a phone). Of course, he never calls back. But this same volunteer, Bonnie Lewis, has the bit in her teeth. So she calls

Sinatra's lawyer, finds out where he is in Vegas, and calls him cold out there. Very cold. Negative on Sinatra. Bonnie then discovers that Garfunkel is in Europe and Simon is for Badillo. Peter and Paul are missing in action, but Mary's for Lindsay anyhow. Bonnie pins a notice up on the *Hair* bulletin board asking any of the cast to come do their thing for Mailer. Nothing. One of the black volunteers says he knows the Jefferson Airplane. Great. So he goes to Boston in search of the group, and we never hear from him or them again. A wild-looking man comes up to me at headquarters. "What about fire?" he says. Not about to be caught out in squaresville, I say, "Great. Fire. Where are they playing?" "Playing?" he says. "I eat fire. It's been a tradition passed down through my Indian ancestors."

So there we are, with Viveca Lindfors and one fire-eater. And nothing from Norman and no Namath from Breslin.

The Fillmore East cancels.

MONDAY, JUNE 2:

An unknown package drops in our laps. Every Monday night the Electric Circus runs something called the "Electronic Ear" series, which is organized by Tais Lathem. She had called to tell me that the electronic psychodrama scheduled for this Monday was Robert Ashley, the "Wolf Man," and would we like it to be a benefit for Norman? Everything over $400 (for the Wolf Man's expenses) would be ours. That was the first thing she said I understood. And with visions of shredded dollar bills from the fund raisers that never came off, I accepted. At least this one would happen.

It happened. It really happened. The crowd started arriving around 8:15. Bonnie and I were doing our button act downstairs while the rest of the volunteers mixed and mingled upstairs trying to make the expected audience of three hundred bigger than the fifty who actually came. CBS and the CBC were covering Norman that night, and a crowd of fifty for a really "hot" mayoral candidate was not the sort of television coverage we needed.

Stan Freeman and Dennis Wright, managers of the Circus,

wandered downstairs. "Do you know the sort of audience that comes to the Electronic Ear?" they asked.

"They look like the walking dead," I said.

They laugh. "You've got all the village intellectuals," they said. "Like the NYU professors, philosophers, and downbeat poets." Very funny. We couldn't *give* the buttons away. The audience walked by us as if we were invisible, the coldest group this side of Ice Station Zebra. They had come to a concert, *not* a political rally.

So when Norman arrived, the handwriting was already frozen into the wall. Norman could have been talking to himself in the shower for all the reaction he got out of the mummified Village esoterics in front of him. So Norman, his ego chilled, gets mad. "You know," he says, "I didn't want to come here tonight. I don't like you or your neighborhood. But I approve of your right to have a neighborhood." And he stalks off into the night.

While the Wolf Man plugs in, we race to the till to collect our profit. It was everything over $400, remember? The total take at the door was $317.

I remind myself never to work in a political campaign again, and go home.

TUESDAY, JUNE 3:

The day the Fillmore East isn't.

The night of the one $25-a-head cocktail party that works, given by the wife of a Democratic money man. She evidently invites all her relatives, is satisfied with the "celebrity" she's asked for (Gloria Steinem), and in spite of the Breslin no-show, raises $500. At last.

The New York *Times* music reviewer gives Norman equally panning time as the Wolf Man. There is an ominous silence from headquarters.

But I have no time for reflection. I talk to Nathan's about the hot dogs, and the liquor man about setups. I talk to the printer about the invitations, and line up volunteers to send them out as they come off the press. I check our final countdown on talent with the

Circus. We've got Tom Paxton, The Anonymous Artists of America —which features John Steinbeck, Jr., playing the flute—the cast from *Graffiti,* and Pulsa, which is a light show from Yale. The Circus winces, but I remind them that Mailer and Breslin alone filled the Gate, so the Circus vetoes only Pulsa because they evidently take twelve hours to set up, and in the process have to tear down all the Circus equipment and computers. Computers yet! Anyway, Pulsa is already on the invitation, so I decide to ignore it.

The Circus party is the most organized party of the campaign, and for the first time, I feel anticipated triumph surging through my almost defunct nervous system. Interest is running high among all the uptown trust funds I've talked to, they all think it's going to be the most "in" do of the season, and I am already counting the thousands of dollars we're *finally* going to make.

The call comes in from headquarters. Laird Cummings, then head of the campaign, says, "I wanted to tell you before you read it in the *News.*"

"Read what?" I say.

"What Norman called the Circus."

"What did Norman call the Circus?" I begin to tremble.

"A warmed-over cancer," he says.

"What about the party?" I say.

"No party," Laird says. "Mailer has cancelled." No party. Canceled. The injured ego won't return to the scene. The whole hysterical time I've just been on another fool's errand.

I've finally learned. I quit.

MONDAY, JUNE 9:

The night the Electric Circus isn't. I'm packing for the seashore and practicing little smiles in the mirror—it's been such a long time.

WEDNESDAY, JUNE 11:

P.S. The last-ditch fund-raising party which must be duly noted though I had nothing to do with it. This one was given by Dr.

Scarrone, the diet doctor, at his East Sixties Spanish-tiled town house. Audrey Maas ran it. The tab was $50 a head, and two days before the party, they had received three checks. I snickered from a distance. But in the last instance, the bare midriffed, dangle earring set couldn't stand not to be part of the scene, and about one hundred people showed up. That should have meant $5000. But, in panic, the committee was selling "twofers," and a large majority of the guests claimed they were presses and got in free, so the take was around $3000. Nice people.

Good old Bonnie Lewis was there, running hors d'oeuvres trays back and forth to the kitchen like someone from the Finnish Employment Agency. It seems when they arrived in the morning to set up the party, the butler had locked away every glass, platter, and tray in the house. He was obviously a Mario man. So they had to go to Service Delicacies and rent all the equipment, buy all the food, and spend the rest of the day in the kitchen, sticking toothpicks into hot dogs. Audrey's only remark at the end of the party: "Next time they should hire a caterer."

Norman and Jimmy showed up (there were his prerequisite three cameras there) to face a crowd ranging from the cream of the *Women's Wear Daily* set to Shirley MacLaine, Sander Vanocur, and the surprise house guest, King Peter of Yugoslavia. (Now there's an influential vote.) Norman was on soda water and his best behavior, and he talked nice to all the cameras, microphones, and midriffs until he was heckled by the lady author of *The Pretenders*. But he didn't swing. He just told her he couldn't stand lady writers. And he left. Jimmy spent half the time with a strained smile on his face being talked at by eager women, and the other half on the street with the boys, drinking by the front door.

So I left. Jimmy says, "Good luck, kid." I say, "Keep the faith." And my campaign is over.

WEDNESDAY, JULY 23:

I lie like a giant turtle in the sand, waiting for my baby. People still want to talk about the Mailer campaign but even the memory exhausts me. It was the most addled, frustrating six weeks I have ever fought my way through. And I have vowed never to take on another back-room job in a campaign. There were those who followed Norman on the campaign treks around New York, who talk glowingly of the crowds he turned on in Coney Island, of how he excited the blacks in Brooklyn. There were those who mulled over his position papers in his house in Brooklyn Heights, and who rode in the campaign car listening to the candid articulateness of a writer running quite seriously for mayor of New York. That was the Mailer of the "fifty-first state" and "power to the neighborhoods." My Mailer was the otherworldly clog in everything I tried to do for him. Send me a purist any day to revere. But God forbid I should try to raise money for him.

We would have made $20,000 easy at the Circus, dammitall.

SHOOT-FOR-THE-MOON MAILER
An Interview with Norman Mailer
on the Literary Life and Practical Politics

LETICIA KENT

In his tenth book, *The Armies of the Night,* Norman Mailer described himself as "warrior, presumptive general, ex-political candidate, embattled aging enfant terrible of the literary world, wise
father of six children, radical intellectual, existential philosopher,
hard-working author, champion of obscenity, husband of four bat-
tling sweet wives, amiable bar drinker, and much exaggerated street
fighter, party giver, hostess insulter," and so on. Thus far he is also
a film maker and winner of a National Book Award and a
Pulitzer prize, both this year for *The Armies of the Night.*

Last May Mailer entered New York City's Democratic mayoral
primary, running on a platform of giving statehood to the city and
power (self-determination) to its neighborhoods. It was, said the
New York *Times,* which at the beginning looked upon Mailer's
candidacy as something of a joke, "the first time the fundamental
reorganization of a great American political entity had been made
the central theme of a campaign for major office."

On the twenty-second day of the campaign, I visited Mailer in
his own neighborhood and found him eating breakfast on the top
floor of his Brooklyn Heights house. As he ate, he scanned the
spectacular view of New York Harbor, Lower Manhattan, and the
East River. Competing with the view and partially obscuring it was
an enormous, zany, colorful model of a visionary city he once built
with Lego blocks. Sitting there in dungarees, Mailer looked rough,
like an ordinary seaman—maybe a wiper. But the peremptory rat-

a-tat-tats of his voice-within-a-voice (like hard candy with a soft center) were obviously the wiper's captain's. So were his exquisite manners. After a while I asked him these questions:

KENT (*Dealing in generalities*): Politics seems to run all through your works. But how does running for office fit into your life scheme?

MAILER (*Averting his eyes, his blue eyes*): To be brutal about it, I guess a guy who wrote about sex all his life would finally have to have sexual intercourse. (Laughs at the reporter's expense.) This is the proof that I'm a politician because it's the remark every politician makes: I finally began to feel it was my duty to get into politics. There's no substitute for it. If you have certain ideas, you have to embody them. It's the only thing that people trust. You can write books for people for two hundred years and you can't move that stone, that boulder around the corner. Because it's easier to write a book than to express through your actions. And people never trust anything that's easy when there's something that should be done that's harder.

KENT: Then do you think that books are ineffectual?

MAILER: No, I think they do a lot of good. They prepare ground. But finally you have to till the ground. To use another metaphor: Books fertilize the earth; they are not the garden. They're not the end of the effort, they're only the beginning. No utopia will ever come into existence because a number of great books have been written.

KENT: But utopia is not what you're after, is it?

MAILER (*Amending it*): Oh no, I'm not after utopia. That is, my idea of utopia is a carnival or a market place or a groovy library or knowing that Las Vegas is in Coney Island, even if I don't go there. Not a model city. I mean, you can't even get a sense of liveliness in a city by having great books or even good books written. Finally, people have to go out and create that liveliness.

KENT: Why do you particularly want to be mayor of New York?

MAILER: New York contains a magitude of all the ills of America. So if we can change it from a city that has these ills into one that has begun to solve them, then the entire country will follow us.

KENT: Doesn't campaigning tend to corrupt your literary style?

MAILER: For the first few days, I kept bleating piteously, "Oh, my style, my style!" But I really don't like the literary world in which I've been one way or another for all my life. I think it's a terribly spoiled and complacent world. I'm not really fond of literary people. There's much too much of the hothouse about us all. When you've got a world that's disintegrating around you, if you're a man and you're leading a life that is self-protected to a degree, you really can't feel too agreeable about yourself. So I got over bleating about the loss of my style in a few days. God willing, I'll get it back.

KENT: Has campaigning revealed things about the city that you couldn't learn in any other way?

MAILER: Yes, that the people in this city are better than I thought they were. They're livelier, smarter, stronger, funnier, and more decent.

KENT (*Aside*): It seems an expensive and time-consuming education.

MAILER (*Soliloquizing*): Another thing I've learned is that there is extraordinary potential in politics with a really vigorous, simple, attractive idea. You know, people love ideas in politics. Politics, if you will, is the philosophy of the poor and of the disenfranchised. Every man, I believe, is his own philosopher. And politics offers the possibility of thinking philosophically, whether one's aware of it or not. One of the things that's so hideous about liberal-technological ideology is that it takes the philosophy out of politics. One's obliged to think as a mechanic rather than a philosopher, a mechanic with a dull, unwieldy machine that has a tremendous terminology and very little grace. There's one thing to be said for conservatism, real conservatism—not the military-industrial complex and let's-bomb-the-hell-out-of-Communist-China, but the kind of conservatism that believes finally that society is founded upon certain deep prejudices and principles which derive from the Lord. It is that every man has his appointed place, and judgment is in heaven, so that, if you are rich, you may conceivably have to suffer, pay more for that fact than the poor pay, so that being poor may be a state of grace. These are all conservative notions, are philosophical notions. You know, they have marrow and strength to them. One can disagree with them, but then one's engaged in a profound philosophical argument which, indeed, at its best, is the argument between left and right. Because the left says in answer: "That's not true. Devils run the world. God is not in His appointed place." There's a theological argument at bottom between left and right. It's one I find profound and fascinating. I mean, I live with it all the time in my own mind.

What I'm getting at is that politics is interesting when you're dealing with philosophy—implicitly—when your arguments always open ethical and even metaphysical questions.

KENT: You once wrote a column suggesting that the Democrats draft Ernest Hemingway for President and you said: "The glimmer of hope on all our murky horizons is that civilization may be coming to the point where we will return to voting for individual men (or individual women) rather than for political ideas."

MAILER (*Forbearingly*): I don't agree with that any more. I think you have a happy politics when the man and the idea are wed and people are attracted to both. If the idea is good and the man's no good, that's not good. If you have a man and there's not really an idea, that's President Eisenhower. Sometimes you have neither a man nor an idea, that's President Nixon. Of course, I preferred him to Humphrey for a simple reason, which is Humphrey was a weak man with a dead idea. And I thought that was even worse. The best thing that can be said about the absence of a man or an idea is that the country then begins to reveal its true lineaments. It does it just as a hideous piece of architecture, a hideous piece of dull, flat, modern office building reveals the internal anatomy of a ten-million-dollar bill. So at least we know where we're at with

Nixon. I mean, Nixon is our objective correlative, which Humphrey wouldn't have been.

KENT: Does anything about the conventional politician impress you?

MAILER (*Expansively*): His stamina. I've got stamina and it's the thing in myself I'm proudest of. I don't like myself when I run out of stamina. Campaigning is hard work. You work twelve to sixteen hours a day, seven days a week.

KENT: At one time you called yourself a Marxist-anarchist.

MAILER (*A trifle impatiently*): Well, now I'm a left-conservative, I'd say, and that means on the one hand, I'm a man on the left; on the other hand, I believe in certain conservative principles. The main conservative principle that I believe in is that man must solve his problems through his own agency, that his problems cannot be solved from without and above. From Bolshevism right down to the liberals, there's that long line of arrogant, smug, complacent believers (He feigns pomposity): This-correct-program-must-be-indoctrinated-into-the-people.   When-the-people-perceive-the-wisdom-of-their-leader, they-will-begin-to-work-toward-a-better-society.   And this, I think, is just absolute nonsense. Old Russian radicals say it's *kvatch,* k-v-a-t-c-h (Laughs). The answer is that a good society, by which I mean a society that doesn't kill you any more than it creates you, resides in the coactivity of our potentialities. But these potentialities are not to be determined from without, not to be determined by intellectuals, not to be determined even by wise men. They're to be delivered. You know, great and good government consists of placing the fewest impediments in the way of people developing themselves. So in all these ways I say I'm a conservative.

But I feel that we inherit a world situation which the conservatives did as much as anyone to bugger for two hundred years. For conservatism depends upon a moderation of greed. If there's excess in human greed, then you have an evil society. We've had just that for two centuries. So I think even before we can begin to attack our problems that way, we've also got to attack one fundamental problem, which is that the poor don't have a bloody chance the way things are today and that we've got to find ways to fund them, ways different from, say, the scandalous welfare programs of the liberals.

KENT: You were once asked, "If you were forced to do something other than writing to earn your living, what would you choose?" You replied, "One of a hundred different things. Just so long as I didn't do any of them for the rest of my life."

MAILER (*More angry than forbearing*): I don't want to run on my record. I'm not running on my record. Let's forget everything I ever wrote because some of it supports what I'm doing now and some of it doesn't. Life goes around corners, particularly modern life, which is so abrupt and discontinuous. It's part of the disease of modern times that a man can't start plowing a furrow and take it up over hills and dales and at the end of his life have it said: "He plowed a straight furrow." Nobody alive can do that any more. There are not only rocks in the fields, there are mines in the fields. Sometimes you get exploded into another direction. And on top of that, the field is disappearing.

KENT (*Firmly*): I'm looking for the thread. Nearly everyone is saying you're not a serious politician. But I think there is a thread that runs through.

MAILER (*Holds his temper*): Oh sure, there's a thread, but what I mean is that I'm not sure we can find it quickly or even that it's worth finding. It's a narcissistic activity to explore one's own threads.

KENT (*Intrigued*): But much of your writing has been narcissistic. Has politics made you less so?

MAILER (*In a gruff voice*): Yeah, yeah, I'd say so. Finally it makes you modest. And maybe one reason I'm in politics is that I'm tired of myself that way. I'm tired of myself as my own laboratory. After all, I've been in that laboratory for twenty years now.

KENT (*Points to Lego construction*): You seem preoccupied with physical planning, with visionary projects like Lego City. Isn't this inconsistent with your antiutopian approach to politics?

MAILER (*Groaning*): Oh, don't call it "Lego City." It sounds like Lefrak City.

KENT: Mailer City?

MAILER: No. No (A moment of uncomfortable silence). None of my ideas is the least bit visionary. They're all very practical. The only thing at all visionary is the assumption that people will be interested in getting power back. That's what most critics don't believe. Well, we'll find out. If we win the election, then the idea will have proved to be not visionary, but practical. If we do very poorly, then I'll have to agree, yes, there was something visionary about it—not in the idea, but in the fact that I thought I was the man who could embody the idea. That may have been the aspect that was impractical.

Norman Mailer went down to defeat in the New York mayoral primary on June 17, but, as he hoped, his ideas for turning the city around are still in the air. Writing on the editorial page of the New York *Times,* Tom Wicker conceded that what Mailer had done was to "dramatize a fundamental issue, not only for New York but for America, in demanding a 'new beginning.'" Meanwhile, Mailer is studying up on the men who shoot for the moon.

MAILER—BRESLIN

PETER MAAS

I remember the precise moment that I decided to support Norman
Mailer for mayor and Jimmy Breslin for City Council president.

It was on April 11, 1969, and I was in the Windsor Room of the
Biltmore Hotel covering an announcement from Robert F. Wagner about whether he was going to get into the Democratic mayoral
primary. During the past months the more candidates I had observed girding up for the race, the more it appeared that I—and the
city—had seen it all before. The mere fact that there had been a
breathless wait for Wagner to declare himself one way or another
showed us just how far we hadn't come.

Now among those closest to him, Robert F. Wagner enjoys the
reputation of being something of a wit. He put it on public display
in the Windsor Room when he officially expressed his desire to
move back into Gracie Mansion. Wagner, who is sixty years old,
had spent practically all of his adult life in New York politics; he
had been an assemblyman, a city housing commissioner, city planning chairman, borough president of Manhattan, and then mayor
for twelve years until he decided to step down in 1965.

Thus in the Windsor Room, after announcing his candidacy for
an unprecedented fourth term, Wagner was asked what he thought
was the city's most urgent need.

"I think," he said without a moment's hesitation, "it needs new
leadership."

"Oh," said one of the hangers-on in the audience, "he is in rare
form today, I can tell you that!"

Who could argue?

Right at the start of his formal statement, Wagner had everybody
in suspense. For a second it sounded as if he were about to eschew

public life forever and enter a Trappist monastery. "After intense contemplation and self-examination and prayerful consultation with members of my family," he declared, "I have decided to stand again for nomination and election as mayor."

The letdown some might have experienced after such a spiritual opening was quickly dispelled by more Wagnerian wit. Noting his "arduous years" of previous service, he disclosed the real reason why he was running once more. It was, as he said, because, at liberty after a brief career as LBJ's Ambassador to Spain, he had recently found himself "importuned by increasing numbers of ordinary citizens to come back to the mayoralty."

This unforgettable prose, I learned, was drafted by Julius C. C. Edelstein, who used to be Wagner's intellectual-in-residence, the kind of fellow Lyndon Johnson always hoped Eric Goldman would turn out to be. While Wagner was going around town talking to "ordinary citizens" like Brooklyn boss Meade H. Esposito, he also carried with him in another pocket a second, shorter statement by Edelstein that said he was not going to run for mayor after all.

This was classic Wagner—and we had seen that before too. If he doesn't know what he is going to do—or even if he is going to do anything—how can anybody else be sure? He had used the same tactics in 1965. The day before he announced that he would not seek re-election, I happened to be with the late Senator Robert F. Kennedy. "What do you think Wagner is going to do?" I asked.

"I think," Kennedy said, "he's going to run again."

I couldn't help noticing that morning that the Wagner supporters who were in the Windsor Room to greet their hero were not exactly what you would call young. "It was like it always was," a fellow with CBS said. "They're all four years older, that's all."

The question of youth inevitably arose. Wagner allowed that if elected he might have a few appointees who were over thirty. After pausing for appreciative chuckles, he also said that he thought he looked a little younger than Mayor Lindsay. He then qualified this somewhat mysteriously by adding, "Certainly I act a little younger." It was a detail I hoped he might clear up as the campaign progressed, but he never did.

The proceedings at this point in the Windsor Room were interrupted by a bony lady, about fifty, sporting a gold Wagner emblem, who cried out shrilly, "She's more handsome than she is." Considerable confusion resulted—even Wagner turned quizzically toward the bony lady—until it was established that she was favorably rating Wagner's wife Barbara over Mrs. John Lindsay.

As Wagner called from the podium for new leadership for the city, he was flanked on his right by a man named Walter Coleman. Coleman was there possibly as a symbol of continuity with the past, since he had been heard to exclaim earlier to an acquaintance, "Just like old times, huh?" A florid, heavy-set man who was Deputy Commissioner for Marine and Aviation under Wagner, Coleman was as alert as a Doberman pinscher. He loves nothing more than to usher a candidate through a crowd, stand at a door checking credentials, or otherwise act in a security role.

As Wagner announced his candidacy, I had already started playing a new game called "What does it mean?" All you needed was your own frame of reference.

"It meant," Gloria Steinem told me, "that with Nixon in the White House and Wagner running, it's 1957 all over again."

"It means," said John Chancellor of the "Huntley-Brinkley Report," "that John Cameron Swayze will be back."

For humorist Ralph Schoenstein, it meant nostalgia. "I like to feel," Schoenstein said, "that I made a major contribution to Robert Wagner's greatest political defeat"—and at the time his only one—"when he ran for the U. S. Senate in 1956 against Jacob Javits. It was the height of the calypso craze, and the Wagner people asked me to write something for a sound truck in Spanish Harlem."

Schoenstein's song was a rare gem in the mediocrity that usually marks municipal politics. It went, as he recalls, like this:

> *Robert F. Wagner is de best man for*
> *United States Sen-ator.*
> *De representation dat you want you will get*
> *With Robert F. Wagner in de Sen-ate.*
>
> *When you're alone in de voting booth*
> *Important thing is tell de truth*
> *And say de only candidate for Senate job*
> *Is Wagner, name of Bob.*

According to Schoenstein, this helped to solidify the entire Span-ish-speaking community behind Javits. "It helped," he said, "to kill the calypso craze too."

My notes indicate that in declaring himself in, the former mayor was mostly modest. "I do not pretend," he said, "that I am so uniquely equipped that I can through the exercise of my own powers solve all the problems of New York City."

A touch of arrogance—which would mark his subsequent cam-paign and defeat—did creep in. "I must apologize to the other candidates [in the Democratic primary] for the time required for soul-searching." Roughly translated, this meant: "Well, Herman, Mario, Jim, and so forth, you've had your fun. Now forget it."

As I listened to Wagner's words, I thought that nothing better illustrated the Democratic Party's bankrupt state in the city. As wily a politician as the town had ever known, he was a product of the bosses and yet turned right around and made bossism the winning issue in the 1961 campaign.

He was a conciliator, and possibly conciliation was what we needed now. But the city was also falling apart. It desperately needed fresh approaches to horrendous problems, and there was nothing in Wagner's record to indicate that he brought them with him. Indeed, when he departed City Hall a little less than three and a half years before, he left with a "do nothing" reputation and a $250-million deficit in city financing.

Was this the white knight we had been waiting for?

There was, of course, our City Controller, Mario Procaccino. But the only thing that is not conservative about Mario is his oratory. I will never forget him addressing a fund-raising dinner in the grand ballroom of the Americana Hotel a few days before the 1965 municipal election. Extolling one of his fellow candidates on the ticket, Frank O'Connor, Mario reached ever higher in search of superlatives until he found himself frantically searching for a way to end it all. He succeeded. "Frank O'Connor," he boomed, "grows on you like . . . like . . . like cancer!" So the thought alone of Mario on City Hall steps flailing away for a punch line in greeting, say, an astronaut, was enough to drive you up the wall.

There was James Scheuer, the Bronx congressman, elected as a reform liberal, still purporting those views, yet with a book timed to come out just before the primary about safety in the streets. The appeal was a bit blatant. To put it mildly, the Scheuer image was—and remained—blurred.

There was also Herman Badillo, the Bronx borough president, who laid claim to being the only true liberal in the race. Now having covered politics for a while, I expect politicians to be, ah, evasive, but I also expect the ones I'm for to do it with a little style. Badillo lost me the day he announced that he would not accept the backing of any of the local bosses, especially that of Brooklyn's Meade Esposito, after having solicited such support, including Esposito's, and having been turned down.

All these candidates, whatever their ideology, had a common denominator. They were conventional—and boring.

Then, suddenly, there was hope of rescue from complete ennui. I refer to a new slate on the scene, which featured Mr. Norman Mailer as Democratic candidate for mayor and Mr. James Breslin for president of the City Council. You could see at once that it had a nice ethnic balance. The nicest thing about this, however, was that it came about by accident rather than design, in itself a historical first in city politics.

Both men were heavyweight candidates. Mailer's expansive, vested middle needed only a great gold watch and chain to complete the picture, but he was shortly to go into training for his series of articles for *Life* magazine on the Apollo 11 moonshot. Similarly, Breslin, having been stricken with pneumonia during the winter, had forsaken cigarettes and strong waters, and, bent on reducing his girth, could be found every morning jogging up and down Far Rockaway Beach.

The idea of Mailer and Breslin occupying City Hall seemed pretty far out—until you took a look at the other aspirants.

The whole thing, I learned, originated with Jack Newfield, *The Village Voice* political writer and activist. "I felt that all the liberal candidates were inadequate," he said, "and I figured I wasn't alone. Nobody had a better feel for the city than Norman and Jimmy, and I couldn't think of anyone who could better expose the shabbiness of the other candidates or could offer some good radical solutions for the city."

Thus, around the middle of March, Newfield called Mailer and said, "Norman, you ought to run for mayor."

Mailer didn't pay much attention to it. Then, a couple of days afterward, he got a call from Noel Parmentel, who used to be with William Buckley on the *National Review,* and whose politics is as far away from Newfield's as you can get. "Norman," Parmentel said, "you ought to run for mayor."

Mailer started thinking about running for mayor.

Breslin, meanwhile, had from time to time thought about running for City Council president. Once asked why, he muttered, "It's getting tougher and tougher to get a cab back to Queens, and it'd be nice to have a car."

Would he require a phone as well?

"Nah," he replied after a reflective moment, "I don't want any phone. *They* would know how to find me." *"They,"* it must be noted, are usually frantic editors trying to locate the whereabouts of Breslin and/or his copy.

Underneath Breslin's cynical façade, however, there beats a great deal of outrage about what is happening to the city, and he wasn't kidding when he pondered "the fun of exposing some of these clowns."

The two men joined one another at a meeting in Mailer's Brooklyn Heights house at the end of March. I was present along with about twenty other invited guests, including Parmentel and Newfield, Gloria Steinem, black militant Flo Kennedy, Pete Hamill, and Yippie leader Jerry Rubin.

It quickly became apparent why Mailer had called such a diverse group together. The only possible chance for his candidacy, he said, was a left-right alliance. "The hope is," he observed, "that a few sparks from the fires on the right and on the left will fly up and form this coalition."

The scene was dramatic. Mailer spoke from a semicrouch, his face shadowed. Behind him was a spectacular view of Lower Manhattan, glittering without a thought of a ghetto. It was the same kind of a view movies in the thirties featured when the big Broadway producer took the girl fresh from Indiana over to the window and said, "Baby, this is my town, and if you play your cards right it can be your town too."

It also became quickly apparent that Mailer, if he was to assume the candidacy, would do so seriously, although some of those present had thought of it simply in terms of laying bare the gut problems of the city. "Illuminating the issues is a lot of crap," he said. "If you're going to get into this thing, you do it to win."

Allowing that he still was eager to run, he listed some of his faults as a campaigner. "After the third intelligent question," he said, "I get a pained look in my eyes. After the four hundred and fiftieth dull question I tend to get violent."

There was, moreover, the fact of his probable absence from the city during most of the primary, since, having committed himself to the *Life* series, he might have to spend most of his time in Houston. Even though this didn't happen, there was a general agreement at the time that he could duck back into town for occasional television appearances and that Breslin could take up the slack. Indeed, being in Houston, as Mailer himself noted, had some advantages when you considered the rival candidates.

On the plus side, as well, was his physical appearance. Mailer, who is now forty-six, occasionally looks like a young David Ben-Gurion, especially when he dons his rimless glasses. "Lindsay," he said, "is too tall and too good-looking for the city. He's built on a national scale."

There was some give-and-take. Flo Kennedy suggested that Mailer and Breslin run on a ticket headed by Adam Powell. "A white man shouldn't be the top candidate," she said. "It should be Powell."

Breslin, seated in an armchair beside Mailer, ended this phase of the discussion. "We're supposed to be nuts," he said, "but Powell isn't even reliable."

Jerry Rubin broke in emotionally to know why Mailer and Breslin had to run in the Democratic primary. Why didn't they run as independents? "I don't care about these people," Rubin said. "Why have anything to do with them?"

Mailer was on his feet at once, glass in hand. "Jerry," he said, "why not make the machine spiritual . . . make *it* hum?"

Someone asked Mailer what he would do in office. "I'm completely ignorant of the entire internal affairs of the city," he said. "I'll learn on the job and report to the people every day about what I've found out. What to do with New York? You have to take it back to the people, left and right, black and white. Once you're in office, you're accountable."

It was obvious that Mailer and Breslin would make a splendid team. It would be worth the price of admission just to watch the opposition squirm.

In the ensuing primary campaign, Jack Newfield and I served from time to time as co-press secretaries for Mailer and Breslin. This service was not without its moments.

There was, for example, the rally we had at a Greenwich Village nightclub, the Village Gate. This was our first big fund-raising affair, and things didn't quite go as we had planned. It was there, you may recall, that Mailer took the microphone and, after surveying the fashionable East Side crowd which had decided to make the rally the "in" social event of the evening, suddenly unburdened himself of a number of choice phrases not normally heard in public.

As it happened, I was not present at the Gate when all this took place, having left a few hours earlier for Puerto Rico to try to get rid of a bad case of laryngitis. As far as my voice was concerned, however, I might as well have stayed in town.

The first call came around 4 A.M. It was from Breslin, who, with considerable emotion, sketched what had occurred.

"Jimmy," I croaked, "where are you now?"

"At home," he yelled, "under the covers."

The next day I got thirty-eight phone calls to Puerto Rico on the same subject, some outraged, some gossipy, some perplexed, but each embraced the same theme—how could Norman have done such a thing?

When I got back to New York a couple of days later, I saw Mailer and asked, "Norman, how could you have done such a thing?"

"Well," he said, "the devil dealt me five cards and I picked the wrong one."

At a subsequent strategy meeting to ascertain what the post-Village Gate damage might be, it was Mailer who, in summing up, set the tone for the whole campaign. "Oh, come on," he said, "if we were professionals, we'd be saying that we were finished. But we're not professionals. We're amateurs, and we'll just roll with the punch and come back fighting."

A lot of people can be forgiven for thinking that with a couple of tigers like Mailer and Breslin, getting proper coverage of their candidacies would be a cinch. I guess that's what Newfield and I thought too, or else we would not have volunteered. But as it turned out, the ticket's reputation in previous arenas did not make things easy.

"The whole idea is a joke," a friend said to me. "How can you possibly work for those guys?"

"Take a look at the other candidates," I replied with some heart; "that's where the joke is."

The local press did not share my sentiments, and in the pre-announcement stage, so important in building momentum in an election, only *The Village Voice,* Newfield's paper, and *New York* printed the possibility of Mailer and Breslin running for office. Apparently it was too mind-bending for other editors around town to face up to the thought that two writers, equipped with imagination and concern, could conceivably contribute any fresh solutions to a city that resembled nothing so much as a terminal patient in a cancer ward.

Thus at 3 A.M. one morning it was a Tokyo newspaper that called me about them, another time the London *Standard,* then the Toronto *Star,* the Washington *Post,* the Boston *Globe,* and so on—not the New York *Times,* the *Daily News,* or the New York *Post.*

In an effort to rectify this, another historical first in city politics took place. Newfield and I invited Richard Reeves, the local political editor for the *Times,* and Sidney Zion, a *Times* reporter whom we had heard might be doing a Sunday feature on Mailer and Breslin, to lunch at Toots Shor's.

The point was to impress upon them the seriousness of our

campaign, the fact that our two basic issues—making the city the fifty-first state and returning real power to the neighborhoods—had extraordinary validity, that both members of the ticket were not in it for a lark, that we had rented a headquarters, and that, even as we spoke, hundreds of committed volunteers were out rounding up the necessary petitions.

Over coffee Reeves allowed that he was convinced and would henceforth assign coverage of Mailer and Breslin as he would any of the other candidates. Just then the waiter brought the check and by accident deposited it on a plate in front of Zion. It flopped there for some minutes like a great codfish. Finally Newfield said, "Sidney, that's the new politics. The reporters pay."

An incredulous look crossed Zion's face. Almost hypnotically he reached into a pocket for his wallet and forked over the cash, muttering all the while to Reeves, "Are you going to okay this?"

Thereafter the *Times* did cover Mailer and Breslin regularly, although it placed the announcement of their candidacies well back in the paper while according Mrs. Ellie Guggenheimer page-one treatment when she became one of Herman Badillo's running mates. The trouble with the *Times,* we quickly discovered, is that it is too vast an operation, and regardless of a particular editor's intent, our fate in the end rested on the caliber and insights of the dozen or so reporters who followed Mailer and Breslin at various times during the campaign. The same spotty results appeared on the editorial page. The first editorial in the *Times* mocked the prospect of either Mailer or Breslin seeking public office. Newfield and I promptly sent off a suitable reply, although the only sign that it ever arrived was a form letter noting that our letter was one of many the *Times* received every day and unfortunately did not have the space to print. Later on, both Tom Wicker and Russell Baker, editorial page columnists interestingly enough based outside New York, cheered the ticket. Obviously visitors to the cancer ward could see a good deal more clearly how sick the patient was.

Coverage by the *Daily News* was spasmodic at best, and the *Post,* with a monopoly position in the afternoon, was even worse. The *Post* did carry the announcement that Mailer and Breslin were in the race, which was really mandatory, and then consistently ignored them. A *Post* reporter explained why. His editor, he said, told him that the paper was not in business to advance the careers of former employees, meaning Breslin.

We were nonetheless having an impact. I discovered this when representing Mailer and Breslin for their television debates. Whenever I made a suggestion about the format, the representatives of the other candidates automatically banded against me. It was a great morale booster. What was good for us was bad for them.

In the end the *Post* finally took serious note of us. Mr. James Wechsler wrote that had it not been for Mailer and Breslin, Herman Badillo would have been the Democratic nominee. But the polls showed that if the election had been held ten days earlier, Mailer and Breslin would have gotten almost twice as many votes. It was Badillo who took votes away from us in the last hours of the campaign—and what we ended up with was ours alone.

As a Wagner strategist observed the day after the election, "The trouble was that you fellows just peaked too early."

Ah well, we were amateurs after all. Next time we'll know better.

DIARY OF A MAILER TRAILER

JANE O'REILLY

One fine Sunday morning last May I got into a car with a photographer from *LIFE,* a literary columnist from Chicago, a reporter from the *Yale Daily News,* and a person who in political campaigns is known as The Driver, and we all rode out to the Howard Beach Jewish Community Center to hear Norman Mailer, Pulitzer prize-winning author and candidate for mayor of the city of New York. Howard Beach is on the line between Brooklyn and Queens. The houses look as though they were built for a showroom out of toothpicks and bits of styrofoam and balsa wood. It is a place where the developers rolled incredible, possibly plastic grass out over the dunes of Jamaica Bay, plopped identical houses in rows on top of each square of the incorruptible turf, and planted spotlights amidst the shrubbery for nighttime revelations of the proud achievement of the owners of these $18,000 villas.

It was ten o'clock in the morning, and they were serving bagels and lox and cream cheese. Perhaps forty men and a few wives were waiting for Mailer and his running mate, James Breslin, political columnist and candidate for City Council president.

One of the men told the columnist from Chicago that what New York needed was a mayor like Daley. Accountants and schoolteachers and appliance-store managers live in Howard Beach, and they are strong on the law-and-order issue. Breslin spoke first. He is a big man, and he worries a lot, and is often moved to outrage. He looks at his audience sideways, as though he isn't sure they, or he, can take what he has to say. This morning it is too early for him to comfort them with his famous humor, he lays it on straight: "They are lying to you. They say what we need is more police. The police aren't going to solve this problem. We must control our lives. As long as everything is centralized, nothing will happen."

Mailer is introduced and politely applauded. He is dressed in a marvelously tailored pinstriped suit, a white, rather old-fashioned shirt—his campaign clothes—and he isn't sure of the early-morning vibrations in this prefabricated synagogue-*cum*-community center. One hand in a coat pocket, standing three quarters to the microphone—his usual fighting posture, both exhortive and combative—he says: "What we have in New York, what has come to New York first, is the problem of the technological age. The problem of the society which is built on a machine rather than a conception of the human spirit."

After he spoke, the audience asked questions: political questions about Mailer and Breslin's program and how it could work. They didn't ask why they were running, or if they were serious, and they apparently didn't think they were listening to a literary curiosity come to entertain them on a spring morning. They treated Mailer and Breslin as candidates who might have an answer to some of their problems. There were nine more campaign stops that day, and those questions would be asked at other places, but mostly in the press car. We actually were spending a fine spring day observing this literary curiosity, the writer as candidate (MAILER as candidate), and it was our professional duty to wonder why and what for and what did it all really mean?

About a month before, in mid-April, when Mailer decided to run for mayor, he was quoted (which is usually a very different thing from saying "he said") as saying: "This is a dangerous thing for a writer to do, I'm going to try to think creatively in public, out in front." Mailer isn't just any writer, and the press came pouring into town, partly on the wise assumption that there might be something said worth listening to, and partly to catch the show—Free Mailer, Come and Get it! Always good copy!

The show toured the five boroughs daily, and I caught it whenever I could from the back of the campaign car. Let other people write about the impossible Mailer, the "fireworks salesman," the mean drunk. By the June primary, Mailer had become My Hero, and it pleases me to portray him as flawless. Mailer is the man who is permanently out in front, the scout for our times, always miles ahead down the path testing the trail for traps and false prophets and illusions, confronting with his own spirit the villains and fakers and wrong turnings; always ahead, dimly glowing with evangelical fervor, exhorting us to come on, press on; stop sniveling and posturing; stand up and march like men with souls.

The day that began at Howard Beach I was not inclined to admire him. No middle-aged Bronx housewife had a more tight-lipped image of Mailer as Public Sinner albeit Greatest Living American Writer. In retreat from the sure sense that things are indeed getting worse, I had been reading the comforting cadences of Jane Austen, and not Norman Mailer. But, media glutted, I read *about* him; newspaper accounts of marriages and binges; highly reasoned and tortuously wordy literary essays by other New York writers, who essentially complain that Mailer's behemoth personality is burning up all the creative oxygen around. "Norman," not the real Mailer but some secondhand version, is a constant whisper at New York cocktail parties—someone has always just been to Provincetown, or to a party at the fabled penthouse in Brooklyn Heights. Girls are constantly sighing: "Oh, Norman Mailer, I met him once, I made such a fool of myself." There is something about him—a combination of charm and shyness and fierceness and fame—that makes people, men and women, fling themselves into his presence like moths into a candle. There is no real evidence that Mailer continuously invites or enjoys these physical and mental challenges. He does not suffer fools gladly, but he has such sympathy for the spectacle of someone making a fool of himself, that if he can, by sheer magnetic force, he will make him stop. Some of his friends are people no one else can tolerate, and one of the reasons is, they are tolerable around him. He insists on his own perception of a person, and some people respond by improving. Others markedly do not.

That first day on the campaign I would ordinarily have made a fool of myself, and asked a lot of dumb and bitchy questions, except that by good fortune I had such a terrible toothache I couldn't talk. Also, I was terrified of Mailer. I had seen him twice before, and neither was a soothing experience. The first time was in April, when I went, in a mood of tentative mockery, to a campaign organizational meeting. There were dozens of people milling around busily, all energetically carrying on overlapping conversations and repeating directions and committee allocations to each other. There were some former Kennedy people, and some former McCarthy people, some people who would work for anybody with an idea, some writers, and some people to whom it was important to pretend that they know the "real" Norman better than anyone.

The real Norman looked just like his pictures, maybe a little fatter. His eyes are so intense that the expression shows even in a photograph. But his voice was surprising: words rumble and bubble and jump out, in a variety of accents; New York, faintly southern, all g's dropped (as in "Ahm talkin'") when he is particularly shy. Rising from his chair occasionally, he tried to give encouraging directives to the oblivious workers. "We have got to get some sense of everything moving upward in this campaign. We will levitate at some point . . . or we won't." "We are going to allow these people to find some interest in their lives." "New York either gets an imagination, or it dies." He then snarled, an icy snarl, at one of his most efficient campaign aides: "DON'T TALK WHILE I AM TALKING."

I sniffed, and went home muttering about the liberal death wish and the fate of New York intellectuals who have no grasp on the realities of life. People even dumber than I was were saying, "He's a writer, and writers should write." Smarter people were calling up to ask if they could help. A week later I went to the press conference Mailer and Breslin held to announce their candidacy. Very nice, very straightforward, very interesting. New York should be the fifty-first state and get out from under Albany's thumb. Power to the neighborhoods. Fine.

Then, on May 7, there was a rally at the Village Gate, which was very hard to explain away to the "Norman Mailer couldn't possibly be serious because obviously he is off on the ultimate ego trip" skeptics. The rally began at midnight, $5.00 admission, and the place was jammed. Campaign buttons saying "Vote the Rascals in" and "The *other* guys are the joke" and "No More Bull Shit" were all around. Jimmy Breslin, looking especially anguished,

made a very funny speech. "What brings fat James Breslin to the
Gate on a night when he could be in a smaller bar with fewer
people who couldn't check his lies? People ask if we are serious.
The first day I thought we were doing a little dealing in politics
between books. The second day I thought it was a good way to
straighten out. The third day, Norman arrives with a TIE on. This
city is run by people who think everything is O.K. if things are
O.K. on Wall Street, in the 17th Congressional District . . .
while the East Bronx falls down." And, "Our claim is that we're
going to put the English language back into politics."

Mailer had been to some earlier fund-raising parties. By the
time he got up to speak, his mood, and the audience's mood, had
soured. Other speakers had not been as gently outraged as Breslin,
and at least half the crowd was there for blood. The Greenwich
Village cannibals, the "Fang Club" somebody called them, like the
mechanical dolls in *Barbarella* with sharp little pointed-steel teeth
clicking and snapping, they were there to tear Mailer apart; just as
they tear him apart at dinners and cocktails and in small literary
reviews.

He attacked back, in the style that later in the campaign came to
be known as "The Old Mailer." "Listen to me, 'cause I'm talkin'
hard," he said, hard, his nose twitching with distaste. "If you're
comin' to work—WORK. Leave you ego at the door. Keep quiet!
. . . Don't come to be entertained, we're in this very deep."

There was a girl crouched on the floor beneath the platform, like
a particularly hideous illustration from an underground newspaper.
She was beating steadily on the stage with a huge stick and shouting
FUCK FUCK FUCK in rhythm with the stick. She was obscene,
and so was Mailer, and the half of the audience that had come to
see vintage Mailer roared and hissed and spit back. The other half
of the audience, the ones Norman was addressing when he talked
about "If you are coming to work—WORK," was perfectly respectable, dimly do-gooder, willing to donate bits of money and time,
but essentially unrelating to the city or the crisis except in the most
comfortable way. They had given little dinners for each other before
the benefit, and they were shocked and embarrassed. Later, Mailer's
campaign staff laboriously explained to him that he had hurt the

people who were really working for him, and he apologized and said he understood he was cruel to those rich pigs who came in late and—still later—he called it the night he made a fool of himself. But, what he said at the Gate was true, and for some there was catharsis in the insult.

The next day I called a friend who was working hard for Mailer, and I said: "What on earth is really going on?" She said, "We are doing it because the Democratic Party in New York is in a desperate situation and we need to spread some ideas around." But Mailer was running for mayor. He said: "I'm not running an educational campaign because I think an educational campaign saps the spirit and creates a false superiority in the defeated." He was right again, of course.

When we left Howard Beach I got into Mailer's car. The day was clear and springy, and we drove along the edge of Jamaica Bay, "Where particularly hardy New Yorkers go swimming," said Mailer. There were people riding horses along the water's edge, and Sunday fishermen, and people enjoying nature, just as they do in Cincinnati and Malibu Beach, but not at all the way they do in my Manhattan-bound image of New York City. All day we drove through neighborhoods in Brooklyn and Queens and the Bronx, through parts of the city where life has roots and continuity. There are miles and miles and miles of New York, and every possible life style, except agricultural. (No, even that, there are still farms on Staten Island.) The city is governed by Albany, where, said Breslin: "They think Bedford-Stuyvesant is a new breed of dairy cattle." If New York City were a separate state, it would be the sixth largest. Of course, I think to myself, what an obvious idea, how strange that none of the other candidates have suggested it.

We drove through a section of Brooklyn with small one- and two-story row houses; ugly, but friendly in the morning light, with careful aluminum awnings and silver balls in tiny front gardens, and orange-painted store fronts. Comfortable lower-middle class. "Now this is what I call a neighborhood," said Mailer. "This is the sort of place I grew up in." "You did?" I said, disappointed. He laughed. "You thought I grew up in some slum," he said. I certainly did, I thought EVERYBODY who grew up in New York had to fight their way out of a tangle of fire escapes. I thought the tree that grew in Brooklyn was the only tree.

Another synagogue. Everything in it is labeled, "Donated by . . ." The chairs donated by the Glick family, the window from the Goldstein family, the microphone from Mr. Schwartz. Mailer tells them: "We are running on a powerful notion, the notion of New York as the fifty-first state. We are offering the city a chance to reconsider, we are offering a chance to dig and explore and debate and see where we are going. What we are saying, is, there is no need to destroy ourselves." A man in the audience says: "There are people, other people, who are trying to keep the city alive. I see complete ANARCHY in your neighborhood concept." Applause; *this* neighborhood's concept seems to be a sort of gang warfare with gun battles and street barricades against "them"—the people in Harlem and the South Bronx and Bedford-Stuyvesant. Mailer smiles, the smile of the emerging politician, and says; "OK. Now let's talk about it. I don't mean ALL power to the neighborhoods, I mean as much as is compatible with the needs of the city." By the time he leaves, they are still suspicious, but interested.

About five o'clock, Mailer dropped into two fund-raising parties. Afterwards, the whole pack of us, press, campaign manager, advance man, and candidate, went to a West Side hotel where, under different auspices, "Swinger's Socials" are regularly held. ("Passive man wants to meet two strong blond dominating women.") This evening some kind of Reform Democratic club, not swinging, was meeting in an airless, ugly room, filled with people who seemed to have taken literally the columnists' advice to lonely people: "Join your local political club and meet people, get involved." Mailer talked about the mechanics of Power to the Neighborhoods: "They will forge themselves, deliver their own forms out of their conflicting needs." Part of the Mailer-Breslin platform was a plan for a monorail around New York City, and free electric jitneys in Manhattan. No cars allowed. "It will give New Yorkers a certain sense of liberty swinging from one bus to another." There was polite laughter. New Yorkers right now have so little sense of liberty that they cannot even imagine the exhilaration of free buses. "This city either gets an imagination or it dies," the candidates keep repeating. Now I see what they mean. The meeting was followed by a tango-dance exhibition. We did not stay.

Political clubs all look the same: full of folding tables and ancient chairs, drifts of leaflets on the floors and ashtrays that have been forever full, little old ladies who bring boxes of cookies and packs of cigarettes and make nests in the desk drawers. That night we drove through the cool May twilight to another club, miles and miles into Queens, along New York's version of the numbing All-American highway, Queen's Boulevard. Endless blocks of pizza parlors, parking lots, automobile showrooms, chandelier modern. One reporter swore he had driven down it one night with Mailer, who was muttering to himself: "I don't want to be mayor of this evil, evil city."

Twelve midnight: We are going to a bar. Just a bar, not one of the in places where people whisper "NORMAN was here last night." Norman says he isn't too crazy about those. By now I'm calling him Norman. I'm very happy, there are six men and me, and it is very late and everyone feels justified in staying up later because we've all been through a long day together and, besides, while Norman keeps talking, we are theoretically still working. I keep drinking brandy—for my tooth—and I say something calculatedly self-deprecating about how I was pleased to be with the grownups, but I was afraid I had taken up somebody else's position in the car. With just the barest hint of a twinkle Norman says: "You are ageless . . . and without position." He grins fiendishly. Now I see why they say don't lie around him. Don't even adopt a slight, comforting little pose.

The men talk about stories they have done about athletes: Sonny Liston and Cassius Clay and Jim Brown. They talk about the sheer physical presence of those guys: All of them describe a moment of truth when they were plain scared. Mailer's presence has the same frightening effect on writers, male writers. "Norman's going to read this," they think, paralyzingly, their professional egos at stake. For women, it isn't quite such a challenge. We, the women I know working around him, and me, aren't even sure he takes us seriously anyway. "He exalts women spiritually and puts them down intellectually," somebody said. For some reason, with Mailer it is endearing instead of infuriating. Probably because we are so busy trying to meet his real challenge to us; we are trying to be proto-typical WOMAN.

For men, getting Mailer down in words is like wrestling the big one into the boat. The results are often very contradictory, verging on incoherent. Probably the only person who can write about Mailer is Mailer. Even describing his face is like trying to capture exactly the effect of light on a particularly profound body of water. Some-times he looks menacing, and his lip curls back like an angry dog as when he talks about the dis-ease (he pronounces words literally, as well as using them literally) of the twentieth century. And then, in the split second before Wolfman takes over, the lines around his eyes crinkle up and the threat is a joke, shared. In the course of one sentence he can be brilliant, obscure, naïve, kind, attacking, ar-ticulate, and demonic. He is deeply engrossing, terribly funny, and almost totally impossible to remember accurately when you are not with him. It makes complete accuracy in reporting difficult.

Still at the bar; two o'clock in the morning. One of the reporters, relentlessly searching for Mailer's essence, said: "HOW could you have written *Armies of the Night* without taking notes?" And Mailer said: "It's funny, when I checked my facts I found I had remem-bered most of the night. I didn't take any notes because I didn't plan to write anything. But when I got on the plane back to New York I had a sudden Epiphany." He grinned, and spread his arms, and we could see him sitting in the plane, expanding with a vision. We laughed and talked about how "Epiphany" would replace "existential" in intellectual slang, and we all planned to have crea-tive Epiphanies as soon as possible.

May 26: A new girl is riding in the press car, tall, blond, just back from free-lancing in Vietnam. Norman goes into his ritual ten-minute man-woman thing: "You look like you hunt, do you hunt?" he asks her, cozily. Yes, she hunts, with various kinds of guns. I hate her. "I fish," I say, hopefully. He laughs, his mood is good. All evening he deals with petulant questioners, lightly, in-tuitively, truth through tact. It's the same night that Breslin faces a hostile, long-winded girl who questions him while her large dog howls. Jimmy resists his natural instincts, and inquires politely:

"Madam, has that dog had his shots?" He deserves to carry the assembly district for that.

There is a brief unpleasantness during a small benefit appearance at the Electric Circus. Intellectual cannibals again, and Norman asks for questions instead of giving his rousing street-corner speech. "I hate the Electric Circus, I hate the architecture, I hate what it stands for. It's a trap." (A rather inconvenient aversion, since Village campaign headquarters are in the Electric Circus building.) "The whole Village is a trap, isn't it?" someone asks. "Well, it isn't nourishing," says Mailer. Out of six stops tonight, the *Times* tangentially covers only the Electric Circus appearance, with a drama page review: "First the audience . . . witnessed a psychodrama of another variety, "The Campaign," starring Norman Mailer. While TV cameras captured the bizarre scene . . ." Later, Breslin will say truthfully, "Most of the reporters in New York are $240 a week shipwrecks."

They are waiting for Mailer at the Women's League of Voters. They are really with him, tolerating the other candidates in tonight's debate, but applauding wildly for Mailer. A man about thirty-five, with a drooping mustache, claps, and his mother, in stony disapproval, jabs him with her elbow. The son strokes his mustache fiercely, in defiance. Mailer begins: "The acquired experience of the past is useless for New York because New York is the first victim of the twentieth century, what I called the dis-ease of the technological society. To wit, all the ills of the world were assumed at one point by technology, which proceeded to pipe them out the back of the car in the form of exhaust and they've come back: the greed, the exploitation, the iniquity (spoken letter by letter, with fangs showing) of capitalism have come back to the city in the form of smog." Applause. There are many little old ladies here, with firm hats and firm opinions. They agree with Mailer on the Vietnam war—a subject he doesn't get into because this is a mayoral contest. If there are no votes here, there are no votes anywhere.

Memorial Day weekend the campaign went to Aqueduct Race Track and Coney Island. I missed it, but the tall beautiful blonde went. Today, June 3 (??) there is a lunch-hour walk around midtown Manhattan: from the CBS building to Rockefeller Center, up across

Fifty-seventh Street and down Third Avenue to P. J. Clarke's pub. Jimmy and Norman, wearing bachelor's-buttons in their buttonholes —donated by the St. Patrick's Cathedral flower fair—walk down the street, hand out. Volunteers fan out around the block, leafleting, urging, "Come and meet Norman Mailer, Pulitzer prize-winning author and candidate for mayor. Come and meet Jimmy Breslin, candidate for City Council president."

At that hour, at that time of year, the people on Fifth Avenue are half Swedish models and Middle-Western tourists, but there are enough New Yorkers, and enough step up to shake hands. They have heard of Mailer, but KNOW Jimmy, who has spent years writing columns in their cause. His walk was one long series of regards sent to sisters-in-law, inquiries about the family back in Flushing. It sounded as though he had gone to high school with half the people on the street. "How's it goin' Jimmy," they said. "Not bad, same old thing," he said. "Say, he's a handsome guy isn't he? What a big fella," they said, pleased to meet Breslin and see that he was handsome. They were shyer about Mailer, asking for autographs and telling him they had read his books.

That day there were packs of reporters, several elite columnists, and at least two complete television crews. It was June 3, and finally the press seemed to have decided that this was a *serious* campaign. Up until then, the three local papers had been running stories, with a few excellent exceptions, that were inaccurate, misleading, out of context, and "made us look like monkeys," said Mailer.

Mailer was not easy to cover. He speaks so quickly there is no way to catch what he says exactly, and he speaks with such unexpected turns of language, a sort of shorthand of his writing, that he is impossible to paraphrase. And, unless he is carefully struggling through an interview, he often doesn't answer questions at all, throws off one-liners, or answers them four hours later.

He patiently suffered through daily interviews, explaining slowly what he thought about the city, trying to answer tedious questions without snapping. If people tried to get his opinion on subjects other than the mayoral race, he referred them to his books, saying, "I've written about it so much better than I can say it here." One day, when I had collected a lot of questions, I tried to have a straight interview. He said: "Whose questions are those? They aren't real questions, they are dull, stupid questions. Why do you need an interview, you've been here two weeks. Why are you so greedy? You reporters all have tapeworm, and the tapeworm is dialogue." He had grown fangs again, but I copied down everything he said so dutifully that he laughed.

For most of the other reporters, he contained himself, not that it did much good. They would arrive, saying: "I guess they are always drunk, late, and obscene, huh? Crazy guys, what a wild idea." And then they would begin to dimly realize that this campaign was something between Norman Mailer and Jimmy Breslin and the people of New York. Rarely did they manage to carry their new perception back to the city desk. They would take the easy way and play it for laughs: "Norman Mailer considers the solution to crime to be spiritual: He is sort of the left-wing Billy Graham."

Verbally, Mailer was hard to catch. But the *concept* shouldn't have been beyond the reach of most journalists. Even so, one reputedly competent man murmured at the end of two weeks on the assignment: "But, WHY is he doing it?"

He was doing it, I think, for spiritual reasons, partly. "We are paying our dues to this city," he said, and Breslin said. The way to do it was to go out and challenge, personally, the disease of the twentieth century where it lived: by confronting the tired and numbed people and making them think and prodding them to get a sense of themselves. He gave more than he got, and he seemed to thrive on it. "I'm not tired," he said toward the end of the campaign. "My stamina is good and getting better all the time." Every day he seemed to be cheerier, happier, and firmer about what he was saying. There was a suspicion that he had been bored before the campaign began.

On Fifth Avenue, the people were not yet greeting the candidates as saviors of their city. A woman darted up to Breslin and said, hissing, "That's all we need, an illiterate for City Council president, and a pervert for mayor." She said it twice, to make sure. "Beautiful," said Breslin. She may have called Mailer a pervert because he has gone on record in favor of sex, and has had four wives. But everyone is entitled to at least two marriages these days, and certainly Norman Mailer is entitled to four. One of the press group's favorite things to cluck about (reporters are really old men at heart, gossips, all of them), was the fact that Norman's wives seem to get along with each other. As though that were undesirable and somehow shocking. But there he is, way out in front, once again.

The women on Fifth Avenue were frightening. They scuttled along, girded for war with the Return for Credit Department; eyelids painted brilliant green over the webs of age. Once in Queens, Mailer said: "The women out here are real women, their lives center on their home and children." I thought that was Mailer, the Last of the Great Romantics, speaking. He didn't seem to notice their fingernails bitten down to the quick, or their wigs at ten in the morning, or the petulance that had settled on their faces. But when I really looked at the examples of womanhood on Fifth Avenue, stared them in the face while I urged them to shake the candidates hand, I saw what he meant. They were ravening beasts compared to the housebound ladies of Queens. Norman Mailer is a cumulative experience.

Lunch at P. J. Clarke's. There is a long table full of reporters and campaign aides, and Norman and Jimmy pick up the bill— again. People seem to think this is a Rockefeller running. A grizzled city-desk type is hunched over the end of the table, interviewing Norman. "I'm not looking for a revolution at all," he says. "I'm looking for its exact opposite. I'm lookin' for a way to give people in this city a sense of their own political power. Until we give power back to the neighborhoods, nobody will have a sense of what it is to gain or lose. I say I'm running as a left-conservative: It means the conservatives are right that man must solve his problems through his own agency, but you can't ask the other half to do it until they have their own agency. I'm talking about economic funding for the other half, and that's left."

That afternoon Mailer speaks at a special meeting for *Time-Life* employees. He is really rolling along, by now he REALLY knows what he would want to do if he were mayor, and he moves through the subjects of welfare and discriminating trade unions and finally to crime as a result of the greater evils of society. "Crime becomes a way of life, it becomes the one way a man may express himself." They ask about his position on CCNY. Mailer was the only mayoral candidate who spoke out in favor of the black students at CCNY who were demanding, last spring, separate and open enrollment for blacks. ("I didn't even have to think about it," said Mailer at the time. "It seemed right.") It was a position that shocked the fair, liberal-white sensibilities of the people who learned those liberal sentiments at CCNY in it's great days during the depression. Beneath the liberal façade, they simply believed that letting in many black students would SPOIL the university. "Lower standards."

Mailer said, to *Time-Life:* "Well, you all are *very* serious about CCNY. The idea of the pearl having its standards adulterated, eh?" He stopped, and said as an aside, "It's awful to think of a pearl having its standards adulterated." Earlier, another night, he had said, "These black people have been promised in the last twenty years over and over and over and over that they would be given opportunities to have education, free education, for their needs. They were denied, cheated, and tricked for two centuries in this country. Finally they seized the opportunity, they *forced* that recognition that they should have double admission at the college, and I say fine, I cheer. What no one says is, what are they going to do if those kids don't go to college? Let 'em stand on the street and shake their dice and wait and jive talk and figure out how they can spoil the city? They have the wit to want to get into college and I say bless 'em." To *Time,* he added: "We have to recognize that everybody in this city is paying for the sins of their fathers. And, realize, when WHITE boys can't get into CCNY, then we will finally get those community colleges, and not before."

Outside the lecture room at *Time* there was a reception room with a yellow-and-black-tile floor, and long tables spread out with drinks. No one standing outside the hall touched a drink until Mailer finished. There were ripples of girls going through: special *Time-Life* girls with Hampton tans and very short skirts. One of the photographers said: "They made me want to just grab hold with both hands and bite their thighs." I asked Norman what he thought of their fuckability quotient, if the question didn't offend him. He said: "Yes, it would offend my notion of the mystery."

The day's campaigning continued. A fund-raising party in a too carefully decorated West Side apartment. A debate on the Lower

East Side where the people were stolid, welcoming. There were sleeping children in the audience, and a few hippies, and some who looked as though they had come over from the old country in 1860. Norman liked it there, it reminded him of another part of his childhood, and when he had to leave to go uptown to another meeting, he hurried through it and raced back downtown. "I think I can get 'em," he said. "The devils are running in this campaign," he was saying to the audience, as one of the devils walked in through the stage door. The poor man never had a chance. In response to Mailer he said things like: "I don't use liberal in the pejorative sense. We don't need simplistic nonsense. We are in a crisis of liberalism. If competent, tough, effective liberalism doesn't work, then we are in trouble." I don't think the people he was speaking to had actually realized that liberalism had already failed until that moment.

"I'm not a liberal," said Mailer. "I don't believe in gentle progressive steps. This city is half insane by now and we have to do something. John Lindsay is a nice fellow, but he is too good for this city. He is so tall and we are all so small and ugly. He should be president, the problems would be simpler." He talked about Sweet Sunday: "Since at bottom I'm a mystic, I'm still for shutting off the electricity, but it won't happen until New Yorkers get their heads cleared, and get tired of TV."

Afterwards, outside, it was dark, and it was good. A man came up in the crowd, wearing a yarmulke and work clothes, and said: "Mr. Mailer, would you give me your autograph, and your favorite verse from the Old Testament. I've read a couple of your books and they have given me a lot of pleasure in life." The crowd gathered around to see if Mailer could do it. He wrote something slowly in Hebrew, and then he corrected the end, and they sighed with relief. Later, in the car, he said he had written, "In the beginning."

On June 5 I met Mailer and Breslin in Joe's Restaurant in downtown Brooklyn. Jimmy was swearing under his breath at some political enemies sitting across the room. Norman had gotten up at six to shake hands outside subway entrances. Norman and I were supposed to have an interview, but that was the day he snarled about tapeworm, so I sat there and ate their olives and asked about the beginning of the campaign.

In April ("My God," said Breslin, "do you know how long ago that seems?") they had gone to about fifteen local colleges to see if they had any support. They said: "We are feeling around, if you want us to go for it, we will." At Union Theological Seminary, Jimmy made them feel ashamed of their education, they felt guilty at not having street smarts. They asked Norman to read aloud the passage from *Miami and the Siege of Chicago* where he describes the Republicans, ("They scourged themselves with WASP self-Hate," said somebody who was at UTS).

At Queens College, Mailer and Breslin climbed up fourteen floors to talk to the kids who had seized the building. In Queens, one of the big political issues in the campaign was the fact that the snow had not been removed for two weeks after last winter's blizzard. "What would you have done about it?" they asked Mailer. Imbued with the revolutionary spirit of the fourteenth floor, Mailer put his hand on his hip, leaned forward, and said: "I would have PISSED on it." Somehow in print that doesn't look as captivating as it was.

I wondered if he was ever asked questions about his books, his "body of work," his philosophy. "They don't treat me as a walking body of knowledge because there is no reason why they should. I'm a frightfully ignorant man. I'm an amateur philosopher," he said, scowling. One of Mailer's favorite mottoes is "Once—a philosopher, twice—a pervert." He says a girl told it to him, he thinks it is from Voltaire, and he is pleased thinking so, and he trots it out prefaced by "I would remind you that . . ." But he delivers it with an emphasis that reads as though he meant once upon a time a philosopher, sure to end up a pervert twice. The recipient of this philosophical nugget usually stands nodding in bewilderment, which gives Mailer a chance to get away.

After Joe's Restaurant, we went to Bedford-Stuyvesant, the particular ghetto section of Brooklyn that was the center of Robert Kennedy's prototypical slum program. It is a really beautiful part of New York, full of trees and magnificent old brownstones, which Mailer took great pleasure in pointing out. Brownstones can be saved he said, housing projects simply crush the soul. The group, press, and/or leaflet passers, stood on a central street corner, in front of the Club Baby Grand. I had never noticed before that we were all white, or at least we were that particular afternoon.

Norman had said: "We are scarcely a household word in Bed-Stuy," but then, almost none of the other candidates ever appeared there at all. People, mostly young black men, stopped and talked and wanted to know what about it. Norman, who was shorter than most of the men, looked straight into their eyes and spoke levelly, straight ahead, which was physically impossible. His face was compassionate, concerned, he told them what he would do and what they would be able to do if there was neighborhood control. Everywhere he spoke, the middle class stood up and said, "If the neighborhoods have control, what about Bed-Stuy? What's to keep them from getting most of the money?" He answered: "The idea won't work unless black neighborhoods get more at first, in order to build their own economies. The liberal and the left in New York have to consider over and over that the black communities have to have the chance to get their thing together."

So there the candidates were, on a June afternoon, explaining what it would be like if the firemen and policemen and garbage men were from the community, and if the community could decide for itself what to do about its schools and its parks and its traffic. They talked about their platform which called for the community to take over the renewal of dilapidated housing, to train itself to do the work, (which would also by-pass discriminating trade unions). A very tall black man, wearing an African robe, asked Jimmy a question about police. Breslin stood very close to him and looked up into his face, craning his neck back and said, very low, pushing the words into the man, pushing the reality, the recognition out between them where it might do some good: "You know by now the white man isn't going to do *anything* for you. You've got to have your own police." The man nodded. He knew, but he didn't know anyone else knew.

That day I was carrying a copy of *Armies of the Night*. We were all constantly sneaking around with unread Mailer works. Norman offered to autograph it, and I was pleased. As we drove to his house, he thought and fidgeted, and finally wrote down: "To

Jane, with all fine lights to the lady, Norman." Thank you, I said, what does it mean?

"I thought it sounded nice," said Norman. My Pulitzer prize-winning autograph.

The best thing about being a Mailer Trailer; aside from my life being changed, my perceptions unclogged, and my knowledge of New York extended beyond the surrealistic and dis-eased island of Manhattan, was that Norman did, indeed, make me feel like a lady. That afternoon, he was on his way home to change and then drive out to Rutgers to receive his first honorary degree. He asked if I would like to come up. I had once heard him describe another candidate as "a gentleman, someone I would invite to my home." I felt privileged.

Everybody at headquarters that afternoon was absolutely outraged by what they called the Pulitzer prize-winning jingle. Someone had donated money for radio spots and the staff wrote a series that they considered sharp, impressive, educational, and moving. Norman threw them all out and insisted on using his jingle which had been partially inspired by a man who had pressed a small piece of paper into his hand on the street in Bedford-Stuyvesant, on which was written, "You've seen the rest, now vote the best, Mailer-Breslin and the fifty-first state."

Canvassers were out ringing doorbells, carrying notes from the major position papers, and some directions, one of which was: "Under the present status of this city, the same style of life is being forced on both the lion and the ox, and that, as the poet Blake said, is oppression." At their last press conference, Mailer and Breslin presented a "Miscellany of Ideas for the 51st State." Vest-pocket neighborhood colleges. Free bicycles in all city parks. A referendum calling for the fifty-first state and subsequent constitutional convention. Day-care centers and nurseries. A central farmer's market offering ethnic foods of all varieties. Rebuilding our dilapidated neighborhood water fronts as water-front housing. Investigation and abolishment of loan companies and city marshals. Craftsman training in gardening. And so on. Think about it. People laughed and laughed, as though civilizing steps were forever beyond them, but as one of the slogans said: "If you think the 51st state is a joke, New York may die laughing."

They didn't win of course. Mailer came in fourth in a field of five. Jimmy ran well. They had hoped to do somewhat better. The night of the primary, people came to headquarters. "It wasn't the sort of party that Norman Mailer usually attends," said one of the newspapers. They were always saying things like that. How did they know? One time a reporter asked: "Don't you find this grubby; aren't these people you would avoid in your personal life?"

"It isn't the same," he said patiently. "You see a blank stare when they meet you. Then you tell them who you are and what you are trying to do, and their eyes light, and you know you are relating and somehow it all seems to matter."

Mailer and Breslin thanked the volunteers. Norman said: "I came up with the fifty-first state idea. I thought it was a powerful idea. I'll see if it has real growth potential." Jimmy said: "I will now drink in public. I am mortified to have been part of a process which required the closing of the bars." And then he said: "Please don't stop here. I think most of you know what you have to do."

The next day Norman went back to editing his movie, *Maidstone,* and then went to Houston for the moon flight. Jimmy went to Westhampton to write.

After one of the meetings in a synagogue, two men who had been standing in the back started laughing and shaking their heads. "They are really crazy with that power to the neighborhoods stuff," said one. "Imagine giving power to Harlem!"

"No, wait a minute, Herbie," said the other man, "he's talking about giving power back to US too." Mailer and Breslin, by sheer force of will and argument, had opened up that one person, that day, to a new idea. I guess that's what we all have to do.

CANNIBALS 10—CHRISTIANS 0
(or I Was a Right Wing Plot for Norman Mailer)

NOEL E. PARMENTEL, JR.

I am indebted for a title assist here to Mr. Jack Newfield, columnist for the *Village Voice,* contributor (at least at this writing) to *Life* and author of a stylish and best-selling encomium to the memory of that noted civil libertarian and New Left activist, the late Robert F. Kennedy. While Newfield is tight with Eldredge Cleaver, Abbie Hoffman, and Professor Herbert Marcuse, my own admittedly *outré* political tastes have led me up the labyrinth ways and garden paths of Barry Goldwater, John Tower, and Bill Buckley. Still, we are friendly and it was over dinner at Casey's (a sort of space-age Café Society Downtown) that we created, fomented, incited, and abetted the now-legendary Hip Coalition (of left and right) dedicated to the proposition that Norman Mailer should run for mayor of New York. Or so it seemed.

What Jack did not realize, until he hastily debarked a third of the way through the campaign, was that Norman Mailer was a Right Wing Plot, hatched some time earlier by me and a nameless but Machiavellian jurist, to be referred to here as the poor man's Felix Frankfurter. This was to have been the greatest Trojan Horse operation since Washington, D.C. CORE amalgamated poor Joe Mitchell's Seaboard White Citizen's Council. But like most Right Wing Plots, especially those engineered by same nameless jurist and myself, this ended an unmitigated calamity.

But one can forgive Newfield his gullibility, accustomed as he was to the company of such Beautiful People as Dick Goodwin and Adam Yarmolinsky in the rarified air of UN Plaza with the heady dialectic of Steve Smith, Bill van den Heuvel, and Carter

Burden as counterpoint. My own experience in the New Politics has been limited to boozing in the Algonquin lobby with Warren Hinckle and a Negro seer from Baton Rouge.

But I am a veteran of Norman Mailer campaigns. I was to be a press secretary (with, I believe Seymour Krim and Allen Ginsberg) almost ten years ago when Mailer first thought he might run for mayor as the existential candidate and as a psychic outlaw. But except for a position paper on introducing jousting tournaments into the Police Athletic League curriculum to head off juvenile delinquency, the campaign never got off the ground. And only a year ago last summer, while summering in Easthampton, I served in the boiler room on *Maidstone* (jocularly referred to as *Bête du Jour* or *Super 8½*), a cinematic run-through of the presidential campaign of Norman T. Kingsley ("the American Buñuel" according to the script) and still mercifully unreleased. As a hopelessly hooked buff of political exotica, I had observed Mailer's political *persona* from close range for almost a decade. But his name was now on everybody's lips. He had just written *Armies of the Night,* the best and most original piece of political journalism I have ever read and a fitting match for his great novel—our great Hollywood novel—*The Deer Park.* He had shamed the academic/literary bureaucrats into giving him his due (they had ever despised him—he was their better —they knew it) and won the triple crown, the Polk and National Book awards and the Pulitzer prize. There was serious speculation about him as Nobel laureate. It seemed to be Norman's year. But while he had written perhaps the best books of our time, he had definitely produced its worst movies. The essential Mailer was still with us. With these thoughts in mind, Newfield and I went to work, with the aid and abettance of the subject's monstrous ego. In fact it was easy work. Norman was a pushover. He even grumbled every time I told him he had no realistic chance of winning. For him, Lightning Could Strike. Fine. For Newfield (who could not have had any idea of Mailer's *realpolitik*) it was Breakthrough, Liberation, an end to such tawdry clubhouse hacks as Paul O'Dwyer and Herman Badillo. This was the Real Thing. Fine. Let him be Schlesinger. I would be Larry O'Brien.

My strategy was for Mailer to run fairly strong, over 100,000 votes, almost all from Hugh Carey, the Kennedy candidate who would run as an out-and-out liberal, thus assuring the nomination of Bob Wagner, the captive of the reactionary Johnson-Humphrey clique, who would chase Procaccino, Badillo, and the others out and defeat John Lindsay. In one brilliant coup I had checkmated the Kennedy *putsch* in New York and put an end to Lindsay as a presidentibili. Very simple. I felt like Lee Pressman must have felt communizing a union.

In addition to my own shortcomings as a theorist and Newfield's *naïveté* as regards the politics of our tiger, there were a few other chinks in our *armoire,* namely the *ad hoc* group which met at Mailer's tower of babble to discuss his candidacy. There is no way to describe that *entente cordial,* but many of us who followed the campaign regret that Richard Leacock did not carry through his threat to make a *cinéma-vérité* film of this political happening. If Thomas Pynchon were to write a political novel he might be interested in this caucus, composed of equal parts of Reform Democrats, Goldwaterites, Tammany Regulars, Crime Fighters, Black Panthers, Village Voicers, Mailer's Rat Pack, Junior Jet Setters, Muckrakers, Maoists, and a few Irish lads who appeared to have slipped out of an O'Casey tenement to rush the growler.

Compounding this campaign committee was a phenomenon which I have observed over the years which can be isolated as the Mailer Syndrome, a vast, complex, even cosmic put on/put down composed of feigned or actual psychological and rhetorical devices such as gynecology, dypsomania, coporolalia, astrology, scatology, anti-Semitism, ————lepsy, glossolalia, and proctology. This Syndrome can appear, without warning, from any vantage point and the Subject is able to have at you and/or himself from almost any angle. I have personally known it to manifest itself like a presence or a familiar from bar stool, arm chair, television screen, lectern, Steenbeck, book page and from a movieola, where I once observed Norman barking back at a dog.

He is plenty tricky here and I have known him when. But, although I am a bit of a stick about cussing, I have invariably been amused to see him, as Sy Krim put it, "put his index finger

up the system and still crack the headlines and bank the bread."
Here is some Mailer verse planned for a poetry reading:

> To tell the sad dreary truth
> it was a Jew
> Almost I came with him
> almost
> was pissy
> but sweet
>
> A Jew
> You
> Dear Kike
> I wish you were a dyke.

For which pains he got the hook. (Actually the curtain was rung
down.) And the place? The Poetry Center of the Young Men's/
Young Women's Hebrew Association. Here's another from the Syndrome, an aside, actually a position in regard to pollution control
by predisposal of raw sewage by chemical methods in home toilets.
Arguing tortuously of human engagement in technology, he gets you
from civic engineering to the problems of alienation and depersonali-
zation with "Man should smell his own shit." Or in the middle of
a discussion of marriage: "By the time they're eighty, a couple
should die fucking." (This last a fleeting reminder of those halcyon
days of yore when the game was Norman Mailer Meets the Sexual
Revolution. At this point he was, for a short time, hooted about
town as the Mockie de Sade.)

Not to be overlooked here are Mailer's credentials as Marxist
dialectician. (I refer here to Chico, not Karl.) He does all accents
badly. His Irish is Crown Heights Behan, his southern, White Horse
Willingham. One dreadful evening, after watching Norman's Weber
to Merv Griffin's Fields, a viewer was moved to send the following
telegram: "Your British is Yiddish. Your Erse is Worse." (The
only writer in recent memory who shows up worse than Mailer on
the tube is New York *Times*man Sidney Zion, who should be
required to provide subtitles for his video appearances.)

But regardless of the Mailer Mystique, we had a unique, highly individualistic candidate running on an exciting platform. I personally felt that Mailer and his ideas about the city merited at least the consideration of anyone who retained any love or hope for New York. And in spite of the odd combinations and potential cannibalism of the campaign committee, their togetherness represented the greatest pool of talent and energy available to any candidate for public office anywhere. We were on the brink of something historic, a revolutionary challenge to politics as usual. The New York *Times* noted, "If Mr. Mailer does well, some of the rules may be changed. It is conceivable that his candidacy could broaden national concepts of politics, politicians, and government."

Such send-offs from such august quarters were beginning to have their effect. People all over New York, in fact all over the world, were suddenly talking about the Mailer candidacy and its implications. But all was not beer and skittles yet. There remained one major area of potential trouble, in fact, disaster. This was the credibility of the Mailer campaign. If he were taken seriously he would get a large vote and make his point. If, on the other hand, people tended to think of his candidacy as a joke, just another Mailer caper, then a catastrophe was in the making. It was essential to any kind of effective showing that his campaign be taken seriously, that it not be treated as a gag. To solve, therefore, the crucial problem of credibility we came up with a master stroke. We put Jimmy Breslin on the ticket.

In my own defense I should add here that Jimmy was not a unanimous selection. I vociferously objected to running mates in general and Breslin in particular. There was nothing personal in this. I have known him over the years and, while a little of his neo-Runyan goes very far with me, I have friendly feelings toward him personally. (He is also, when he eschews the garbage, a good writer. A column of his, "The Way Things Are," was one of the best newspaper pieces I ever read.) But I saw ruin. I saw the whole effort being dismissed as a yuk. I saw Mailer's 100,000 votes being cut in half. I saw Breslin running ahead of Mailer, thereby fatally blunting our point. In short, I saw the run-of-the-mill ruination that is ever the fate of a Right Wing Plot.

But mass masochism was the order of the night among our little grope group. Except for Buzz Farber, a road-company Paul Morrisey, and the world's fifth worst actor (just behind Carole Lynley, Jane Fonda, John Gavin, and Mailer himself), I received no support from the Hip Coalition. Newfield was particularly eloquent here, seeing in Jimmy a man of the left who would give the ticket some badly needed political direction. (He had begun to get the picture about Mailer who learned to red bait at the feet of Jean Malaquais, and who has been known to repeat Henry Wallace's oft-quoted line that "the trouble with the common man is that he's too damn common.") Newfield was right. Jimmy went left and behaved very creditably toward the end, coming across as a veritable Vito Marcantonio. Mailer made the best of a bad bargain, wistfully musing that maybe Breslin might nail down the doorman vote, a remark touching in its innocence, but indicative of Mailer's *aperçu* of lower-middle-class *Zeitgeist*. And I was again easily voted down when I favored an all-out attack on Badillo who, along with Procaccino, had refused to follow Carey's example of knuckling under to Wagner. Badillo loomed very dangerous to what, after Breslin, remained of the Mailer vote. Badillo, personally or politically, would not stand up under close scrutiny. But I stood alone as a "racist" and "bigot" for pushing for an attack on Badillo's jugular. (Farber, the other racist and bigot, had taken his crash helmet and gone home.)

Being a good loser, therefore, I turned on to the general tone of the campaign which I suggested Terry Southern direct. I was a strong supporter of Gloria Steinem's short-lived bid for comptroller on the ticket which I suggested we market as Son of the Fugs (there should be no problem of rights here since Mailer had, after all, invented the word) with the possibility of an LP as well as a single each by Norman, Jimmy, and Gloria. And I was frequently observed passing out lapel buttons with such legends as:

VOTE THE RASCALS IN

THE OTHER GUYS ARE THE JOKE

Breslin's participation, which proved even more of a disaster than I predicted, was greeted with whoops of delight by both press and public. There was no further chance for Mailer to be taken seriously. "Cute as a button they are, just like a pair of little butterballs," was one you heard often and indeed they were, looking as *gemütlich* a pair of Paddy Chayefsky figments as ever enbussed for Kutshers. A newspaper description of a news conference: "Mailer, somber as a mortician in his three-piece blue pinstripe, served notice that he wasn't fooling around . . . The prize-winning novelist sweated heavily . . . the frizz of a hairdo . . . was stiffly matted with an overdose of pomade." Or "Breslin . . . waddled in . . . 50 minutes late, looking like a Queen's Hoss Cartwright in his black mohair suit. As to Lindsay: 'He's too tall.'" (After the elongated Miss Steinem was eased off our slate, we had the shortest ticket ¡since the Beam Team, a fact that was to plague both the candidates and the photographers. Neither Norman nor Jimmy would stand on a box, so many of the shots showed only a cluster of mikes.) One of the pictures that did come out, a candid shot of Jimmy with a glass, was captioned, "Breslin oils his tonsils before speaking." More coverage, "Breslin, terming the rest of the candidates 'bums and nuts,' predicted a runaway victory. When it was suggested that he might have some trouble shaking his reputation as beer-hall vivant . . . Breslin sneered 'That's silly . . . that's stupid. Look, I been through all this, I ain't takin' anything from you guys.'" Still another reaction to the ticket came from one of New York's finest at the police department's John Jay College of Criminal Justice. "Are you serious?" a policeman asked. "What would happen if you are elected and you go ape some night and Breslin goes ape too?" The latter apparently had misgivings of his own later in the campaign. At a last minute summit of the ticket, hastily assembled in the Russian Tea Room, he beefed, "The campaign is getting serious and we'll make fools of ourselves." But Breslin's finest hour came after Mailer in his cups "went ape" one evening at a "fund-raiser" at the Village Gate, where he lustily treated his audience of potential fat cats to a number of fine old Anglo-Saxon suggestions, instructions, and exhortations. Fleeing the scene, Jimmy is reliably reported to have called Jack Newfield

about four in the morning to complain, "Jesus Christ, what did
you get me into? You guys got me runnin' with fuckin' Ezra
Pound."

That particular Village Gate affray aroused considerable comment,
almost unanimously unfavorable to Norman. I was there and I think
by and large the audience richly deserved what it got. With
notable and honorable exceptions it was a tacky bunch. Pushy,
loudmouthed climbers, and flunkies. Like the poor they are always
with us. One can view them almost any evening or weekend, slither-
ing around Elaine's or Casey's or polluting the beaches in the
Hamptons. Sleazy and weaselly, low-class hustlers, and sycophants.
I have noted these *canaille* entering through the front door of the
houses of people who know better, like George Plimpton, Bill
Buckley, and Norman Mailer. Their house, their game. All the
evening needed was a foursome of Jane Holzer and Jerry Schatzberg
and Mr. and Mrs. Jacob Javits. It would require the services of
Daumier or Rowlandson to do justice to these creatures. (David
Levine is too soft-hearted but Diane Arbus might have a go at it.)
Yet we live in an incredible time when such like are indexed in
books with titles like *The Beautiful People*. God save the mark.
Whatever Mailer's faults are, it must be intolerable to him to be
patronized and condescended to by such scum. This is a long over-
due "Well-Done" for his performance on the side of the angels at
the Gate.

One generally unreported incident of the campaign which may
be of general interest to social anthropologists was the Right Wing
reception for Norman hosted by Douglas McKelvy, wealthy aesthete
and recluse. McKelvy's claims to political fame include being photographed in Hyannisport putting Nixon stickers on his automobiles
the day John Kennedy was nominated (McKelvy is the Kennedy's
summer next-door neighbor on Cape Cod, where his baronial digs
make the Compound look shabby indeed); he put even money
on Barry Goldwater to win the presidency in 1964; and being the
world's greatest imitator, bar none, of the vocal qualities of Mrs.
Aristotle Onassis. Among McKelvy's guests for this fete was an
amiable lecher, who had abandoned a successful career in engineering to devote full time to the activities of the League of

Christian Laymen; there were two attractive East Side matrons who, as heads of New York for Goldwater, organized a midnight raid on the offices in the Graybar Building and seized and removed the files to a Park Avenue apartment. (If it had not been for the foresight of these belles, Goldwater might have lost New York.) Now comes a brilliant economist who has been, in season, high priest of Ayn Rand's quasi-religious grope group; *guru* to the dissident group of Henry Georgians; and author of that never to be forgotten line, "Roy Cohn is the American Dreyfus," a great moment in American political dramaturgy. On this particular night he appeared to be a Black Panther, but has since become a Maoist. He has had everything but the whooping cough.

Most of the gang were for Marchi at the beginning ("The dullest dago in Staten Island," growled one skeptic), but they were all for Mailer at the end. Like UFO crewmen, we recognize each other. It would have warmed the cockles of Newfield's heart to see this mutual-admiration society in action. On the strength of this new-found (or newly acknowledged) bond between Mailer and the Right Wing, most everybody got drunk (these are old-fashioned folk), and there were a couple of incidents. Mailer had made the mistake of arriving with Dick Goodwin, a high-echelon Kennedy brain truster; Richard Tuck, a low-grade flunky for (believe it or not) Pierre Salinger, and Tuck's girl. Tuck did not make much of a hit. He was finally told that he had about ten seconds to decide whether he would leave by the door or the window (the party was on the second landing of McKelvy's town house). His girl was welcome to stay. He scurried out (with his girl) and was last seen out on the street howling obscenities up at the Right Wingers *and* Mailer.

Goodwin fared somewhat better. A girl who arrived with one of the midnight raiders, and who identified herself as a writer about sex for a new Luce publication as well as a connection of Chicago Mayor Richard Daley, freaked out and began to scream at Mailer. She had to be restrained and led into another room where Goodwin who had lost interest in the dialogue went in to comfort her. The last I heard of either one of them, they were together out in Antioch, Ohio, where Goodwin was lecturing the youth of America on the moral leadership of Teddy Kennedy. I am proud and happy that I was able to bring them together.

It was interesting that no one at the gathering thought to invite Bill Buckley. The feeling was that as the pet Jew of the establishment, Buckley had become impossibly square and mellow and would not think of doing anything as exciting as endorse Mailer which could only endanger his hard-won respectability. (After the primary, the feeling of this group was that a few days campaigning by Buckley gave Marchi the Republican edge and that if he had run himself this year he would have defeated both Lindsay and Procaccino, that Bill Buckley would be the next mayor of New York.)

But what happened to Mailer? It was not merely his manic compulsions, his self-destructive bent. It was not only his bad judgment, say, in hoping Breslin would get the doormen and hackies. (These types quickly recognize Jimmy's *ersatz* average with the *echte* of Procaccino.) Mailer should have conceded the doormen and hackies to Mario. Spengler cannot play at Tartuffe. He should have gone after the tenants and the fares, the almost 70 per cent of eligibles who did not bother to turn out. There was the Mailer vote. And there is where he failed. These were simps who must know whether it was ape or agape. Seeking to be Padraic Perse, he somehow came across as Bummy Davis.

But it was a gas while it lasted, and for a couple of months New York was alive again. For one brief shining moment there was Babylon. Now go back to Cole Porter, ahead of his time again.

> Broadway's turning into Coney
> Champagne Charley's drinking gin
>
> Old New York is new and phoney
> Give it back to the Indian.

They say a man is gauged by the enemies he makes. For my money this makes Mailer aces. He did not score among either the Brooklyn Jews, the Bronx Irish, the Queens Italians, the Bedford-Stuyvesant blacks, the Barrio Puerto Ricans, the East Side Episcopalians. None of them liked him, not the self-pitying black-bottom, not the whining, backlashing white lower-middle, not the smug middle, certainly not the zombie top. Not one of these social Typhoid Marys likes Mailer. Not one. He can't be all bad.

Election night, at his Plaza suite, after Mailer knew he had goofed and failed, I meant to say to him what Carroway shouted at Gatsby. I say it now: "They're a rotten crowd. You're worth the whole bunch." And Walker Percy, in *The Moviegoer,* said it so: "You're damned right we're better than they are. And don't think they don't know it." I think these things of Norman Mailer. I think what a brave man he is. I think what a good friend he is. But do not judge him too quickly. He's a pain in the ass.

NOTES FROM THE CANCER WARD

GLORIA STEINEM

Twenty years from now, when the New York air is pure poison and only a few squatters wander on foot across the George Washington Bridge, a reporter will come to interview us, the refugee New Yorkers, in camps set up for us outside Seattle or St. Paul.

"Why didn't you leave sooner?" the reporter will ask in honest bewilderment, much as Jews were asked why they failed to leave Germany. "Didn't you see the warning signs? Transportation couldn't move, air pollution was shortening your lives by ten years, whole blocks of buildings had been abandoned by the landlords, there were bonfires in the streets of Brooklyn, old people on welfare starved to death in their rooms and were found only by the smell, power black-outs came more and more often, races fought each other for a few feet of living-space . . ."

He trails off into silence, realizing that we don't believe it even now. Kids and scientists and a few sane men had been reading us that list for years, after all, and we paid no attention. Even politicians had blamed each other for a few such ills, though within gentle limits. No man ever got elected by predicting doom.

"We didn't think it could happen," we will tell the reporter. "We thought New York had always been here, and always would be."

"We didn't want to change our city."

"We liked the toughness of it, the survival of the fittest—and the wiliest, and richest."

"It was the greatest city in the world," we will tell him. "A place of infinite opportunity, infinite risk."

Then the reporter will go off, shaking his head in disbelief, to write a moralistic story on the Fall of New York, and we will be left in our camps, eyes glazed with memory like every group of refugees since Gaza.

We will sit very still, and we will tell each other stories of what once was New York. "This city," E. B. White wrote, "which not to look upon would be like death."

It was a gray morning in late March that Jimmy Breslin, Peter Maas, Jack Newfield, and I converged on the offices of *New York* magazine to deliver our respective manuscripts; and went out for a self-congratulatory, wake-up cup of coffee with *New York*'s publisher. (There must be well-organized writers who don't stay up all night before deadlines, but I don't know who they are.)

By the time coffee had given way to an early lunch and beer, self-congratulation was wearing thin. Soon we were back to the usual political talk, underscored by gloom and doom about the city, and speculation on the mayoral primary coming up in June. Procaccino crying and using all the antiblack, anti-Puerto Rican code words; Scheuer talking law-and-order while claiming to be Eugene McCarthy's heir; Wagner droning ineffable, impenetrable Wagnerese; Carey courting Wagner while claiming to be Robert Kennedy's heir; Badillo trying hard to get as far left as the Republican we've already got: No, things weren't looking too cheerful for those in the Democratic Party, or to the left of it.

In fact, we'd all been looking forward to working for Herman Badillo, a probable Democratic candidate, but we'd got discouraged after talking with him at a meeting arranged by Norman Mailer, who was then supporting him. Badillo seemed a good man, but one devoted to tinkering, to changing a school official here or streamlining some bureaucratic process there, but not to challenging old concepts. He promised less to change the quality of life in the city than to reduce our expectations of it. ("Slum clearance isn't possible now," he said, "so let's just concentrate on essential services. Lindsay increased expectations, and that made trouble.") Most of all, Badillo, a first-generation Puerto Rican himself, had an old-fashioned ethnic view of things that sometimes antagonized the more politically independent second generation. "If they don't vote for me," he said that night in Mailer's living room, "they aren't Puerto Ricans."

We muttered about this sad state of mayoral affairs, staring morosely into beer mug or coffee cup. Even publisher George Hirsch, the only Republican present and a young liberal who would probably support his friend John Lindsay again, wasn't pleased at the kind of primary it would be. With all of Queens at Lindsay's throat for his alleged favoritism toward blacks and Puerto Ricans, he would have to run cautiously. It promised to be a campaign with no ideas at all.

Unless, of course, Mailer could be persuaded to run. Jack Newfield had talked to him, and he hadn't said no. We sat for a minute, savoring the beautiful absurdity of it. Four-times married, famous peace marcher, defender of the young, braver of any available lion's den, confessed wife-stabber at one low point of his life, best writer and probably best political or any kind of mind in America at several high points: he might just be the big excessive visionary who could turn this big excessive city on its ear.

Not that he could win. There was never any illusion of Mailer's winning. But, as Peter Maas pointed out, campaigns sometimes change American minds as much as elections; the McCarthy and Kennedy campaigns proved that. Mailer could plant a lot of ideas— about common goals of the black and white poor, for instance, as Bobby Kennedy had; or a left-right coalition on urban problems —that might take root and grow.

As for Mailer's running mate, Jack had that figured out, too. His candidate for city council president was Jimmy Breslin.

Which was the first that Breslin had heard about it. Jimmy grunted enigmatically, looking as if he'd been hit in the chest with a hockey puck, and continued to sip sorrowfully at his mug of beer.

The rest of us had no such hesitation. Mailer, the wild-eyed Jewish, Harvard-bred, intellectual-activist; combined with Breslin, the tough, street-bred, would-be Irish cop—a perfect coalition for New York. As we all knew and as his readers probably suspected, Jimmy secretly reads books. (Rumor had it that he was currently packing a copy of Hannah Arendt's *Banality of Evil*.) But his ideas, at least as radical and humane as Mailer's, were couched in unphony, shit-free street language that Queens and Red Hook could take to heart.

"You know, we could fix them political bums so they never knew what hit them," said Jimmy, hitting the table with a hamlike palm. "Even if we only did it for a day—just held one of them phony hotel press conferences to announce our candidacy, and played it very straight—we could tell more truth about this city than politicians ever heard."

He fished in his pocket for a dime, and went off to telephone Mailer, a man whom he scarcely knew.

"I think," said Jack Newfield, watching Breslin lumber toward the pay phone, "we've got a candidate."

One candidate. At a very New York lunch in the Algonquin (editor of *New York Times Magazine* at one table, Arthur Schlesinger and Marietta Tree at another), I listen to Norman Mailer explain his immediate commitment to write a book on the astronauts and the moon shot, and his unwillingness to enter the race unless he could campaign full-time.

"New Yorkers are tough old birds when they're in trouble," he said. "If we declared ourselves and then didn't campaign seriously, they'd never forgive us."

Maybe he's right, but by now the possibility of inserting any ideas at all into the primary seems better than leaving it to the professionals. I get off on the wrong foot by talking about an "educational" campaign, even if, as it now seems, Mailer would have only five or six days in New York, and would just fire off press releases while astronaut-watching in Houston for the rest of it.

I get further off on the wrong foot by trying to explain why women's political groups won't support him. His mystical resistance to birth control and to repeal of the abortion laws seems unrealistic, especially to poor women. He thinks about that for awhile. Legal abortion, he decides, is preferable to birth control. "At least that way women *know* they're murderers."

I silently write off the women's groups, and wonder if the whole thing is worth it. Imagining Mailer storming through New York like an excommunicated Old Testament prophet, and Breslin's black-Irish rages against Establishment injustice, I decide again that it is.

"Somebody's got to run," I say finally, "or we'll all die a little more during the primary. We'll all die from the neck up."

He looks at me sharply, and seems tired. "All right, you won that round. But I've got to figure out the energy it takes. You burn up a lot of writing out there." He's talking out of bitter experience. I must look as dismayed as I feel (we'd been too selfish to think of the big and little humiliations such a campaign would cost him, much less the price to his work), because he adds that it's something only he can decide. He'll think about that, as well as whether or not the astronaut book can be put off, while he and Beverley spend some time in Provincetown.

"But if I run, I try to take it. You don't kid around in a cancer ward."

After a big pre-Provincetown meeting in Mailer's living room, Jimmy is some combination of worried and admiring. "Norman," he says seriously, "scares the shit out of me. I think that fucking bastard wants to win."

I am beginning to know how Jimmy feels. I've got problems of my own.

At the first meeting, someone suggested semiseriously that there should be a woman on this visionary ticket, and why didn't I run for controller. Jimmy, worried about the prospect of running with someone as risky as Mailer ("You guys got me running with Ezra Pound," was how Breslin put it), went as far as to say he wouldn't run unless I did.

At lunch with Mailer, some small approving reference was made to a third spot on the ticket. I assumed he was being humorous and/or polite.

At the third meeting, a forty-person affair in Mailer's living room, there was actual pressure toward running as controller; most of it coming from a black lawyer, Florynce Kennedy, who said neither she nor other women activists, in or out of the Democratic Party, would work for the ticket otherwise. The pressure continued through two more meetings. The result: I'm desperately looking for a replacement.

The medicinal purpose of this campaign can only be served after all, if it's used as a platform. And to do that, the candidates have to get up in front of live audiences and talk; preferably well. It's only in the past year or so that I've been able to show up for television talk shows (I used to cancel out the night before, ending up on several TV producers' black lists), where kindly interviewers go out of their way to keep you from looking like a fool. Standing up to give whole speeches unaided is the stuff of nightmares. As for volleying hostile questions, five minutes of that and catalepsy would set in.

All of which I tried to explain at the third meeting, while Breslin gave me the incredulous look of a born storyteller, and Mailer muttered darkly, "You can learn."

There are some traditionalists in our fast-growing group, however, who believe that any woman other than Margaret Mead or Coretta King would make the ticket look frivolous. I don't agree, but I pretend to; they get me off the hook. Fear makes strange allies all over town.

I *am* off the hook. Mailer and Breslin make a fine left-right package. Therefore it's been decided that adding a Negro, a woman, or a Puerto Rican would be old politics and cynical.

During two weeks of worrying about it, however, I've learned a lot about the job. A controller audits all city funds, keeping an eye out for stealing and waste; he manages a city employees' pension fund that is twice as big as any private fund; he has four votes, as many as the mayor, on the Board of Estimate, probably the only group of men with an overview of the city. Thus the controller should be as skilled and creative a money manager as any of the big fund operators on Wall Street; he should be a reformer, using his office as a social instrument to pressure banks and businesses into ghetto investments, integrated work forces and the like; and he should be a leader who could tap New York's gifted financial community for investment advice.

In real life, however, we often get an Eskimo from Staten Island, or some other combination that balances a political ticket. Probably, an office of such expertise should be appointed, not elected at all. In the meantime, studying the practices of our current controller, Mario Procaccino, takes away much of the modesty with which a would-be controller (male or female) might approach the job.

In a cancer ward, it isn't who can perform the function properly, but who can function at all.

Our campaign headquarters is on Columbus Circle, a large barren room formerly occupied by Eugene McCarthy's campaign.

Coming to open it for the first time tonight, I found more than a hundred volunteers lined up in the rain. There were McCarthy kids, Kennedy kids, a bartender from the East Bronx, half a dozen lawyers, several teachers, and a scattering of assorted professional people, mostly young. All of them worked patiently and cheerfully on the donkey-task of filling out cards for petition-signing. I had supposed that some were just there to see the Celebrity Candidates, but they kept working long after Mailer and Breslin were due to arrive, even absorbing the Kafka-esque regulations about what was a valid petition signature, and what was not.

The voter's name had to be exactly as registered, for instance, down to the choice between middle name and initial. "Street" could not be abbreviated to "St.," and pencil wasn't accepted. Petition-carriers must know the signers personally, or approach them in their homes. Each signature sheet must have a cover sheet with attached names typewritten on same. . . . The regulations went on endlessly, deepening the suspicion that it was a process invented by incumbents for the purpose of keeping the insurgents out. ("Don't worry," said a sixteen-year-old boy cheerfully. "We went through crazy stuff like this in New Hampshire, too. The Establishment doesn't know we have the patience to beat them at their own game.") Joe Ferris, (a teacher) and campaign worker who was directing all this, consulted in whispers with Laird Cummings, another campaign worker who had been through petition-signing to get candidates on a ballot before.

"Good news," Joe announced, beaming. "Ballpoints are legal!" Appreciative laughter, and one shout of, "Yes, folks, it *is* 1984!"

Breslin arrived, and answered questions on two main campaign points—making New York City the fifty-first state, and decentralizing it to fit the slogan, "Power to the Neighborhoods!"—but he looked uncomfortable behind his enormous cigar.

It wasn't until Mailer arrived—fresh from a rally on a college campus, television cameramen struggling to keep up—that the occasion took on an existential glow.

Standing on a table, Mailer grinned delightedly at the political pungencies rolling off his tongue. "The Democratic Party hasn't had a new idea since 1932," he said. And, "I tell you, if we pull this thing off and get elected on our platform of the fifty-first state, it will be a political miracle. The men in Washington will be *on their knees!*"

Then Breslin caught fire, too, telling how black people could run their own neighborhoods for the first time in history, and enunciating his campaign slogan with such dead-pan force that it brought down the house. "If elected," he said, wrapping his mouth around the dental New York t's, "I will go to Queens!"

The man standing next to me laughed and applauded. He had worked in this same room during the McCarthy campaign, as had I. "We're going to lose again," he said, "but I don't care. This time, we've got a candidate."

A formal announcement of candidacy this morning, with both Mailer and Breslin rather stiff, explaining their platform with care. The reporters, however, seem more interested in eliciting an obscenity. After much questioning, often condescending or hostile, they press Mailer for a campaign slogan. "No more bullshit," he finally says, grinning. And so they print that. Or rather, they print what they can, and add lascivious dashes.

Thanks to the hard work of Alice Krakauer, a former McCarthy aide, the candidates have been booked into every campus in the five boroughs and some on Long Island. They are going into the neighborhoods and social centers and synagogues now. Their individual styles have begun to take shape—Breslin consistent and entertaining; Mailer alternately obscure, self-conscious, or brilliant—

but they're taken more seriously in the out-of-town press than in New York.

They're also taken more seriously by real people with real problems who have never heard of Mailer or Breslin than by that book-buying public which presumably has.

Press aides Jack Newfield and Peter Maas are trying to shame reporters into printing the candidates' ideas, but there's nothing that can be done about certain Reform Democrats and celebrity-hunters of the upper-middle class. Collectively, those groups have come to be known as The Cannibals. They come to say they've been there, and listen for ammunition to prove the new ideas wrong.

Mailer wrote somewhere that the very rich adapt their speech to politics by imitating movie stars. If Norman himself is an example, the very intellectual imitate southern crackers; well, maybe Virginia Populists made husky by bourbon and branch water. Only in Mailer's case, it's cheap bourbon and New York tap water, because he occasionally clips and chlorinates a word, letting the southern accent slip; and he almost always cuts off ends of sentences in the manner of Kennedy family orators and others to whom broad-gauge political speechifying is not a natural thing.

He did it on "The Tonight Show," his first television appearance of the campaign. He did it when he announced his candidacy. I believe he does it most whenever nervousness attacks. (Tonight in a Lower East Side Democratic club, with various students and Puerto Rican students really listening to his ideas, he did it least of all.) As some actors come to comedy with a Jewish-sounding cadence, Norman comes to politics with a southern accent, and an imaginary watch chain across his vest.

I missed the famous Village Gate benefit (at which Mailer said "fuck" a lot, yelled embarrassments, and generally let fly at the high percentage of Cannibals in the audience), but it now appears to have been a Good Thing. At least, the "serious" primary candidates took it as evidence that Mailer couldn't possibly be serious, and therefore didn't challenge the legality of Mailer-Breslin petitions.

Since challenges on all those fine points of legal names and abbreviations can take weeks to stagger through the courts, Our Low Point (as the Gate evening is now called by campaign workers) could be written up as a brilliant tactic.

Could be, but shouldn't. Even in California where I was the morning after, I got seven phone calls from Mailer-Breslin supporters who believed in the campaign's ideas, had worked hard, and now wanted to know who the hell Norman thought he was. Even Joe Flaherty, a good writer and former longshoreman who was one of his closest campaign aides, woke Mailer up the next day to lecture him on how outrageous he'd been. ("I didn't want to listen, but Joe just kept boring in," said Mailer afterward. "You have to love a man for that. He really cared.") It was destructive, it hurt the campaign's platform, and we're all a little fearful that it will happen again.

Still, I wish I'd seen the faces of The Cannibals.

Buttons used in the campaign:
"51"
MAILER & BRESLIN: POWER TO THE NEIGHBORHOODS
THE OTHER GUYS ARE THE JOKE
VOTE THE RASCALS IN
TAKE A CHANCE
NO MORE BULLSHIT
WALL STREET FOR MAILER—BRESLIN
I WOULD SLEEP BETTER KNOWING NORMAN MAILER
WAS MAYOR

Buttons almost used in the campaign:
MAYOR MAILER
GIMME JIMMY
LANDLORDS FOR MAILER & BRESLIN
TENANTS FOR MAILER & BRESLIN
FREEDOM FOR MAILER & BRESLIN
I WOULD SLEEP BETTER KNOWING NORMAN MAILER
WAS IN GRACIE MANSION

Not all the spirit has gone out of this campaign.

But it is getting remarkably serious.

Jimmy has seen so much decay and suffering in the streets that it comes out like a litany. "Manhattan is proud and glittering, but that is the face of the city. Down in the neighborhoods, down in the schools that are in the neighborhoods, New York is slashed and bleeding from someplace deep inside. The South Bronx is gone. East New York and Brownsville are gone. Jamaica is up for grabs. The last thing this city can afford is a politician thinking in normal politicians' terms. New York either gets an imagination, or the city dies . . ."

Norman has learned so much with that gigantic brain of his that it's quite possible he now knows more frightening statistics, more rehabilitated drug addicts by their first names, more neighborhood gut-issues, and more slum landmarks by sight than any other living human.

He is kind, and so perceptive that one can see him being honorable in ways that the beneficiary will never understand. (Or couldn't know about. Jimmy is sometimes late or absent for their joint appearances, but Norman never betrays him. "He is caught in traffic," Norman will say, and he conveys such sympathy for the plight that the audience nearly apologizes to the delinquent Jimmy on arrival.) He takes everybody very seriously at a level slightly above their own, and thus makes them a little better than they are.

How does this square with surly, insulting, paranoid Mailer of occasional parties and the Village Gate? I don't know. But perhaps we should accept his theory that you pay for everything, that you must be willing to sink down as far as the heights you would learn how to climb.

As for me, I look at them campaigning their hearts out in these last few days, and am sorry I helped persuade them to do it.

The second-worst occupation in the world is fund-raising from individuals. The worst occupation in the world is fund-raising at parties.

We have lost. Standing in the crowded headquarters, we catch Mailer and Breslin concede for the cameras. They have learned a lot, and taught a lot. Fresh air and ideas are floating into New York nooks and crannies where they've rarely been before.

I still have my recurrent fantasy of fleeing the city like Jews from Germany. But not quite yet. There are neighborhood projects to support, and campaign-born coalitions to explore, and some candidates to support.

As Breslin says, "If I'd known how dumb the other guys were, I might have tried it much sooner."

New York is still a cancer ward. But some of the patients are smiling.